Fundamentals of
Sailing,
Cruising,
and Racing

Fundamentals of
Sailing,
Cruising,
and Racing

Revised and Updated Edition

Steve Colgate

CEO, OFFSHORE SAILING SCHOOL, LTD.

W.W. Norton & Company
New York • London

For information about permission to reproduce selections from this book, write to
Permissions, W. W. Norton & Company, Inc., 500 Fifth Avenue, New York NY 10110.

Diagrams by Ellen Goodman
The text of this book is composed in Adobe Garamond
with the display set in Centaur Italic and Adobe Garamond
Book design and composition by Ken Gross
Manufacturing by The Vail-Ballou Press
Cover photo: Offshore Sailing School

Library of Congress Cataloging-in-Publication Data

Colgate, Stephen.
    Fundamentals of sailing, cruising, and racing / Steve Colgate.
    Rev. and updated ed.
        p.   cm.
    Includes index.
    ISBN 0-393-03811-4
    1. Sailing   2. Sailboat racing.   I. Title
GV811.C563   1996   95-25208
797.1'24—dc20   CIP

ISBN 0-393-03811-4

W. W. Norton & Company, Inc., 500 Fifth Avenue, New York NY 10110
W. W. Norton & Company Ltd., 10 Coptic Street, London WC1A 1PU

0 9 8 7 6 5 4 3 2 1

Contents

Preface

The language of the sea is a traditional one and very chauvinistic. Women rarely went to sea in the golden age of sailing ships and for a woman even to be aboard was considered by many superstitious sailors to be extremely unlucky. Times have changed and many women and men are enjoying sailing. Nevertheless, in writing this book, I have in many cases found it hard and awkward to use words that include both male and female. So where I have described a skipper or crew in male terms, please be assured that I know full well they may be female and I'm using the terms in a general rather than specific manner.

Author's Note

This book was really started in 1964 when I formed the Offshore Sailing School Ltd., researched the existing "how-to" sailing books, and found that none were written with the proper progression to augment a sailing course. Over the period of the next few years I developed a basic sailing manual, starting from a few mimeographed sheets, until a compact 138-page manual was printed in paperback by the school and sent to each student enrolled in the basic course. Then we expanded the scope of our courses at Offshore Sailing School to include cruising and racing courses, which also needed their own course manuals. This book is a compilation of all the course manuals, with changes and additional material. The emphasis in this book, as it is with our courses, is to give practical, simple explanations about the sport of sailing.

Offshore Sailing School, Ltd.
16731 McGregor Blvd.
Ft. Myers FL 33908
(941) 454-1700
(800) 221-4326
FAX: (941) 454-1191

PART I

Fundamentals of Sailing

Introduction

The appeal of sailing is its variety. Sailing is called a sport, but it's far more than that. To many, it's a lifestyle.

I can best describe such a varied and difficult subject through a few of my own experiences. I started sailing at the age of 10, and have sailed competitively for 50 years and expect to sail the rest of my life. A friend raced small sailboats until she was almost 80 years old, and a 66-year-old man won a silver medal in the 1968 Olympics. There aren't many sports which can cover such a life span so effectively.

What makes people want to sail? It's not that it's all delightful; in fact, many times it's downright uncomfortable. It's the moments that make it great. For ocean cruising, it's the moment at night when the full moon rises brilliantly above the horizon and sends a pathway of glittering diamonds right to your boat. Or the moment at night when dolphins come streaking toward you like torpedoes, leaving a trail of phosphorescence 20 to 30 feet long. It's frightening moments such as losing a rudder at sea and having to steer with sails alone, or when a ship with towing lights crosses your bow at night and you can't find the tow. It's when you're young and indestructible, sailing a 50-year-old wood boat in heavy seas, the lighting system shorted out, no radio, a leaking fuel tank, waterlogged lifejackets, pumping like mad to keep her afloat, and the moment the next day when the wind and seas subside, the sun shines brightly, and you've survived.

In coastal cruising, it's being safely anchored in a protected, snug harbor, watching an incredible sunset while succulent steaks sizzle on a charcoal grill off the stern. It's waking to the smell of frying bacon. It's the thrill and challenge of navigating in fog when you can't see the bow of the boat from the stern; everything seems hushed and eerie and the crew talks in low voices for no good reason except that it seems like someone's listening.

Or in racing, it's the moment when you've won. It's the exhilarating, noiseless speed as the boat surges down a large wave. And it's the mental concentration needed to squeeze every last fraction of a knot from the boat.

In short, sailing can provide peace, tranquillity, excitement, mental and physical challenge, contentment, camaraderie, solitude—fulfillment for almost any age and any personality.

Why, therefore, don't more people sail? Tradition is one reason. Sailing is steeped in tradition since it's one of the oldest methods of travel in the world. Yet it's this tradition that somehow makes it mystical in the eyes of the novice—strange words and strange concepts. Add this to the traditional feeling that it's a rich man's sport (even though this is no longer true) and many people don't even attempt to learn sailing. Adventure books about sailing around the world single-handed or living on the life-raft from a sunken yacht for months in the Pacific don't help prove that sailing is for everyone, not just a special adventurous few.

There are almost 8,000,000 outboard boats in the United States and every person who can afford even a 20-horsepower outboard motor (not even the motorboat itself) can buy a sailboat such as a Sunfish for the same price— and not have to pay for gas! Sailing is within the reach of just about everyone and is no longer only a rich man's sport.

◆ I ◆

General Terminology

Let's take some of the mystery out of sailing. As we talk about it we will use and describe traditional words. Most of the language of the sea has been developed over the centuries for clarity and descriptiveness. Attempts to change it usually end in confusion. For instance, we take for granted that "port" means left and "starboard" means right. Port is easy to remember because both "port" and "left" have four letters. But we seldom think about the derivation of starboard from the Old English word "steorbord" or "rudder side." Early Teutonic ships had their "steering boards" or rudders on the right side of the boat as you faced forward. This meant that the left side of the boat was clear to lay against a wharf and may have been the derivation of the word "port," the left side when facing forward from the stern. Even the word "stern," the rear part of the sailboat, probably came from the Old Norse word "stjorn," meaning steering. The bow of the boat (the forward part), a bow and arrow, archery, and other words came from the Old English word "boga," meaning an arch or something that is curved. It's not surprising that these words are retained in sailing since most words in the English language are derived from older usages. Any set of unusual words is difficult to master, but since they are constantly being used in sailing, it's of utmost necessity that the new sailor make an effort to learn them.

A remarkable number of people nowadays go right out and purchase their first sailboat without knowing a thing about sailing or the terminology. They may end up buying the correct boat for their purposes, but it certainly will be difficult for them to narrow down their choice from written descriptions without understanding the words used.

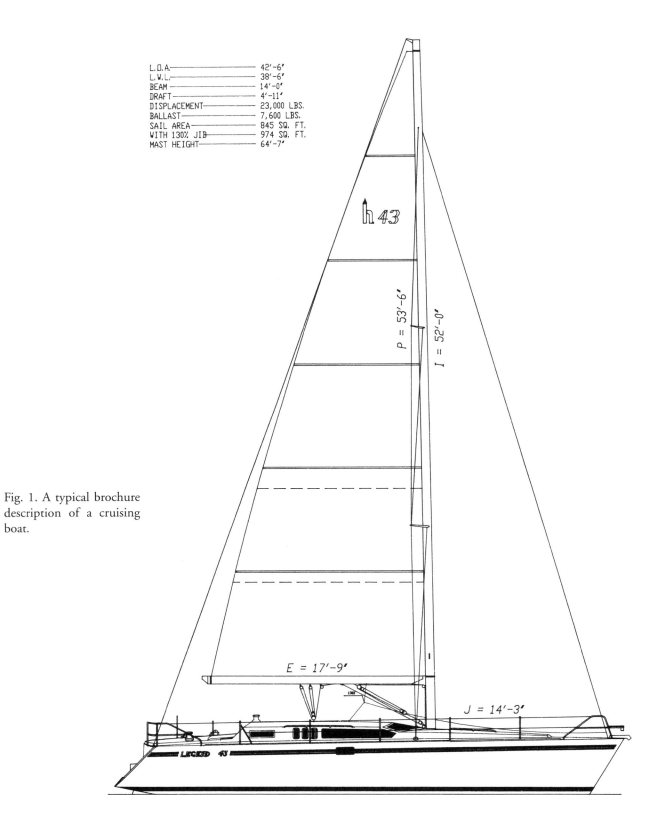

L.O.A.————————— 42'-6"
L.W.L.————————— 38'-6"
BEAM —————————— 14'-0"
DRAFT —————————— 4'-11"
DISPLACEMENT————— 23,000 LBS.
BALLAST———————— 7,600 LBS.
SAIL AREA————————845 SQ. FT.
WITH 130% JIB————— 974 SQ. FT.
MAST HEIGHT————— 64'-7"

h 43

P = 53'-6"

I = 52'-0"

E = 17'-9"

J = 14'-3"

LEGEND 43

Fig. 1. A typical brochure
description of a cruising
boat.

Hull Terms

Figure 1 is a reproduction of a portion of a brochure for a 43-foot sailboat built by Hunter Marine Corporation in Alachua, Florida. The "LOA" stands for "length overall" or the straight-line length of the boat from the stern to the bow, not including any bowsprit.

"LWL" is the waterline length of the boat measured in a straight line from the point where the bow disappears underwater to the point where the stern does the same. Actually, the waterline is the line scribed or painted on the boat, which is the level of the water when the boat is floating normally loaded. LWL therefore, really means "load waterline," though when used as a dimension it is measured in a straight line rather than along the curve of the hull.

The next dimension on the list in Figure 1 is "beam," often abbreviated as "BM." Beam is the maximum width of the boat. If it is able to just squeeze between two pilings, as in Figure 2, the pilings touch the boat where the beam is measured. If the boat is widest at its sides, rather than at deck level which is more usual, the boat is said to have "tumblehome." The sides of the boat above the waterline are called her "topsides" (not to be confused with "going topsides," which means going on deck from down below in the cabin of a yacht. Never say "I'm going downstairs" when going down the "companion-way" ladder that leads into the cabin of a boat from on deck. Say "I'm going below," which is short for going "below-deck" or under the deck).

The next dimension, "draft" or "DRA," is a most important one. It is the distance from the waterline to the lowest part of the boat. (Figure 3 shows how this and other dimensions are measured.) The Soling class sailboat in Figure 3 draws 4 feet 3 inches. She will touch bottom in 4' 3" of water if she is upright. (Note that if you are discussing a particular boat, the feminine is usually used.) To avoid going aground in a falling tide and being stranded for hours, you must know both the depth of the water and how much your boat

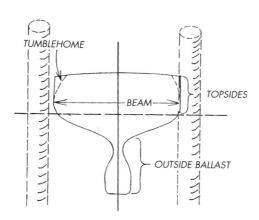

Fig. 2. "Beam" is the widest part of the boat (where it might touch imaginary pilings).

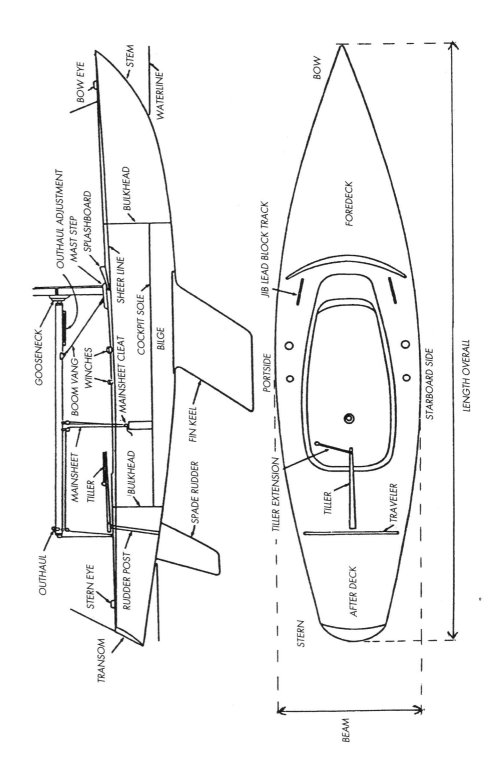

Fig. 3. The parts of a sailboat.

draws. A friend of mine chartered (rented) a sailboat and sailed over a number of locations that showed 5 feet of water on the chart at low tide. He felt marginally safe because he thought the boat drew 4' 6". When he returned the boat to the owner and the story came out, the owner turned white and gasped, "But I said she drew 6' 4", not 4' 6"!" Only the height of the tide had saved him.

The "ballast" listed in Figure 1 at 7,600 pounds is the dead weight used to keep the boat upright. The weight of the tall mast and the force of the wind in the sails make the boat top-heavy and tip it over. The ballast in the keel counteracts this tendency. Unstated here, but usually found in the body copy of the brochure, is whether the ballast is lead or iron (lead is preferable because it is noncorrosive and denser, but makes the boat more expensive). More lead weight can be put in the same amount of space. Also, one should know whether it is "inside" or "outside" ballast. In other words, is it placed inside the molded fiberglass hull or is it bolted beneath the hull?

The "displacement" is the total weight of the boat. If water were solid and the boat lifted out of it, a hole would be left. The weight of the water needed to fill that hole is equal to the boat's displacement. The heavier the boat, the bigger the "hole" it makes in the water. This means it has to push more water aside to move through the water, and more force is needed. It's like a snowplow which needs much more power to push aside snow that's three feet deep than snow that's two feet deep. So given two boats the same size, if one is heavier, the slower that boat will go.

The ballast and the displacement of the boat are often compared to help judge the boat's stability. The higher the ballast/displacement ratio, the better the stability. For instance, the total displacement of the Hunter Legend 43 in Figure 1 is 23,000 pounds and it has ballast in its keel totaling 7,600 pounds, so it has a 33% ballast/displacement ratio. Anywhere from 30% to 40% is reasonable for a cruising boat. A steel hull may have an even lower ratio, but still be very "stiff" (stable).

One other ratio we should mention because sailors use the term all the time is "aspect ratio." It can be used in referring to the keel, the rudder, or the sails. It is the relationship of the height of the item to its breadth. A tall and narrow sail, keel, or rudder is said to have a high aspect ratio, but if the shape is short and squat, it has a low aspect ratio. For the novice, it is sufficient to know that a high-aspect ratio sail is more efficient upwind and a low-aspect-ratio sail (long boom and short mast) is better with the wind pushing from behind.

Rigging Terms

Anyone who has seen a good pirate movie is aware that the old sailing ships were a jumble of ropes and wire to hold the masts upright, to raise and lower the sails, to control the position of the sails to the wind, and to swing around with a knife clenched in your teeth. Modern sailboats also have such rigging

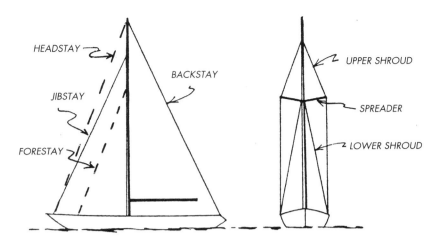

Fig. 4. Standing rigging.

(see Figure 4). The wires that hold up the mast are called "standing rigging." "Stays" are the standing rigging that keep the mast from falling fore and aft (toward the bow or the stern). The "backstay" runs from the masthead (the top of the mast) down to the deck at the middle of the stern. The "headstay" goes from the masthead to the bow. If it attaches a short distance from the top of the mast and runs down at the bow it's called a "jibstay," and if it runs to the deck midway between the bow and the mast it's called a "forestay." Many sailors use these terms interchangeably and aren't careful about the distinction between them.

"Shrouds" are also part of the standing rigging that hold the mast upright. They are wires that keep the mast from falling over the side of the boat. The upper shrouds lead from the edge of the deck to approximately the same level of attachment on the mast as the jibstay. In order to spread the angle these shrouds make with the mast and increase their effective support, most sailboats have metal tubes or wooden struts called "spreaders" on either side of the mast, as shown in Figure 4. The upper shrouds pass through the ends of the spreaders and the compression load on the spreaders bends the mast at this point of attachment. "Lower shrouds" are attached to the mast to counteract this bend. Since these are attached lower down the mast, the angle is wider and additional spreaders are not necessary.

"Running rigging" refers to all other wire and line (most ropes aboard a sailboat are called "lines"). The lines that raise and lower the sails are called "halyards" while those that adjust the position of the sails to the wind are called "sheets." Sheets and halyards take the name of the sail to which they're attached. Thus the *main* halyard raises and lowers the *mainsail* (pronounced mains'l) and *jib sheets* adjust the "trim" of the *jib.* The "trim" of a sail is its position in relation to the wind at any given point in time. However, to "trim" a jib is to pull it in, and to "ease" or "start" it is to let it out, using the jib sheet.

Sail Terms

Though there are hundreds of sailing terms you'll learn later as you sail, the basic parts of the hull, rig, and sails are most important to learn first.

An overwhelming percentage of modern sailboats are called sloops, as shown in Photo 1. They have two basic sails flown from one mast: the "jib," forward of the mast, and the mainsail, or simply "main," aft of (behind) the mast. The parts are named as in Figure 5. The leading edge of the sail is called the "luff," the trailing edge is the "leech," and the bottom edge is the "foot." The "head" is the top corner of the sail, the "tack" is the forward lower corner, and the "clew" is the after lower corner. The dotted line in Figure 5 indicates the straight-line direction from head to clew in the mainsail shown. Any material that falls outside (aft) of this line makes the sail convex. This excess material is called "roach." Concave sails, such as many jibs, have no roach. However, they do have a leech, the material between the head and the clew, just as every sail does.

The foot and luff of the mainsail are reinforced by a rope called a "boltrope." This is one of the few ropes on a sailboat that is called a rope, not a line. The boltrope runs inside the groove of the mast and boom of small boats to attach the sail to those spars. On larger boats, sail slides are often sewn onto and around the boltrope.

Whereas the boltrope reinforces the luff and foot of the main, "tabling" reinforces the edge of the leech and keeps it from becoming frayed and unravelled. Tabling is simply a doubled-over and sewn strip of sailcloth, much like

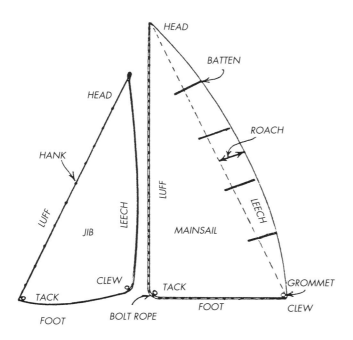

Fig. 5. Parts of the sail.

1. A modern sloop—a single mast with a jib and mainsail.

a hem of a dress. Often a light line runs from the head of the sail down to the clew through the inside of the tabling. This is called a "leech cord" or "pucker string" and, when pulled tight at the clew, reduces leech flutter which occasionally occurs along the trailing edge of the sail.

2. A gaff-rigged schooner.

Because most mainsail leeches are curved (have roach), the excess material will flop over from gravity if unsupported. For this reason, strips of wood or plastic called "battens" are placed in pockets perpendicular to the leech and evenly spaced along it.

3. A modern lateen-rigged Sun-fish sailboat.

4. Lateen-rigged sailboats have been plying the Mediterranean for centuries.

There are a number of other types of mainsails. We've been describing the modern triangular sail. A more traditional sail is the quadrilateral gaff-rigged mainsail, shown in Photo 2. Note that a boom holds up the upper edge. The lateen rig, shown in Photos 3 and 4, is found on some of the oldest sailboats in the world still in use, the Arabian dhows, as well as modern "board boats" like the Sunfish in Photo 3.

Sail Care

Sails power the sailboat. Just as an engine needs care and maintenance, so do sails. They are made of synthetic materials that have very little stretch. A sail-maker sews a particular shape into a sail and doesn't want it to stretch out of shape under the pressure of the wind. If the sail has to have any stretch, the sailmaker wants it to be minimal and predictable. Everyday sail care includes keeping the sails out of the sunlight when not in use. The ultraviolet rays of the sun tend to deteriorate the cloth gradually. Sails should be washed with a mild soap occasionally to get salt and dirt out.

5. Lay the foot of the mainsail on the deck (or on ground ashore) and fold over the window so it will not be creased.

6. Place one hand on the mainsail (inboard side).

7. Pull a fold of the sail over the inboard hand.

8. Continue folding until reaching the head of the sail.

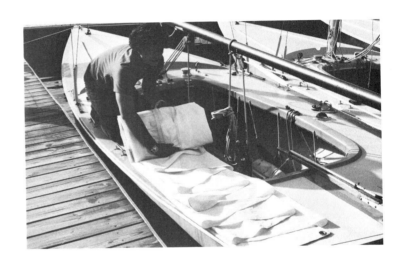

9. Roll the mainsail from the tack toward the clew, so the clew is outside.

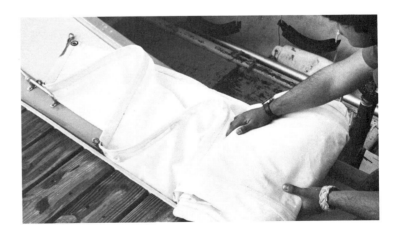

10. Fold the jib in the same fashion, but roll it toward the tack, as shown, since the tack is used first.

When sails are put away after use, some sailors just stuff them into their sailbags. This practice breaks down the filler with which the cloth is treated for reducing porosity and stretch. Thus, the effective life of the sail is reduced. Further, stuffing the sails wrinkles them. It may take as long as an hour of sailing to smooth the wrinkles out. Wrinkles make the sail smaller, a disadvantage in racing. They also disrupt the airflow over the surface of the sail, which reduces its effectiveness as an airfoil.

For these reasons it is a good idea to fold or roll small sails after use. Folding is accomplished by laying the foot of the sail on a flat surface with a crew member at each end. Place a hand on the sail a few feet up the luff and leech respectively, grab the sail even higher up with the other hand, and make a fold of the cloth over the lower hand. Do this continually, accordion-style, until you reach the head of the sail. Then roll the sail up and place it in the sailbag. The clew should be on the outside of the roll for the mainsail, and the tack should be on the outside of the roll for the jib, as these corners are attached first when the sail is next used. A side benefit is that folding results in a smaller, neater package for storing and saves space—a scarce commodity on a sailboat. Follow the steps shown in Photos 5–10.

• 2 •

Starting Out

The first sail you take may hook you for life on sailing. On the other hand, it may make you want never to sail again. So much depends on who you do it with and how pleasant the weather is. Start out with a patient, experienced sailor on a warm, not too breezy day.

Racing skippers may "dry sail" their boats. They store the boat out of the water so slime and seaweed won't grow on the bottom and slow it down. They launch it by trailer or hoist each time they sail. Since even fiberglass boats absorb water, keeping the boat ashore also keeps it lighter and, therefore, faster. Nonracing skippers may also keep their boats on trailers if mooring or docking facilities are unprotected, unavailable, or inadequate.

The Dinghy Ride

If the sailboat is moored (a mooring is a permanent heavy anchor, that isn't picked up when you go sailing and is marked by a buoy), then you have to go out to it in a dinghy. When you step into the dinghy, always step into the middle of the boat and not on the seat. The lower you get your weight in the dinghy, the less tippy it becomes, so sit down before the next person boards. Adjust the fore and aft trim of the boat so it's either level or "down by the stern" (more weight aft), but never "down by the bow" (more weight forward). The "trim" of the boat is the relationship of its design waterline painted on the hull and the actual waterline. The person rowing may ask you to "trim up the boat," which usually means that there is too much weight on one side, making it difficult to row. You are then expected to shift your weight toward the other side so that the dinghy is level.

Never overload a dinghy. Many wintertime drownings have been documented as resulting from overladen dinghies. If there isn't sufficient freeboard, the distance from the edge of the deck to the water, waves can splash into the boat. A large amount of water coming aboard over the side is called "shipping" water, and will cause the boat to become even heavier. The freeboard becomes less as the boat sinks deeper in the water and waves break over the side with more and more frequency until the dinghy swamps (fills up).

Getting Aboard

If you are going sailing on a small centerboard sailboat, be careful not to tip it over when you step aboard. Step in the middle of the cockpit and lower the centerboard immediately for stability. The centerboard is usually stored in the "up" position in a housing called the "centerboard trunk" so seaweed won't grow on it. The centerboard is a metal or wood plate that rotates downward on a pin axis at its forward end. Don't confuse it with a daggerboard, which doesn't pivot but raises and lowers vertically.

Most centerboards are quite lightweight so they can be raised and lowered easily. Therefore, they do little to enhance stability as does a keel (a heavy, fixed weight well below the water surface). When lowered, the centerboard improves stability a little but, more importantly, slows the rolling motion of the boat. If you step to one side of the boat, it won't tip so fast and you can regain your balance before the boat capsizes.

11. Getting aboard from a dinghy is the same for a cruising boat as for a small boat: hold the bow and only one person stands up at a time.

The reason for stepping into the cockpit rather than forward on the deck is again one of stability. Many small sailboats have a narrow, V-shaped bow and a reasonably flat hull aft. By stepping in the bow you push the V-ed portion deeper and raise the flat, stable part out of the water, so the boat tips over.

A keelboat is easier to board because you don't have to worry about capsizing it. When the launch or dinghy is alongside, someone should hold onto the moored boat while others are boarding. A common mistake is for the passenger in the bow to get off first and let the bows drift apart. He or she should be the last off, holding the dinghy next to the sailboat for the others, or should get aboard the sailboat and hold the bow of the launch or dinghy in with the "painter" (the tow line tied to the dinghy's bow), as in Photo 11. When getting aboard, be careful to avoid having your fingers mashed between the launch and the sailboat. If the sailboat has high sides, the safest way to board, particularly on a rough day, is to turn around, sit on the deck, and then swing your legs aboard.

Getting Underway

If you haven't learned the parts of the sail yet, refer back to Figure 5 for the terms that follow. After taking the mainsail out of its bag, locate the clew. If the sail was bagged properly, the clew should be on the outside. The boom will probably have a groove through which the foot of the sail is run. Starting near the mast, one person feeds the foot of the sail into the groove while another pulls the clew out to the end of the boom. A pin or shackle secures the tack corner, an "outhaul" is attached to the clew, and the foot may then be stretched out tight by pulling on the outhaul line and securing it (cleating it).

Battens are placed in the batten pockets. They should fit snugly so they can't pop out. Starting at the tack, trace the entire luff of the sail to make sure that there are no twists. The same results can be obtained by following along the leech of the sail, starting at the clew, as you put in the battens. Attach the main halyard to the head of the sail, looking "aloft" (up) first to make sure the halyard isn't "fouled" (twisted) around a spreader or shroud. A small boat's mast will probably have a groove, so one person will have to feed the luff into the groove as another hauls the sail up. But first, let's get the jib ready.

Always attach the tack corner of the jib first. With practice you'll be able to recognize the tack by its shape since it's often the widest of the corners. A second identifying factor is the sailmaker's label, which is always located near the tack if the boat is going to be used for racing. This is a rule of the International Sailing Federation, the governing body of sailboat racing, and it's prudent for sailmakers to put their label at the tack so the sail can always be used for racing if the owner desires. Another way to determine the tack is to look at the jib hanks or snaps. They usually attach to the jibstay for right-handed people with the opening of the snap normally on the left. So, just by looking at one hank you can tell which way to follow along the luff to the tack.

Further, a good crew will "bag" a jib (put it away in a sailbag) leaving the tack at the top of the bag since it has to be used first the next time. And if you want to be sure you don't make an embarrassing mistake, just write "tack" at the proper corner.

After attaching the tack, start snapping on the hanks from the lowest one upward. It's awkward and unwieldy to start hanking at the head of the sail because you have to hold up the hanks, and with them a lot of sailcloth, while you snap on the ones underneath. Moreover, the sail must be kept low to avoid being blown overboard by the wind. For best control, the sail should be led forward through the legs of the person hanking on the sail.

Next, we tie the jib sheets to the clew of the jib and lead them through the blocks (pulleys) on either side of the boat. The two jib sheets adjust the trim of the jib in and out, and the blocks they run through are called jib "leads." Only one jib sheet is in use at a time. A knot is tied in the end so the sheet won't run out through the block when it is let go. Knots for this purpose, which can be easily untied after use, are the "figure-eight"' knot shown in Photos 12–14, and the "stop" knot shown in Photos 15 and 16. (Of the two,

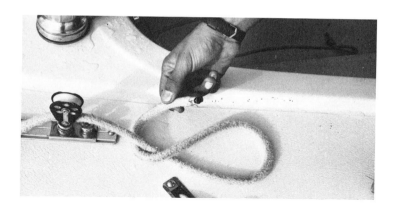

12. Pass the free end of the jib sheet under the standing part (attached to the jib), forming a loop.

13. Pass the free end down through the loop from above.

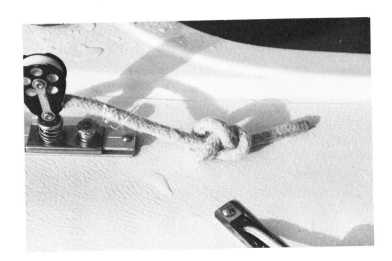

14. Pull tight for a completed figure-eight knot.

15. To make a stopknot, pass the jib sheet twice around your hand, with the free end on the outside. Then cross the end to the inside and pass it under the loops toward your fingertips.

16. Pull the stopknot tight, as shown.

I prefer the latter. It has less chance of shaking out.) After attaching the jib halyard to the head of the sail, the jib is ready to be hoisted. Remember that each corner of every sail must be secured or have something attached to it.

Always raise the mainsail first in any size boat. It keeps the boat headed into the wind like a weather vane, whereas a jib will fill with wind and blow the bow sideways if it's raised first. If the boat is not headed directly into the wind, the mainsail will push against the rigging and bind in the mast groove, making it extremely difficult to raise.

Another reason for raising the jib last is that it makes a dreadful commotion on a windy day. The jib flails around, causing the jib sheets to get tangled, the sailcloth to become fatigued, and the leech of the sail to be battered against the mast and rigging.

It's very important to make sure that all sheets are completely loose when raising sails. This allows the sails to line up with the wind direction rather than fill with air. Lines that hold the main boom down, such as the downhaul, cunningham, and boom vang, must also be released to allow the mainsail to be raised to its full extent. It is helpful for a crew member to hold the after end of the boom up in the air to make it easier to hoist the sail. Otherwise, the person hoisting the sail is pulling up the boom with the leech of the sail.

Dropping the Mooring

Once the sails are up, one would expect that leaving a mooring should be a very simple matter: just let go and you're underway. Not so. Until the boat is moving forward or backward and water is flowing past the rudder, there is no way of steering a boat with a rudder. The boat is "in irons" or "in stays," headed directly into the wind and motionless. Leaving the mooring isn't the only time this happens. Sometimes a skipper attempts to change tacks by turning the boat into the wind and sea direction. If the boat doesn't have enough forward momentum at the time, it can be stopped by a wave and loses "steerageway." It is "in irons," which is a common occurrence with catamarans. When the boat is "dead in the water," the rudder is useless because there is no water flow past it to be deflected.

Since the boat is headed directly into the wind when this happens, the sails are shaking, "luffing." It is necessary to fill the sails with wind in order to gain forward motion and steerageway. This happens when the boat is pointing about 45° from the wind direction. Though the sails aren't filling normally, we can force them out against the wind manually and initiate a turn away from the wind. This is called "backing" the sail. By forcing the jib out to port as in Figure 6a and Photo 17, the wind pushes the bow to starboard. As soon as the boat is heading 45° from the wind direction, we release the jib, it comes across the boat, and we trim it in on the starboard side. The boat is now in position 2 and the sails fill normally.

17. Backing the jib to port will force the bow to starboard.

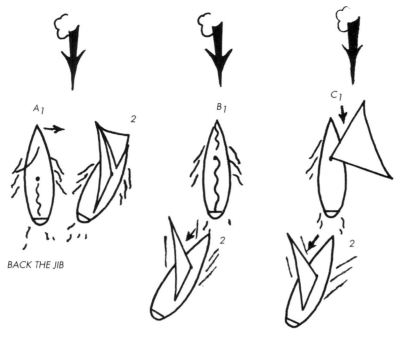

BACK THE JIB

DRIFT BACKWARDS

BACK THE MAINSAIL

Fig. 6. Getting out of "irons."

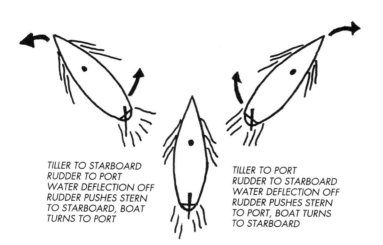

TILLER TO STARBOARD
RUDDER TO PORT
WATER DEFLECTION OFF
RUDDER PUSHES STERN
TO STARBOARD, BOAT
TURNS TO PORT

TILLER TO PORT
RUDDER TO STARBOARD
WATER DEFLECTION OFF
RUDDER PUSHES STERN
TO PORT, BOAT TURNS
TO STARBOARD

Fig. 7. Use of the rudder and tiller.

The same result may be obtained by other, less effective methods. If the boat is drifting backward as in Figure 6b, water is flowing past the rudder and the tiller may be used to turn the boat. Put the tiller to starboard (the reverse of what you'd do if the boat were moving forward) and the stern will steer to port, as in position 2 of Figure 6b. Then trim the sails, straighten the rudder, and you'll start sailing forward.

Some small boats have no jibs. If you find yourself in irons, you must back the mainsail against the wind. Usually, depending on the location of the mast, this pushes your stern in the opposite direction, as in Figure 6c. Reversing the rudder as described above will also help turn a boat that has no jib.

It's very important to be able to control the boat when it is in irons. If the boat turns in the wrong direction in a crowded anchorage, it could easily hit another boat before the skipper has enough steerageway to avoid it. The standard procedure when leaving a mooring is for one crew member to untie the mooring line, but to hold onto it and even pull the boat forward if possible to obtain steerageway for the skipper, while another crew member backs the jib. When the bow is definitely swinging in the desired direction, the mooring is released.

The effectiveness of the rudder increases with the speed of the boat through the water. The boat pivots around a point near its center. Water deflected by the rudder pushes the stern in one direction and the bow turns in the other. Figure 7 shows how this works.

3

The Points of Sailing

The title of this chapter may sound strange to the novice. The "points" of sailing are the terms that describe the direction the boat is sailing in relation to the wind. There are three basic points of sailing: closehauled, reaching, and running—about 45°, 90°, and 180° from the wind direction, respectively.

The problem for the beginner is to know where the wind is blowing from. The wind is invisible and, though the novice may understand from books or the classroom just when a boat is closehauled or on a reach or a run because the wind direction is a nice, clean black line in a diagram, he or she may be hard-pressed to do the same when sailing. We usually ask students the first time out to point toward the wind. Often they are as much as 90° off. Turning the boat tends to confuse them even further. Thus, it becomes imperative that novices learn how to determine the wind direction if they are ever to learn what point of sailing they are on. We urge them to point at the wind every time before making a maneuver the first time out. If they know the direction of the wind before the boat is turned, they will understand what point of sailing they'll end up on.

As an aid, we tie pieces of wool to the shrouds to indicate wind direction. Fuzzy angora wool is the most sensitive in light air, but is not as good as other synthetics when wet. Red is a good, visible color to use. All the novice has to do is look at these wool "telltales," point parallel to them, and there's the wind direction.

Another aid is the "masthead fly." This is a weather-vane type of device at the top of the mast where the airflow is unaffected by other influences. It should be extremely light, because any weight at the top of the mast will aggravate heeling and pitching of the boat. Also, lightness improves the masthead fly's sensitivity in light air and reduces its moment of inertia. In other words, we want it to start to swing to the new wind direction immediately and to stop quickly, rather than swing past the wind direction because of inertia. The test of a masthead fly is to hold it horizontally. If it stays level, as in Photo 18, it's well balanced.

Once the wind direction is clear to the novice, half the battle is won. Sailing is like riding a bicycle—once you've got it, you'll never forget it.

Figure 8 shows the various points of sailing. Note that you can be on a beam reach with the wind coming directly across the side of the boat and yet be sailing in either of two completely opposite directions. In order to further describe the sailing direction of a boat, we say she is on either a port tack or

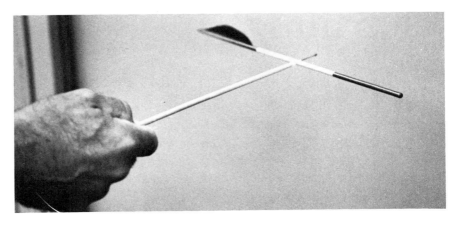

18. A good masthead fly should balance level when placed in a horizontal position.

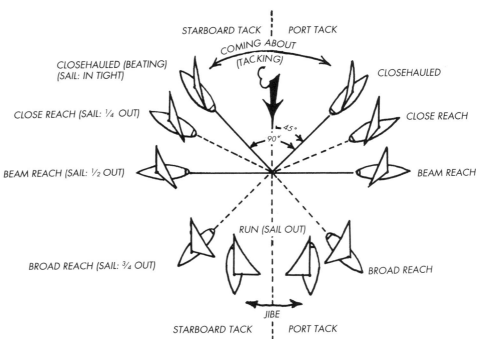

Fig. 8. The points of sailing.

a starboard tack. A boat is always on one or the other tack unless she is in the process of changing tacks. If the wind is blowing over the port side of the boat she is on a port tack, and if over the starboard side she is on a starboard tack. Many people remember it that way, but then tend to be confused when the wind is blowing over the stern of the boat, as on a run in Figure 8. Instead, just remember that the legal definition of a tack is the side opposite to the one which the main boom is on. If the mainsail is on the starboard side of the boat, she is on a port tack. Though it's obvious which side the boom is on when you're reaching or running, because the sails are eased out, it may not be as clear when you're closehauled and the sails are trimmed in tight. In that case, just imagine which side the boom is on if the sail is eased. Another valid way of remembering what tack you're on is by observing which side of the mainsail is "filled" with wind. If the port side of the sail is "filled," you are on a port tack.

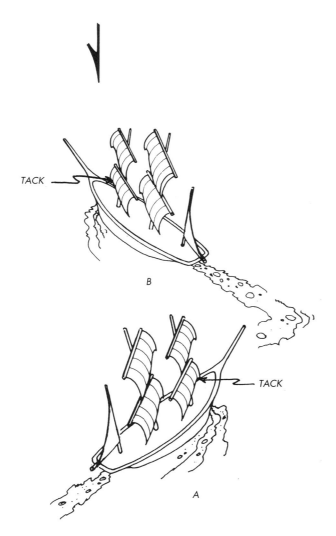

Fig. 9. On a square sail, the forward lower corner is called the "tack."

By now you may have noticed we have been using the word "tack" in three ways. First, the forward lower corner of a sail is called the tack.

Second, a sailboat is either on a port or starboard tack, and, third, a sailboat changing from one tack to the other (through the wind) is in the process of tacking. The relationship between these three usages developed long ago in the days of square-rigged ships. The forward lower corner of the square sail on the windward side was called the tack. In position A of Figure 9, the wind is coming over the port side of the ship, the port half of each square sail is forward, so the port lower corner becomes the tack and the ship is on the port tack. In position B, the wind is coming over the starboard side of the ship, the square sails have been pivoted so the wind can flow over them, and the starboard half of the sail is facing forward. Thus the starboard lower corner becomes the tack and the ship is on the starboard tack. In the process, the ship has changed tacks, a term which has been shortened to "the ship has tacked."

For the reader's interest, the difference between a ship and a boat is that the latter may be carried aboard the former. Don't make the mistake of looking at a yacht and saying, "That's a beautiful ship."

Reaching

The first time out sailing, it is best for the novice to practice sailing on a beam reach (Figure 10). It's a pleasant and forgiving point of sailing—pleasant because the boat doesn't heel (lean over) much, and forgiving in that the helmsman steering the boat can wander far off course without being concerned with an accidental tack or jibe. Practice making a few sharp turns so it will be clear which way the boat turns as the tiller is pushed or pulled.

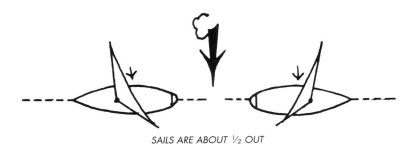

SAILS ARE ABOUT ½ OUT

Fig. 10. Beam reaching (wind is at right angles to the boat).

Point at the wind before making a change in course so you become continually aware of its direction in relation to the boat's heading. If your point of sailing is a beam reach, you will be pointing at the wind directly across the boat, 90° to the boat's heading. On a beam reach, the wool telltales on the shrouds will be flying with their tails pointing toward the mast.

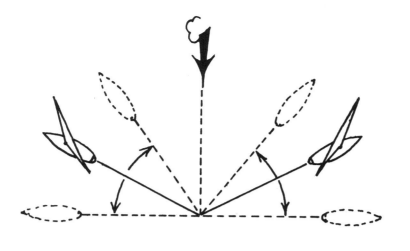

Fig. 11. Close reaching is any heading between closehauled and a beam reach (wind is slightly forward of abeam).

SAILS ARE ABOUT ¾ OUT

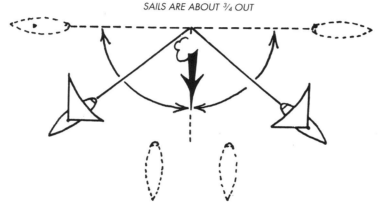

Fig. 12. Broad reaching is any heading between a beam reach and a run (wind is aft of abeam).

Now, after pointing your arm at the wind, turn the boat a little in the direction you're pointing. The boat will be sailing on a "close reach" (Figure 11), or closer to the wind than before. (If you sail further away from the wind, as in Figure 12, you will be sailing on a "broad reach.") The sails will start to flap (luff) and you will have to trim (pull) them in to keep them full of wind. Imagine the sail as a flag flying freely in the breeze. Seize the tail, pull it across the wind, and the flag will fill with wind and stop flapping. As you release the tail of the flag slowly (just as you ease a sail out), the material near the flagpole will start to flutter first because that part will line up with the wind first. So, as you sail along on a reach, the test for proper sail adjustment—"sail trim"—is to ease the sail until it luffs along the leading edge, which is called the "luff" of the sail, and then trim it back in until the luff stops. Note we have used the word "trim" in three ways so far. To trim a sail is to pull it in. Sail trim is the relation of the sail to the wind and may necessitate either trimming or easing to get it right, and the trim of a boat or dinghy is the relation of its waterline to the water in simple terms.

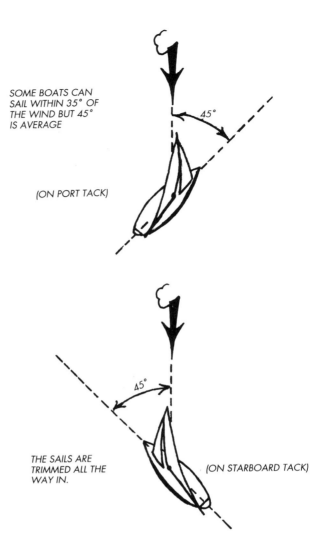

SOME BOATS CAN
SAIL WITHIN 35° OF
THE WIND BUT 45°
IS AVERAGE

45°

(ON PORT TACK)

45°

THE SAILS ARE
TRIMMED ALL THE
WAY IN.

(ON STARBOARD TACK)

Fig. 13. Closehauled (as close to the wind direction as the boat can sail).

Closehauled

By continuing to turn the boat in the direction of the wind, the direction you were pointing in the previous example, you will have to keep on trimming in the sails as they luff. Eventually you won't be able to trim the sails any tighter, because they will be practically in the center of the boat. You are now sailing "closehauled" (Figure 13). It may help you to remember this point of sailing by the fact that your sails have been "hauled" in "close" to the center of the boat. You are unable to sail closer to the wind without luffing the sails, and you are unable to trim the sails in any tighter if they do luff. Whereas on other points of sail, such as a reach, the crew trims the sail if it luffs and the helmsman just steers a straight course, when closehauled it is up to the

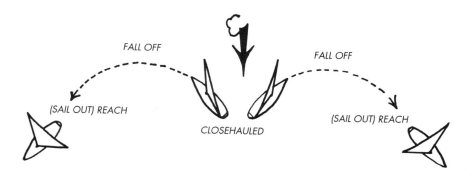

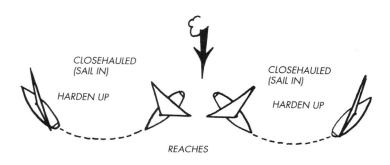

Fig. 14. Changing direction without tacking or jibing is called "falling off" where the turn is away from the wind.

Fig. 15. A turn toward the wind is called "hardening up."

helmsman to adjust the course to keep the sails full. If they luff, he must head further away from the wind to get them full again. This is called "falling off" or "heading down" (Figure 14). To change course toward the wind is called "hardening up" or "coming up" (Figure 15). Any phrase that uses the words "up" or "high" in relation to the course being sailed implies being too close to the wind. "You're too high" told to the helmsman means not to sail so close to the wind because the sails are about to luff. "You're pinching" means the same thing. Phrases with the words "down" or "low" mean the opposite— the boat is being sailed too far away from the wind direction, more broad-side to it.

The point where the sails cannot be trimmed tighter and the helmsman cannot point the boat higher into the wind without luffing the sails varies from boat to boat. Most boats head within 45° of the wind, but some can "point" even higher. Those that can sail within 30° to 35° to the wind (very unusual) are said to be "close-winded." One might ask how we can express in degrees the angle that a boat can sail to the wind. The compass aboard the boat helps give the answer. Just sail closehauled on one tack and record your heading. Tack and record your heading on the new tack. Then split the dif-ference and we have both the wind direction and the number of degrees you are sailing from the wind. For instance, you are sailing due north on the star-board tack. After tacking, you find that a closehauled port tack is taking you due east. You have tacked in 90°. We assume the wind splits right down the middle of the two tacks and that you were sailing 45° from the wind on one tack and the same angle on the other. If the two headings were 80° apart, your boat can point within 40° of the wind when closehauled.

Running

Of the three points of sailing—closehauled, reaching, and running—the last was probably the way sailing got started. Some caveman probably stood on a log in the water and drifted downwind. Then he discovered that by spreading his arms he could go faster. Holding up an animal hide helped even more, but was tiring so he erected a pole to help. Voila! The first sailboat capable of sailing dead downwind only—and the point of sail we now know as the "run" was originated.

Note in Figure 8 that the relation of the main boom to the wind is just about the same on all points of sailing. In effect, you are holding the boom in one position and rotating the boat under it. As we fall off to a run, we ease the sails out to maintain the sails roughly in the same position relative to the wind. We reach a point, as in Figure 16, where the boom is resting against the shrouds that hold up the mast and can't be eased out any more. If we want to turn the boat further, we must swing the boom over to the other side of the boat.

Whenever the boom swings from one side of the boat to the other, crossing the centerline (an imaginary line from the bow to the center of the stern), the boat has changed tacks (starboard tack to port tack or vice versa). When sailing downwind, this change of tacks is called a "jibe." The boat turns away from the wind direction and the wind comes over the stern as the boom swings across. Until you actually change tacks, you are not jibing. Changing course downwind is just "falling off" until the boom crosses the centerline of the boat. Then you are jibing.

As in a number of cases in sailing, there are two commands involved in jibing, the command of preparation and the command of execution. The first warns the crew that a maneuver is imminent and to get ready for it. The skipper says, "Prepare to jibe." Whereupon the crew starts to trim in the mainsheet so that the boom won't have to travel so far as it swings across. If this isn't done and the wind gets on the wrong side of the sail, as eventually must happen if you continue to turn the boat (observe how the sail in position B of Figure 16 is pointing more into the wind), the boom will fly right across the boat and out to the other shrouds. It builds up quite some speed as it goes, particularly in a heavy wind, and crew members have been hurt badly on larger boats in such an accidental jibe. By trimming it in first, the crew keeps the boom under control. As the helmsman sees the boom nearing the middle of

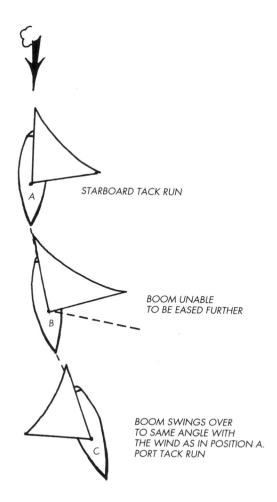

STARBOARD TACK RUN

BOOM UNABLE
TO BE EASED FURTHER

BOOM SWINGS OVER
TO SAME ANGLE WITH
THE WIND AS IN POSITION A.
PORT TACK RUN

Fig. 16. Running (sailing before the wind).

the boat, he gives the command of execution, "Jibe ho," and turns the boat. When the boom crosses the centerline of the boat and the sail is full, the crew eases it out quickly to avoid heeling excessively. On smaller boats or those with experienced crews who know exactly when the jibe will happen, the boom is not trimmed in first, but allowed to swing the full arc (often being pulled to make it swing faster), but this is not a safe method for beginners until they know their abilities and their boat better.

The first-time sailor often gets confused by which way to put the tiller in order to jibe. The mainsail has been eased and is out over the water on the leeward side. Just turn the bow of the boat toward the mainsail and you can't go wrong. Figure 16 shows this being done.

The accidental jibe we mentioned above shouldn't happen if the skipper and crew are aware of the warnings preliminary to it. Figure 17 shows a port tack sailboat on a broad reach. The wind is on the "quarter," or about 45° from dead downwind. The jib is full, which is usually the sign that the boat

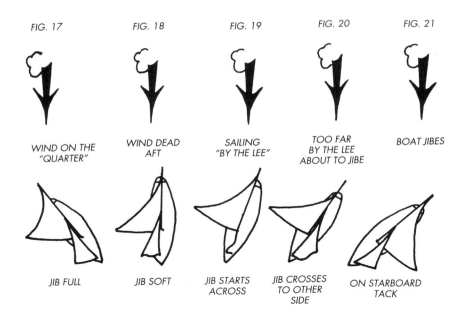

FIG. 17   FIG. 18   FIG. 19   FIG. 20   FIG. 21

WIND ON THE "QUARTER"   WIND DEAD AFT   SAILING "BY THE LEE"   TOO FAR BY THE LEE ABOUT TO JIBE   BOAT JIBES

JIB FULL   JIB SOFT   JIB STARTS ACROSS   JIB CROSSES TO OTHER SIDE   ON STARBOARD TACK

Fig. 17–21. Sailing "by the lee" can cause an inadvertent jibe.

is on a reach rather than a run. As the boat falls off to a run (Figure 18), the jib goes "soft." The mainsail is catching the wind and interfering with the wind's reaching the jib. The jib is said to be "blanketed." There is no fear of a jibe as long as the wind remains dead aft and the helmsman steers a straight course. But if the boat turns further, as in Figure 19, the wind and the main boom are on the same side of the boat. This is called sailing "by the lee." The jib starts to come out from behind the mainsail and cross to the other side of the boat. This is your first warning that a jibe is imminent. Sailing by the lee means that the wind is hitting the leeward side of the boat, which appears to be a contradiction in terms because the windward of anything is that which the wind hits first

Imagine a balloon being carried by the wind just above the waves. The side of the boat it hits first is the windward side; the other is the leeward (pronounced "loo-ward") side. If there are two boats out sailing, the balloon would hit the windward boat first and then fly down to the leeward boat. The reason for the contradiction in the case of sailing by the lee is that the right-of-way rules define the leeward side as that side over which the main boom is carried. A leeward boat has right-of-way over a windward boat, the former being on the latter's leeward side. Since the boom is far more visible than the wind, it is used for the legal definition of the leeward side, even if the boat is by the lee. Of two boats, one beating to windward and one running downwind, the wind hits the latter first so it is the windward boat. The other is the leeward boat, as in Figure 22. Again, the right-of-way rules make it necessary to remember this. Sailors who have been on the water for years sometimes get this confused.

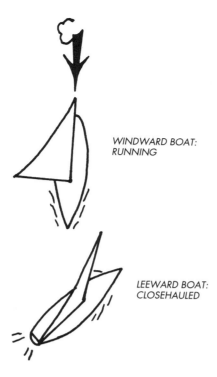

WINDWARD BOAT:
RUNNING

LEEWARD BOAT:
CLOSEHAULED

Fig. 22. The windward of anything is that which the wind hits
first.

If you sail too far by the lee (Figure 20), the wind will fill the other side of the sail and throw it across the boat (Figure 21). The boom will raise up in the air as it follows the sail over, unless it's being held down by a boom vang, a block-and-tackle arrangement that holds the boom down when reaching and running for better sail efficiency. Sailboats of older design used to have short masts (so the backstays were at a low angle) and long booms. A flying jibe, as an accidental jibe is often called, caused the boom to raise up and catch on the backstay. Such an occurrence was called a "goosewing" jibe and was dreaded by all sailors. If the backstay didn't break, the boom was hung up out of reach with the sail forcing the boat over on its side. There was no way to ease the sail and spill the wind out of it, so the boat was out of control and helpless. A traditional fear of jibing has developed even though on modern sailboats, with their short booms and tall masts, it is impossible to catch the boom on the backstay.

Many people, when just learning how to sail, have picked up this deathly fear of jibing. In fact, people have told me, "I know nothing about sailing, but I've heard you should never jibe." This means that rumors are being spread among novice sailors that jibing is something you do only if you can't do anything else. Yet it is a fast, safe way of changing tacks and should never be feared unless the boat is out of control.

Many beginners make the mistake of turning the boat too far in a jibe. It's difficult for them to realize that a jibe is not like a tack, and you don't have to turn the boat 90°. One way to cure beginners of this notion is to head the boat dead downwind. Then swing the boom across the boat, first to one side, then the other, without changing course one iota, assuming the air is light. This points out to the novice helmsman that a large course change is unnecessary in a jibe.

A second basic problem for the novice helmsman is that in heavier air (stronger wind) the boat wants to keep turning and head up into the wind after jibing. While the boom is swinging there's no problem, but when the boom and sail suddenly stop and present a "wall" to the wind rather than flowing with it, the forces build up tremendously. Since most of the forces are out over the water, because the sail is eased way out on a run, the tendency is for the boat to round up into the wind. The novice who has jibed a few times in heavy air and has rounded up into the wind unintentionally learns instinctively to counteract the turning by putting the tiller to windward just as the boom reaches the end of its travel. The reasons are explained later, in the section on balance.

The heavier the wind, the more pronounced must be this tiller movement. It's as if the helmsman were steering the boat to jibe again even before the first one is completed. But, in fact, the boat will sail straight ahead rather than rounding up.

Always remember—the first sign that you're about to jibe is the jib coming across the boat. Having jibed to a starboard tack, as in Figure 21, we can sail any course up to closehauled simply by hardening up.

4

Controlling Your Sailboat

Beating

By now the reader should understand that it's impossible for a sailboat to sail directly upwind to a destination. We can't sail much closer to the wind than 45° so we must zigzag, first on one tack, then on the other, to get there. Each turn we make from port tack to starboard tack and vice versa with the bow passing through the "eye of the wind" (the bow heading at the point of the wind arrow in our diagrams) is called a "tack" or "coming about." A number of these tacks made to sail upwind is called a "beat" or "beating to windward." Figure 23 shows a sailboat beating.

As with jibing, it is of utmost necessity to have proper communication when tacking. The command of preparation is "Stand by to come about," but "Ready about" is more commonly used, since it's shorter. After a crew gets to know a skipper's idiosyncrasies, almost anything the skipper grunts out is enough, such as "Let's do it, heroes." Basically, it tells the crew that they must uncleat the jib sheet so that it can be released quickly when the boat turns. They should also prepare to trim in the other jib sheet. The mainsail, of prime concern during a jibe, is almost totally disregarded when tacking. It has been trimmed in as tight as possible and will swing a few inches across the center-line of the boat unattended as you tack. It is good policy in small boats on windy days to hold onto the mainsheet so it can be released if necessary after a tack or while sailing in crowded areas. A gust of wind can capsize a center-board boat or can put a keelboat out of control by heeling the boat excessively. By releasing the mainsheet the wind will spill out of the sail, causing it to luff and the boat to straighten up. Another way to reduce the wind force on the

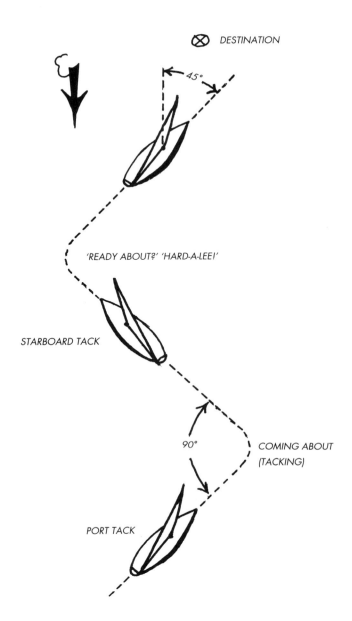

⊗ DESTINATION

45°

'READY ABOUT?' 'HARD-A-LEE!'

STARBOARD TACK

90°

COMING ABOUT
(TACKING)

PORT TACK

Fig. 23. A "beat" is a series of tacks.

sails is to head more into the wind. This is called "feathering" the boat to windward if the sails luff slightly, but in response to a strong gust a full-fledged luff is necessary.

The crew should acknowledge the skipper's command by saying "ready" when they are. Then the skipper will turn the boat, giving the command of execution, "Hard alee!" This term is an abbreviation of "the helm is hard to leeward." In other words, the tiller has been put toward the leeward side of the boat. This turns the boat into the wind. If you point at the wind direction and turn the bow of the boat in that direction, you are tacking (when the bow passes the eye of the wind). "Tack Toward the wind," two *T*s, is a good memory aid.

Certain problems can arise when tacking. If an inexperienced helmsman tries to tack without having enough speed, he may lose momentum midway through the tack because the sails aren't pulling, the rigging and flapping sails are causing a great deal of resistance to forward motion, and the seas are hitting the boat head on. A boat that is stopped midway through a tack and fails to complete it is said to be in irons." As mentioned before, a boat is also in irons when it drops off a mooring. Such a "wayless" boat has no steerageway. Turning the rudder will have no effect. The condition is temporary, because the boat will soon fall off onto one or the other tack. However, unless a crew thinks fast and backs the jib properly, it may fall off on the wrong tack. For instance, perhaps the intention was to tack to avoid hitting a moored boat. If you "miss" the tack (go into irons) and fall unintentionally back on the same tack, you may very well hit the moored boat you were trying to avoid. Your boat will not gain enough steerageway to try another tack until it picks up speed.

Stopping a Sailboat

There are many times when one wants to stop a sailboat intentionally. We mentioned above how a boat can go into irons by accident. Since a sailboat doesn't have brakes like a car or a reverse gear like a motorboat, we must intentionally put it in irons in order to stop it. In other words, we must head it directly into the wind. Just luffing the sails by letting the sheets run free is sufficient to slow the boat down, but will not stop the boat completely. Even when you "shoot" the boat directly into the wind, it will take a while to lose momentum and stop. As shown in Figure 24, the distance the boat travels while it's slowing to a stop is called the distance it "shoots" or "head reaches." In order to be at a complete stop with the bow right next to a mooring buoy, we must estimate how far the boat will shoot and then turn the boat at an imaginary point which is that distance directly downwind of the buoy. We'll call this spot the "turning point." The distance a boat shoots varies greatly with the type of boat and the wind and sea conditions. It is common for the novice to estimate a long distance in strong winds because the boat is sailing fast, and a short distance in light winds when the boat is sailing slowly. Actually, the reverse is true. The stronger the wind, the shorter the shooting distance because the wind resistance of the rigging and flapping sails is so great. Also, seas are apt to be heavier and will stop the boat faster. Heavy keelboats tend to carry their forward motion longer than light centerboarders, so more distance must be allowed for the former.

The angle of approach to the turning point is important. There are two desirable factors: (1) to be able to control your approach speed by luffing or

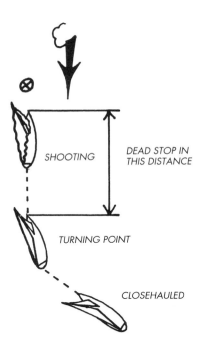

SHOOTING

DEAD STOP IN
THIS DISTANCE

TURNING POINT

CLOSEHAULED

Fig. 24. The only way to come to a dead stop in a sailboat is by shooting into the wind.

trimming the sails, and (2) to be able to control your direction by pointing higher or lower as necessary. The approach that best satisfies these requirements is a reach. If you approach closehauled you can control your speed easily, but if there's a wind shift you may have to pinch or even tack to reach the turning point, so your directional control is limited. A run is even worse. You are unable to slow the boat by easing the mainsail because it is continually filled with air. You can only turn the boat in one direction because the other way will result in a jibe. And it is very difficult to judge where your turning point will be. As the boat is spun around dead into the wind, it will come to an almost immediate stop from the violence of the turn, so the turning point must be almost next to your objective.

On a reach, though, you have both speed control by luffing and trimming the sails and the directional options of heading up or falling off to adjust your approach to the turning point. At the turning point, round up into the wind and let the sails luff completely. Any tension on the jib sheet can cause the jib to back and force the boat over on the other tack. It is best to stay a few degrees (10° to 20°) from being directly into the wind. Then, if you've misjudged your distance and fall short of the mooring, you can trim in the sails, fall off, and continue on for another go-around without getting completely in irons. So adjust the position of your imaginary turning point so the approach will be slightly angled away from any congestion caused by moored boats (see Figure 25).

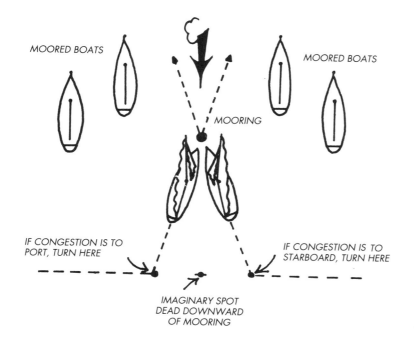

MOORED BOATS

MOORED BOATS

MOORING

IF CONGESTION IS TO PORT, TURN HERE

IF CONGESTION IS TO STARBOARD, TURN HERE

IMAGINARY SPOT DEAD DOWNWARD OF MOORING

Fig. 25. Plan ahead when picking up a mooring so that, if you miss, there will be no moored boats in the way.

19. The owner of this boat may come back to find it capsized (turned over) because he failed to take off the halyard.

There may be a time when there is no option to try again. You are coming in too fast to a dock and must stop in time. Push the boom and the mainsail out against the wind at a right angle to the boat. This acts as a brake and is called "backing the main." It is very effective in slowing the boat.

A mooring pickup in a light wind with a strong current in the opposite direction has to be executed in a completely different manner. Lower the mainsail and sail under jib alone downwind (into the current). Then pick up the mooring buoy and lower the jib. If you try to pick up the mooring in the normal fashion, by shooting into the wind, as soon as the mooring is secure the current will spin the boat around so that it will be heading downwind. The mainsail will be difficult to lower and the boom will be jibing back and forth.

After the sails have been lowered, take them off and fold them. If the boat is going to be used again shortly, the main can be left on the boom, but the halyard should be taken off lest the sail be blown overboard, as in Photo 19. Then, a gust of wind could flip the boat.

Circle of Courses

Now that we've covered the three points of sail—closehauled, reaching, and running—and the two ways of changing tacks—jibing and tacking—let's put it all together in a way that may make more sense to the beginner. By turning the boat so that its wake describes a complete circle, we will pass through all the points of sailing. The sail trim must be changed corresponding to the diagrams in Figure 26 as the boat turns. If you consider the boat as always being on a circle, you can see that it is only a matter of heading toward your desired destination and adjusting your sails accordingly. The only exception is that you must beat to reach a destination directly upwind of you. At all other times you will be sailing on a clockwise or counterclockwise circle, as in Figure 27.

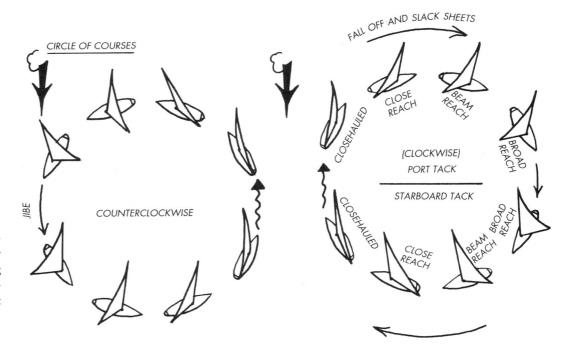

Fig. 26. A sailboat on any point of sailing may be considered on a part of a circle.

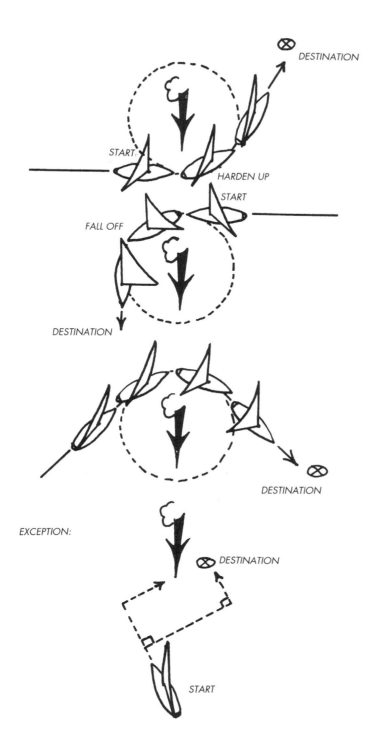

DESTINATION

START

HARDEN UP

START

FALL OFF

DESTINATION

DESTINATION

EXCEPTION:

DESTINATION

START

Fig. 27. Using the circle of courses. To get someplace, just point the bow where you want to go and adjust the sail trim.

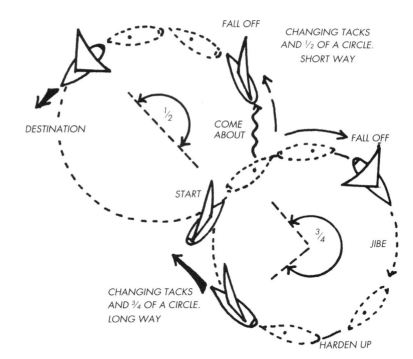

Fig. 28. In most cases, there's a long way and a short way of reaching the destination.

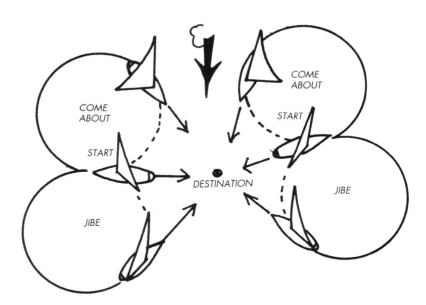

Fig. 29. When the destination is directly behind you, either circle is equally short.

When a tack or a jibe is involved, there is usually a shortest way. Figure 28 shows that if you are at all downwind of your desired destination, a tack is better than a jibe. When the destination is directly behind you, a turn in either direction is equally short. Figure 29 demonstrates this fact.

◆ 5 ◆

The Whys of Sailing

Wind and Sails

It seems a mystery to the person being introduced to sailing for the first time that a sailboat can sail upwind. It's easy to comprehend sailing downwind, with the wind pushing you from behind. Anyone who has been outside on a windy day with an umbrella, as in Figure 30, will have experienced the force with which the umbrella can pull downwind. How, though, does a sailboat move upwind? Part of the answer can be explained again by using the umbrella. If you walk upwind holding the umbrella lightly by the handle, the umbrella seems to lift out of your hand (Figure 31). If you didn't have to keep the umbrella moving forward against the wind, you could let go of the handle and it would float in the air. This phenomenon is caused by the air that is flowing over the curved surface of the umbrella. Airflow produces the lifting effect that makes the umbrella seem to weigh less.

Fig. 30. Downwind, an umbrella pulls you along.

The same principle works with the sails of a sailboat. Try the experiment pictured in Photos 20 and 21. Hold one edge of a sheet of paper against your lower lip so that it hangs down like a bib. Then blow hard, straight ahead across the top of the paper. The paper will rise up as you blow. If the air flows faster over one side of a foil than it does over the other side, the increased velocity in turn reduces the air pressure on that side and produces a suction called "lift." With both the piece of paper and the umbrella, the higher velocity and decreased pressure on the upper side "lift" the objects up.

In the above example, the air is obviously traveling faster on one side of the object than on the other. Why, then, does it work on an airplane wing that is passing through the air presumably at equal speed on both sides? Because

Fig. 31. Upwind, an umbrella tends to lift up out of your hand.

20. Hold the paper against your lower lip.

21. Blow across the top of the paper and the unequal air pressure will cause the paper to rise.

of the curvature of the wing, air flowing over the upper side has to travel further, and therefore faster, than air passing under the wing. It was in 1738 that Daniel Bernoulli discovered the principle that such an increase in velocity means a decrease in atmospheric pressure. In simple terms, this means suction. It is common to diagram this suction as in Figure 32. It acts at right angles to the surface of the sail, and the longest arrows indicate the strongest suction. The higher the velocity of the air flowing on both sides, the greater the suction; and the greater the difference in velocity between the two sides, the greater the suction. Often one resultant force arrow is drawn, as in Figure 33, to indicate the direction and amount of total lift on the sail.

The reason the arrows are different lengths in Figure 32 is because the sail's efficiency as an airfoil varies at different locations. Where the air is

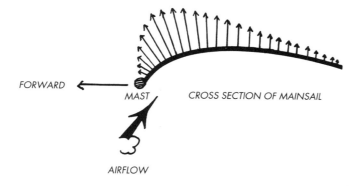

Fig. 32. The forces on a sail (the longest arrows indicate the greatest pull).

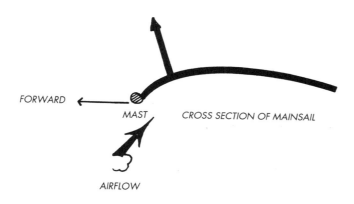

Fig. 33. To make vectoring easier, all the force arrows are combined into one component arrow.

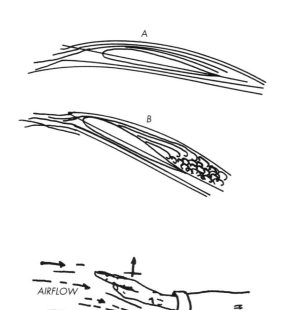

Fig. 34. Cross section of an airplane wing. When the angle is so steep that the air cannot make the turn without separating from the wing, stalling results.

Fig. 35. Hand moves up in opposite direction to air moving down.

flowing smoothly and evenly, the lift is greatest. At the point where the airflow starts to separate from the surface, it becomes turbulent. Burbles develop that reduce the efficiency of the sail and the suction.

Smoothness of the surface helps retain a smooth airflow, but even more important is the angle of attack or "angle of incidence" that the air makes with the airfoil. Figure 34a shows an airplane wing at a low rate of climb, a low angle of attack. The air can flow easily along the wing from the leading edge to the trailing edge. However, increase the angle of attack as in Figure 34b and the air will no longer be able to make the curve without separating and becoming turbulent. When the point of separation has worked well forward, the wing can no longer develop lift and a stall occurs. In an airplane, a stall results in a dramatic loss of altitude. However, a sailboat will just heel more and lose speed.

Other questions arise. What if the airfoil is symmetrical rather than asymmetrical? After all, rudders, keels, hulls, and centerboards of sailboats are all symmetrical, yet they are "lifting" surfaces. It's the angle of attack that helps them develop lift.

Lift, however, is only part of the answer of how a sailboat gets power from its sails. The whole subject is filled with controversy, even after so many years of aerodynamic study, but some of the answer lies in Newton's law: for every action there is an equal and opposite reaction.

Almost everyone has put his or her hand out the window of a moving car with the palm down. When the palm is lined up with the airflow, the hand stays steady. But slant the hand upward so that the airflow hits the palm and the hand goes up (Figure 35). Slant it down so that the wind hits the top and the hand goes down. The slanted hand is redirecting the airflow downward in the first case and upward in the second, and this causes a reaction in the opposite direction.

The sails of a boat do the same thing. The wind comes in at an angle and is bent aft (Figure 36). The reaction to this bending action of the wind is a force that is forward and sideways. Note that I said that the force is forward and sideways. If we could nullify the sideways, all that would remain would be the forward force. And that is the key to the mystery of how a sailboat can sail upwind. There has to be something to resist the tendency of the boat to go sideways, or "make leeway" as it's called.

Fig. 36. Wind direction creates force that is forward and sideways.

Throughout history, many methods have been used. Dutch sailing barges had leeboards that dropped down on either side of the hull to stop sideways movement when the sails were up. Leeboards coming down through the hull, rather than merely attached to the topsides, are found on modern boats such as scows and catamarans. By far the most common method to reduce leeway is the use of centerboards, daggerboards, and keels as described before.

Sail Trim

The objective of almost all sailors is to sail well. Whenever two sailboats are near each other they tend to race. There are optimum trim angles for the sails that make each boat perform at its peak. Unfortunately, the wind isn't visible. If the wind were smoke, we could see it flow past the sails and be able to determine the sail trim that least disrupts the airflow. Smoke visualization tests have been done on models in wind tunnels, so we know the approximate sail trim for maximum efficiency. In recent years sailors have been attaching telltales directly to the sails to show the airflow over them. Such telltales give the most information when used on the jib because there is no mast in front of it to disrupt the airflow. The most practical method is to sew a bright-colored wool strip right through the jib at three or four positions along the length of the luff about 20% and 35% of the distance from luff to leech and aft of the luff. The wool streamers should be from 5" to 12" long, depending on the size of the boat and the distance away from the helmsman. At least the lower ones should be visible to the helmsman in his normal steering position. The streamers should be placed so they cannot touch either a seam or any sail stitching, lest they catch. A relatively hairless type of wool should be used. Angora wool may be best for shroud telltales because it is fuzzy and light, but never should be used as sail streamers.

An easy way to install these streamers in a jib is to thread a sail needle with a long piece of wool. Pass it through the sail and pull it to within six inches of the end on one side of the sail. Cut it off six inches from the other side and tie an overhand knot on each side next to the cloth to keep it from pulling through. With this method you have used only a foot of your wool and don't have to rethread the needle to use it again. Don't be concerned about putting a small hole in the sail. It won't weaken it. Some sailors put tape on each side and pierce through the tape. The tape later starts to peel off and the telltale sticks to it, so don't use tape. Others just tape strips of ribbon to the sails. Again, the tape eventually loses its adhesiveness and the telltales get lost. Moreover, ribbon is more difficult to read correctly. Better yet, have your sailmaker place plastic windows in the sail with streamers on either side.

We have learned that the sail is trimmed properly when it is just about to luff. A tried-and-true rule is to ease the sail until it luffs and then trim it in again until it just stops. The rule is accurate, and was formulated because a luff is easy to see. A stall isn't. A stalled sail looks just the same as one operating at maximum efficiency! The sail is an airfoil and if it is trimmed in too tight the wind will not be able to flow over the lee side of the sail very far before it separates from the surface and becomes turbulent. Then, just as an airplane stalls when it tries to climb too abruptly, the sail loses its lift or effectiveness. With streamers, when the air becomes turbulent on the lee side, the leeward streamer will flutter, indicating a stalled condition. There's very little heading difference between a stall and a luff. A boat that is indicating a stalled jib may need to head up only 5° to 10° before the windward telltale starts to flutter (indicating a luff).

A number of years ago, in 1967, we were using these streamers to help novices steer to windward. A student at Offshore Sailing School, named Dr. Reinhorn, demonstrated that if you pointed the tiller at the fluttering piece of wool, you cured the condition. If the boat is being sailed "too hard" (too low for a closehauled course), the leeward streamers will flutter. Putting the tiller to leeward causes the boat to head up and the fluttering stops. Conversely, if the windward streamer is fluttering, the boat is being sailed too high, almost luffing. Putting the tiller to windward causes it to fall off and again stop the fluttering. Using "Reinhorn's Law," we tell all students to point the tiller at the fluttering streamer. When both pieces of wool stream back evenly, the airflow is undisturbed on both sides of the sail and the sail trim is proper.

Even some of the best sailors in the world use these streamers but tend to rely more on the "feel" of the boat rather than completely relying on the streamers. Though one never wants to sail with the leeward streamers fluttering, there are occasional times when the boat sails best with the windward one fluttering. For instance, in a strong wind and a smooth sea you may be able to pinch a little, carry a slight luff in the jib, and sail faster with the windward streamers jumping. Falling off to the point of smooth flow on the windward side of the sail causes excessive heeling and slows the boat down.

The general idea is shown in Figure 37. Diagram A shows even flow on both sides of the jib and good jib trim for the given course. Just before the sails luff, the windward streamer will jump around, as in diagram B. The leeward streamer will still flow well, but the curve of the sail is obstructing the wind (which is more toward the bow of the boat) from attaching to the windward side. Thus the windward streamer flutters. The solution when closehauled is to fall off, and when reaching to trim in the sail. Diagram C shows the jib when stalled. The wind is hitting the sail more from the windward side and is unable to make the sharp curve around its lee side without breaking away. The solution when closehauled is to head up and when reaching to ease the sheet.

Wool streamers on jibs are very useful when reaching. A racing crew has to "play" the jib constantly on reaches. In other words, they must trim it when

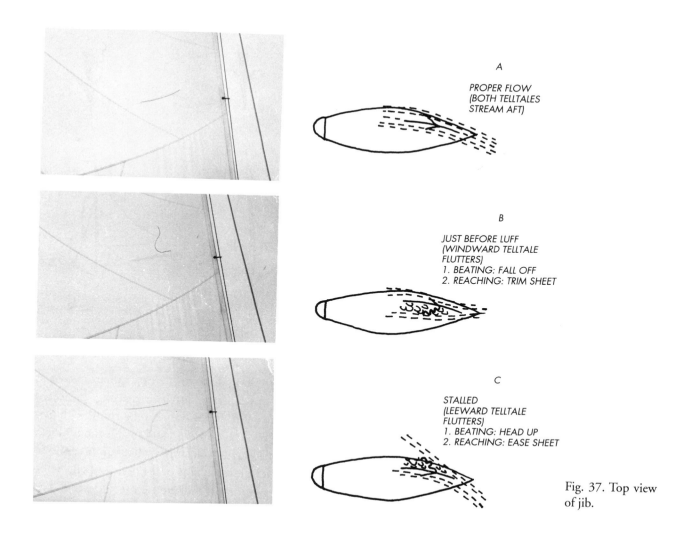

A

*PROPER FLOW
(BOTH TELLTALES
STREAM AFT)*

B

*JUST BEFORE LUFF
(WINDWARD TELLTALE
FLUTTERS)
1. BEATING: FALL OFF
2. REACHING: TRIM SHEET*

C

*STALLED
(LEEWARD TELLTALE
FLUTTERS)
1. BEATING: HEAD UP
2. REACHING: EASE SHEET*

Fig. 37. Top view of jib.

it luffs and ease it when it stalls. Without the streamers, it is extremely diffi-cult to know when the sail is stalled.

There is one time when proper sail trim calls for a stalled condition. When a broad reach approaches a run there is a transition from the "pull" of aerodynamic lift to the "push" of a purely drag condition. The sail shape that creates the most drag will push the boat the fastest. We would like to main-tain airflow over the lee side of the jib as long as possible for better sailing efficiency, but there comes a time when the boat is near a run that the air can no longer make the corner. The telltales on the lee side of the jib start to flut-ter, indicating a stall, and easing the sail no longer gets them flowing aft again. At this point, the amount of sail, in square feet, exposed to the wind is more important than aerodynamic curvature. Just as a larger umbrella will pull you downwind with greater force (Figure 30), a larger sail will catch more wind

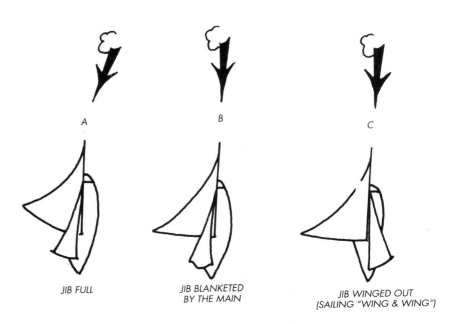

Fig. 38. Winging the jib will help the boat sail faster directly downwind.

A

B

C

JIB FULL

JIB BLANKETED
BY THE MAIN

JIB WINGED OUT
(SAILING "WING & WING")

and be more effective on a run. Anything done to increase sail area, such as pulling the boom down with a boom vang, is said to be increasing "projected area," the area of sail exposed to the wind. For instance, on a run the jib gets blanketed by the main. The main is between the wind and the jib and is blocking the latter from getting any wind. Figure 38 shows what can be done to cure the problem: put the jib out over the other side of the boat and sail "wing and wing," thereby increasing the amount of sail exposed to the wind. The boat will sail noticeably faster.

Another use for wool streamers on the jib is to determine the fore and aft position of the jib lead. The jib lead is usually a slideable block on a short track that may be located and locked in position a few inches closer to the bow or aft toward the stern to change the angle the jib sheet makes with the clew of the jib. The sail is perfectly set if, when the helmsman on a closehauled course pinches the boat a little, the three or more streamers evenly spaced along the length of the luff all flutter on the windward side of the jib at the same instant. This means that the angle the leading edge of the jib makes with the wind is identical at all levels. Look at Figure 39. If the lead is too far forward the jib sheet will be more vertical and will be pulling down harder on the leech of the sail than along the foot, distorting the sail. It will be fairly flat aloft and have a big round belly near the foot. This will cause the lower windward streamers to flutter and is a signal to the crew to slide the lead further aft. If the lead is too far aft, the jib sheet angle will be too low. It will be pulling the foot of the sail tight without tensioning the leech enough. The sail will be flat

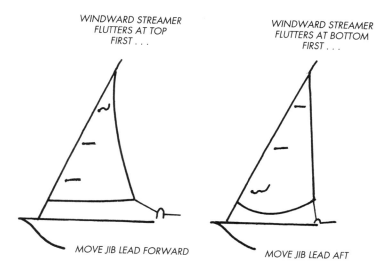

WINDWARD STREAMER
FLUTTERS AT TOP
FIRST . . .

WINDWARD STREAMER
FLUTTERS AT BOTTOM
FIRST . . .

MOVE JIB LEAD FORWARD

MOVE JIB LEAD AFT

Fig. 39. Wool streamers on the jib indicate proper jib lead placement.

below but will fall off to leeward aloft, causing the higher windward streamers to flutter as the upper part of the sail lines up with the wind. So remember the rule: luff aloft, lead forward.

The Slot

If you look at a sloop-rigged (main and jib) sailboat from astern you will see that the jib forms a passage with the main through which air flows. This passage between the main and jib, shown in Photo 22, is called the "slot," and is instrumental in the much greater speed one can sail with both sails than with either the main or the jib set alone. The jib bends and funnels the air behind the main. The restriction increases the velocity of the air over the backside of the mainsail, just as putting a finger over the end of a garden hose squirts the water. Through Bernoulli's principle, this increased air velocity increases the suction and efficiency of the mainsail. The result is called "slot effect." Don't take my word for it; feel it yourself. On a light day, sail with just the mainsail and hold your arms up on either side of it as if you were a soldier surrendering. You will feel a little stronger breeze on the leeward side. Now set a jib in conjunction with the main and repeat the experiment. You will be surprised at how much stronger the breeze is on the leeward side of the main than on the windward side. Not only is the velocity of the airflow increased, but the air is redirected by the jib in a direction more parallel to the surface of the main (see Figure 40). This allows the air to remain attached to the surface of the main for a greater distance before it separates into turbulence. As we mentioned previously, the greater the distance it remains attached to the surface, the greater the lift.

22. The slot—between the main-sail and the jib.

23. The slot narrows when the jib is trimmed too tightly.

Ideal sail trim dictates that the curve of the leech of the jib take the same curve as the surface of the main, as much as is possible. This makes an evenly distributed slot for the air to flow through. If the leech of the jib is pulled too tight, as in Photo 23 (which can be caused by the jib lead's being too far forward or the jib sheet's being trimmed in too tight), then the air will hit a portion of the main rather than flow over it. The slot is being "closed" and

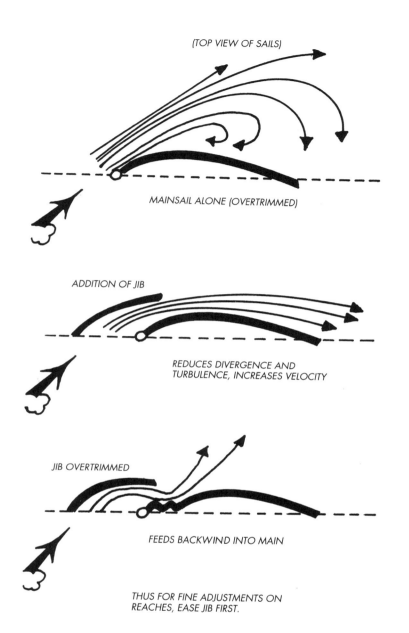

(TOP VIEW OF SAILS)

MAINSAIL ALONE (OVERTRIMMED)

ADDITION OF JIB

REDUCES DIVERGENCE AND
TURBULENCE, INCREASES VELOCITY

JIB OVERTRIMMED

FEEDS BACKWIND INTO MAIN

THUS FOR FINE ADJUSTMENTS ON
REACHES, EASE JIB FIRST.

Fig. 40. Slot effect (top view of sails).

the jib is said to be "backwinding the main" or "feeding backwind into the main" (pronounced "wind" like the breeze, not like "to wind a watch"). The same backwinding occurs when the jib trim is left untouched and the main is eased, thereby closing the slot. Backwind in the main makes it appear to be luffing, when actually all one needs to do to cure the problem is ease the jib. Novices often see the backwind and trim the main, thinking it's a luff, when actually they should be easing the jib instead. Both sails then end up overtrimmed. Backwind is more pronounced on a reach. When the main is eased it goes out over the water, but when the jib is eased it just goes forward. Just the process of easing both sails closes the slot a little. To avoid backwind on a reach, it is best to adjust the jib first and the main second. If the jib is set correctly, and then you ease the main until it luffs, you can be fairly sure that the luff you see in the main is a true luff, not backwind from the jib.

Side Force and Heeling

When the wind hits the sails it causes a resultant force that is a combination of forward and side force. As mentioned before, the keel and hull of the boat offer resistance to the side force but are streamlined in the fore and aft direction so as to offer little resistance to the forward force. The side force is still there and manifests itself in heeling the boat, causing it to lean over. When the boat is closehauled, the force arrows in Figure 41a show that the direction of lift is more sideways than forward because the sails are trimmed in very tightly. As the boat is turned to a reach, as in Figure 41b, and the sails eased, the arrows start to point more in the direction the boat is heading. The result is less heeling and more forward force. Since the energy is being expended more efficiently, a reach is the fastest point of sailing.

This concept is difficult for the beginner to understand because there is so much more "sound and fury" when sailing closehauled. The boat is heeling over, slamming through waves, and the breeze seems stronger because you're sailing into it. As a matter of fact, years ago boat owners thought that a sailboat was sailing fastest when the lee rail was "buried" (under the water). It wasn't until speedometers were invented for sailboats that it was discovered that they actually slowed down when the lee rail was awash. Thus it's natural

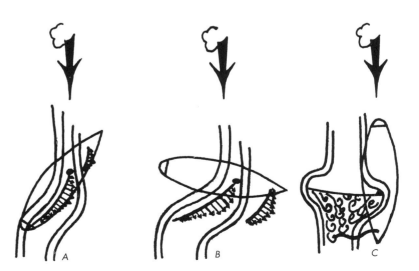

Fig. 41. Sail force causes heeling when closehauled (A), is more parallel with the boat's heading on a reach (B), and is pure drag turbulence on a run (C).

for the new sailor to feel that commotion equals speed. When you fall off to a reach, the heeling is less, the pull of the sails is more forward, and neither the wind nor the seas seem as powerful, yet the speed is greater.

You might expect that a run would be even faster than a reach because you are sailing downwind, down the seas, and the force of the sails is parallel with the heading of the boat. However, for the one important reason, shown in Figure 41c—the turbulence behind the mainsail—a run is slower than a reach. The wind is just pushing the boat and no air is flowing over the lee side of the sail, so no pull or lift is being developed by the main. On a reach the jib is being used efficiently, but on a run it is "blanketed" by the mainsail. In other words, no wind is getting to the jib because the main is blocking it.

It is axiomatic that in sailing there is an exception to every rule. If the wind and seas are extremely heavy, to the point where the boat is overpowered (heeling too much), then a run is a faster point of sailing than a reach.

◆ 6 ◆

More Efficient Sailing

Shifting Winds

Though it may seem as though the wind is steady from one direction, once you have sailed a while you'll realize that the wind is constantly shifting in direction. If you're sailing closehauled and the wind shifts toward the bow of your boat, the sails will start to luff even though the course and sail trim haven't changed. This type of shift is called a "header." It is common to say the boat has been "headed" or "has sailed into a header." Conversely, if the wind shifts more toward the stern of the boat, you will be able to point higher than before (sail more toward the original wind). Such a wind shift is called a "lift." Though most shifts are small, 10° or less, for the purposes of clarification we'll exaggerate the shifts in the diagrams. Figure 42 shows a large shift hitting a boat on port tack. In fact it's so large a header that the wind is pointing right at her bow and her sails would be completely aluff (luffing). To respond to the shift and to keep the sails full, the skipper has to fall off to the new heading shown. Figure 43 shows a wind shift in the opposite direction, a lift for a boat on port tack. Note that she is now heading more directly toward the desired destination upwind, so a lift is a helpful windshift.

A wind shift while sailing closehauled requires a change of course. When reaching, a lift—a shift toward the stern—means the sails may be eased, whereas a header—a shift toward the bow—necessitates trimming the sails to maintain the original reaching course.

Figure 44 shows boats on opposite tacks, one on starboard, the other on port, receiving the same large wind shift. Notice that a header for a boat on

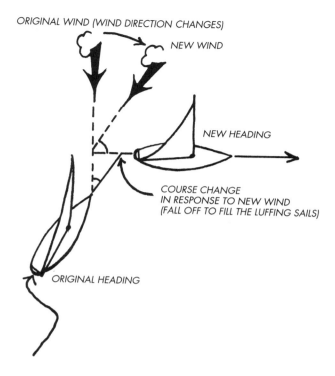

DESTINATION

ORIGINAL WIND (WIND DIRECTION CHANGES)

NEW WIND

NEW HEADING

COURSE CHANGE
IN RESPONSE TO NEW WIND
(FALL OFF TO FILL THE LUFFING SAILS)

ORIGINAL HEADING

Fig. 42. A header (wind shifts forward on the boat).

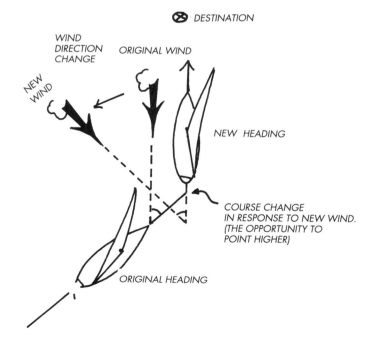

DESTINATION

WIND
DIRECTION
CHANGE

ORIGINAL WIND

NEW
WIND

NEW HEADING

COURSE CHANGE
IN RESPONSE TO NEW WIND.
(THE OPPORTUNITY TO
POINT HIGHER)

ORIGINAL HEADING

Fig. 43. A lift (wind shifts aft on the boat).

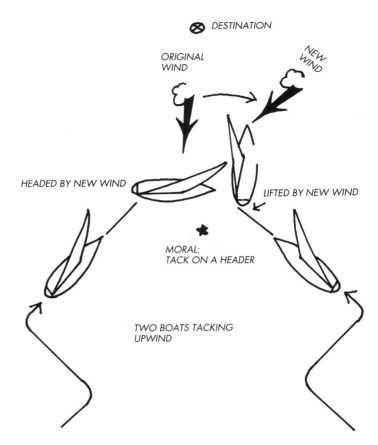

DESTINATION

ORIGINAL
WIND

NEW
WIND

HEADED BY NEW WIND

LIFTED BY NEW WIND

MORAL:
TACK ON A HEADER

TWO BOATS TACKING
UPWIND

Fig. 44. A header for the port tack boat is a lift for the starboard tack boat, so the former should tack.

port tack is a lift for a boat on starboard. Since the lift helps you sail closer to your destination, normally a skipper will tack to the other tack when headed, particularly if the shift is a large one. When racing, sailors almost invariably tack when headed if they want to win.

Up to now we have talked about headers and lifts, shifts in relation to the bow of the boat. The same shifts use different terminology when related to a compass direction. A clockwise shift is called a "veering" or "hauling" wind, and a counterclockwise shift is a "backing" wind (Figure 45). For example, a wind that shifts from north to northeast is a veering wind, while one that shifts from north to northwest is backing. Wind is named after the direction from which it blows. A north wind blows from the north. It's easy to confuse this with current, which is named for the direction to which it flows. A northerly current flows from the south. When a strong current runs against the wind a heavy sea can develop, so don't think you're misreading a sailing guide that says, "In this area, steep seas result from a southerly current during a southerly wind." It means that they are contrary to one another.

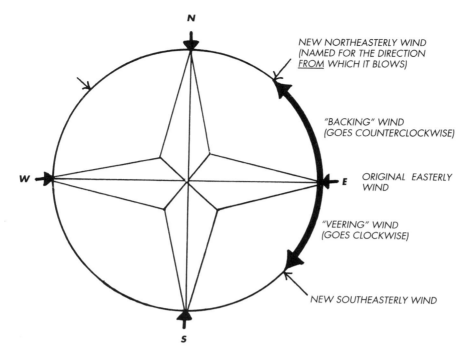

NEW NORTHEASTERLY WIND
(NAMED FOR THE DIRECTION
<u>FROM</u> WHICH IT BLOWS)

"BACKING" WIND
(GOES COUNTERCLOCKWISE)

ORIGINAL EASTERLY
WIND

"VEERING" WIND
(GOES CLOCKWISE)

NEW SOUTHEASTERLY WIND

Fig. 45. Veering and backing winds refer to compass directions.

Apparent Wind

The wind shifts we discussed that refer to the compass, veering and backing winds, are based on the actual wind that is blowing across the water. This is called the "true" wind. The shifts that relate to the boat, headers and lifts, are affected by the speed the boat is traveling through the water. The resultant wind is called "apparent wind." It is a combination of the true wind and the boat speed wind. Everything that shows wind direction on the boat as it sails along is indicating the apparent wind direction. The masthead fly, telltales on the shrouds, cigarette smoke, electronic wind indicators on cruising boats all show the apparent wind. Novices become aware of the phenomenon when they sail closehauled for the first time. They've read that a boat can sail roughly 45° to the wind direction, yet the telltales on the shrouds indicate that the wind is much farther forward, perhaps 25° from the bow. When they tack, they discover it still takes 90° to complete the tack.

To understand apparent wind, imagine you are in a motorboat rather than a sailboat. It's a dead calm day and there's not a breath of air stirring. As the boat moves forward and reaches a speed of 10 knots through the water (a knot is a unit of speed equaling one nautical mile in one hour—it's redundant to say "knots per hour"), the sailors aboard will feel a 10-knot breeze from dead ahead. This is strictly a boat-speed-created wind, since there is no true wind. If, however, the motorboat were heading due east at 10 knots and there were a 10-knot true wind blowing from the north, those aboard would not feel two different winds (the true wind from the north and boat speed wind from the east), but rather a resultant wind from the northeast, a combination of the two winds. This is the apparent wind.

The apparent wind direction and velocity are easy to determine if you know the true wind and boat speed. It's a matter of vectors. For me, however, vectors are a little hard to read, so I prefer to draw out the whole parallelogram for clarity. If your boat tacks in 90°, you know that the true wind is 45° from your bow. Let's say the true wind speed is 10 knots and the boat is sailing at 5 knots. Draw a parallelogram to any constant scale, as in Figure 46, using the above facts. The diagonal of the parallelogram is the apparent wind direction, in this case, 30° from the bow. It measures 14 units so the apparent wind velocity is 14 knots.

Figures 46–50 show the apparent wind direction and velocity on a boat sailing at 5 knots closehauled, beam reaching, broad reaching, and running,

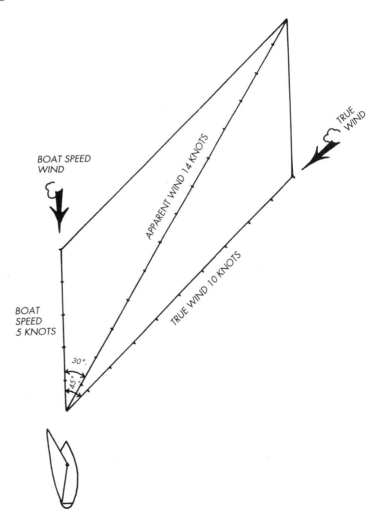

Fig. 46. Apparent wind (close-hauled).

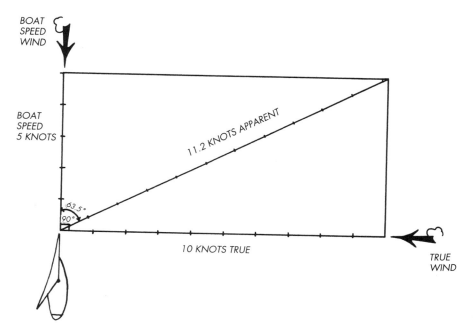

Fig. 47. Apparent wind (beam reach).

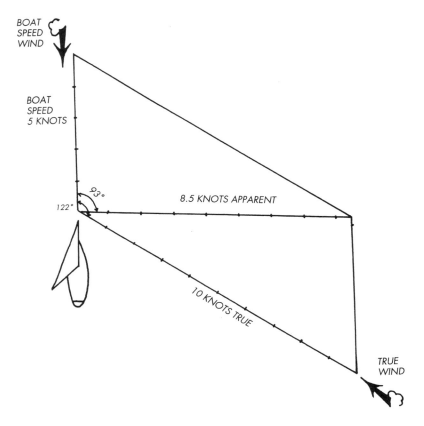

Fig. 48. Apparent wind (broad reach).

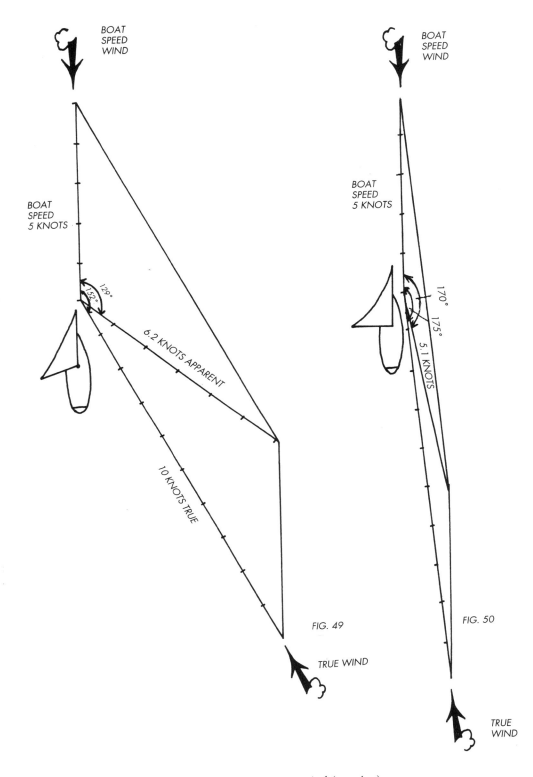

Figs. 49 and 50. Apparent wind (running).

with a constant true wind of 10 knots. This is a hypothetical case because a boat that reaches or runs at 5 knots couldn't maintain that speed close-hauled. Let's assume that the boat is larger, and therefore faster, in the closehauled diagram.

A number of items become apparent when studying these diagrams:

1. Apparent wind direction is always forward of the true wind, unless the latter is coming from dead ahead or dead astern. This fact becomes important in determining when to jibe. In order to reduce the chance of an accidental jibe, most skippers will sail with the wind coming a bit over the side of the boat rather than dead astern. This brings the apparent wind quite far forward. Note in Figure 51 that the boat is sailing at a 25° angle from dead downwind and the apparent wind is forward of that. In order to be sailing at the same angle to the destination after the jibe, the jibe must be made when a 50° turn will head the boat toward the destination. To make such a determination, the skipper must judge fairly accurately the direction of the true wind. Ripples, foam, and streaks on the water give an indication of the true wind direction, but a more accurate way is to sail dead downwind momentarily and see how much the boat has to be turned to attain that point of sail. In our example the turn will be 25°, so we want to jibe when another 25° will point us to our destination.

2. As the true wind comes aft, the apparent wind speed lessens. Though the diagrams make this apparent, it is sometimes very obvious when you observe a motorboat cruising downwind on a light day. The exhaust is blown at the same speed and direction as the boat is traveling and the appearance is that of the Peanuts cartoon character Pigpen, out for a jaunt on a motorboat surrounded by the cloud of soot.

The importance of this reduced apparent wind speed is most noticeable when a run is compared with a beat. If a boat is running downwind at 9 knots in a 16-knot true wind, the apparent wind will be only 7 knots (subtract the boat speed from the true wind speed). The breeze you feel on the boat is very light. On a beat, the boat speed may decrease to about 6 knots, but the apparent wind will increase to almost 21 knots, or three times greater than when running. Even if there were a direct relationship between wind strength and wind force, this would be a substantial increase. However, the wind force varies with the square of the velocity. A 5-knot wind squared is 25. A 10-knot wind squared is 100. So, as the wind speed doubles, the wind force quadruples. In the example above, the wind force is nine times greater when beating than on a run. The amount of sail area that could be carried easily on a run may very well overpower the boat when beating, and you may have to consider shortening sail. Keep this in mind whenever you set sail on a broad reach or a run. You may have a difficult time getting back home when you finally decide to return.

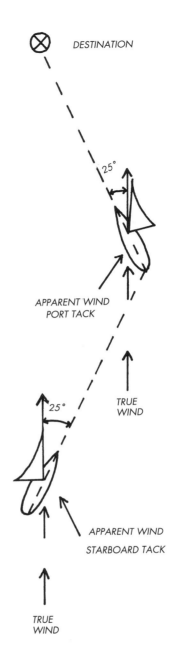

DESTINATION

25°

APPARENT WIND
PORT TACK

TRUE
WIND

25°

APPARENT WIND

STARBOARD TACK

TRUE
WIND

Fig. 51. Knowledge of the true wind direction is needed to determine when to jibe.

3. When the true wind is near astern, a small change in true wind direction will make a large change in apparent wind direction. Compare Figure 48 with Figure 49. A 30° change in true wind direction creates a 36° change in apparent wind. Yet, when comparing Figure 49 with Figure 50, we find that a 23° change in true wind creates a 41° change in apparent wind. Such a large change in apparent wind direction when running makes steering very difficult for the inexperienced helmsman. If he steers slightly by the lee, the apparent wind will swing well by the lee. Threatened with a possible jibe, the helmsman turns the boat the other way, causing a large swing in the apparent wind to the windward side of the boat. To avoid broaching, he steers downwind again and the cycle repeats itself. An accidental jibe can result.

4. When the boat is on a beam reach or closehauled, the apparent wind speed is greater than the true wind. As a matter of fact, the faster a boat sails, the greater the apparent wind speed. The greater the wind speed, the faster the boat can go, limited only by the resistance of the water being pushed aside by the hull. Ice boats attain tremendous speeds because they have minimal resistance to forward motion. They've been clocked at well over 100 MPH in not particularly strong winds. They are basically creating their own wind. Some sailboats are light enough and have a hull shape that lets them skim the surface of the water. This is called planing, and allows the boat to break free from some of the speed limitations caused by the water.

In Figures 46–50 we kept the boat speed constant, the true wind speed constant, and varied the true wind direction. Now let's keep the boat speed constant, the true wind direction constant, and vary the true wind speed, as happens in gusts and lulls.

Figure 52 shows a boat sailing at 5 knots in a 12-knot true wind at 45° off the bow. The dotted extension of the solid 12-knot line indicates a puff or gust that brings the total wind speed up to 18 knots. Note that the apparent wind comes aft. This is always so if the boat speed remains constant. As a matter of practicality, a boat never accelerates rapidly when hit by a puff, so the apparent wind always comes aft.

One rule we've already learned is to head into the wind to reduce heeling when hit by a gust. This spills wind out of the sails and keeps the boat from being overpowered. Figure 52 shows another reason for doing the same thing. When a gust hits, the apparent wind goes aft. To maintain the same angle that the apparent wind made with the sails previously (called the "angle of incidence"), head up a few degrees. If you don't head up, the result will be more heeling and less forward drive. This is particularly important on light days when the increased wind in a gust accounts for a large percentage of the original wind speed. If the wind speed is 2 knots, it's very likely that a puff will increase it to 4 or 6 knots, double or triple the original wind. The apparent wind will come far aft in such a puff compared to a windy day when a 14-knot wind increases at the most to about 21 knots in puffs, or 50 percent higher.

Often the breeze dies for a short time. This is called a "lull" and is shown in Figure 52 as a dot-dash line. Notice that the apparent wind goes forward if the boat speed remains constant. A sailboat doesn't pick up speed immediately in response to a gust, nor does it lose speed immediately in a lull. For ease of remembering which way the apparent wind goes in a gust or lull, imagine

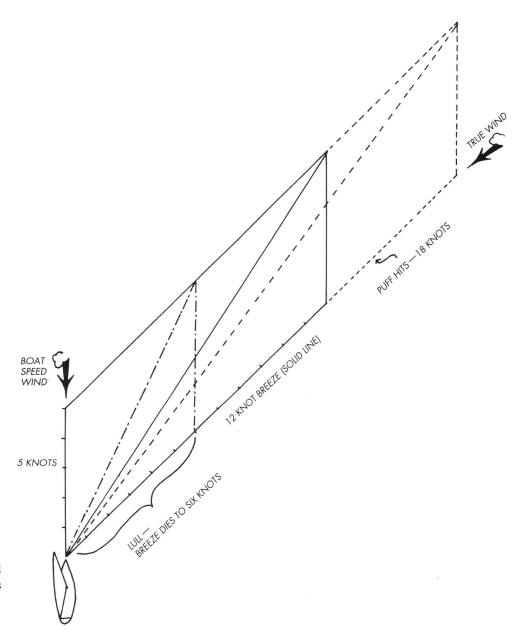

TRUE WIND

PUFF HITS—18 KNOTS

12 KNOT BREEZE (SOLID LINE)

BOAT
SPEED
WIND

5 KNOTS

LULL —
BREEZE DIES TO SIX KNOTS

Fig. 52. Apparent wind goes forward in lulls and aft during gusts.

yourself sailing at 5 knots when the breeze dies completely, as if someone had switched off a giant fan. The wind will be dead ahead and the sails luffing. Obviously, in the absence of any wind the only breeze you would feel would be that produced by the forward motion of the boat.

This happens quite often on light days, particularly to large cruising boats that have a great deal of momentum. The sails will start luffing and give the appearance of sailing too high or too close on the wind. Actually, the boat is only traveling through a light spot or "hole" in the wind. The helmsman must make an immediate decision: Is it a valid wind shift, called a header, or is it just a hole? If it is the former, he must head off to fill the sails. If it is the latter, he could kill what little speed he has by heading off instead of shooting through the light spot with momentum and picking up the breeze on the other side. Unless you can see a puff ahead, the decision is difficult. Usually, the wisest course is to head off very slowly and evenly. If you're still luffing after turning 20° away from the wind, it's probably a flat spot.

One warning—a skipper who reacts precipitously and turns the boat quickly downwind actually aggravates the situation if it's just a hole in the wind. The turn itself forces air against the lee side of the jib, causing it to luff or back. In a short time he will find himself 30° below his previous course, with the jib still luffing because of the turning movement of the boat.

Of course, it may not be a hole, but rather a true header. The boat is sailing a straight course in a light steady breeze and suddenly, because of the wind shift toward the bow of the boat, the jib starts to luff. The skipper decides that instead of heading off to fill the sails, he will tack. As he turns the bow into the wind, the jib will fill as the apparent wind comes aft, due to the turning of the boat. Because the jib has stopped luffing, it can appear that the wind has shifted back to its original direction. The skipper can have the impression that he has been lifted (the wind direction has changed more toward the stern of the boat) when actually it is only the pivoting of the boat that has caused the change. An inexperienced or indecisive skipper will stop his tack in the middle and return to his original course. At first it will appear that he has made the correct decision because, by making the incomplete tack, he has slowed the boat which puts the apparent wind fairly well aft. As the boat picks up speed, the apparent wind will again come forward and he will find himself still sailing in the same header he had before.

Now let's consider other cases where wind speed remains constant but boat speed varies. For instance, if the boat starts surfing down the face of a wave (much as a surfboarder uses a wave), the apparent wind goes forward. Sometimes it goes forward to the point where it will flatten the spinnaker back against the mast and rigging! At other times the boat may slow down for some reason. The apparent wind comes aft and its velocity will increase. As the wind velocity doubles, the pressure on the sails and rigging quadruples.

When a boat runs hard aground at high speed, it is often dismasted because the rig and sails have a tendency to keep on going even though the hull has stopped. But another important reason is that the apparent wind pressure on the sails has increased suddenly. A good example of this happened to *Mare Nostrum,* a 72' yawl, on the 1955 Transatlantic Race from Cuba to

Spain. We had a spinnaker, mainsail, mizzen, and a mizzen staysail (sort of a jib for the mizzenmast) set in fairly fresh winds of about 20–23 knots. The swivel on the spinnaker halyard broke and the chute went streaming out ahead of the boat. Before we could get it aboard, it filled with water, went underneath the bow, and hooked on the keel. This slowed the boat down so suddenly that the top half of the mizzenmast toppled forward under the increased load on the mizzen staysail.

So always remember that whenever there is a change in either boat speed or direction, or wind velocity or its direction, there must also be a change in the apparent wind. A helmsman must be alert to it, and either he must change his course accordingly or the crew must trim or ease the sails.

Now that the reader knows about apparent wind, he should ponder over a little riddle that has made the rounds of sailing circles: Jim and Joe live and work in a town next to a river with a strong 5-knot current. They both sail and have constant fights over who has the faster boat. They finally challenge each other to a race to put the rivalry to rest. The provisions of the race are as follows: (1) it is to be against time rather than against each other; (2) each man can choose his own time to sail it; (3) the distance is from the town down the river to a bridge a number of miles away; and (4) it has to be completed by Friday. Jim is a writer and has a much more flexible schedule. He waits until there is a nice 5-knot following breeze Wednesday afternoon and then makes his run down the river. Joe, on the other hand, has a job which keeps him working until 5 P.M. Each day after work he rushes down to the river, only to find late-afternoon doldrums. The daytime breeze has died. Finally, quitting time Friday arrived, his last chance to race. Again, as in the previous days, there is a flat calm. So, disconsolate, Joe gets in his sailboat and goes down current to the bridge. Who is the winner?

Joe is! Think about it. When Jim sails downwind with a 5-knot following wind in a 5-knot current, he has absolutely no wind in his sails. The apparent wind, which is the combination of the boat-speed-produced wind and the "true" (actual) wind, is zero in this case. So Jim just drifts with the current down to the bridge and has no help from the wind.

Joe, on the other hand, finds he has a 5-knot wind dead on the nose as the current carries him toward the bridge on his windless afternoon. It doesn't take him long to figure out that if his sails are luffing as he heads straight down the river, all he has to do is steer a closehauled course to fill the sails and get the boat moving through the water. Thus, he beats to windward the whole distance the current is carrying him and makes better time than his competitor, Jim.

This is strictly a hypothetical example because it is doubtful that such conditions could be met exactly, but it does show the effect of apparent wind.

Stability

One of the first questions a sailboat dealer gets from a neophyte about to buy a boat is "How tippy is it?" Everyone has seen photos of capsized sailboats and of dinghies heeling over with crews hiking far out on the windward side in an apparent effort to keep the boat from going over. It's really not as bad as it looks. Those crews are only trying to keep the boat more vertical and, by so doing, make it sail faster. If they wished, they could stop hiking, sit normally on the weather side of the boat, and reduce the force on the sails by luffing them slightly. Small sailboats are much tippier when they are dead in the water. They may seem unstable when you get aboard, yet when you start sailing them they turn out to be quite the opposite. It's like trying to balance on a bicycle when it's motionless compared to when it's moving.

We have mentioned that the wind in the sails creates both forward and side forces and that the keel of the boat counteracts much of the side forces, leaving forward force. The keel or centerboard keeps the boat from sliding sideways. A boat with a heavy keel can absorb more wind force than one with a light keel and, therefore, can carry more sail area. More sail usually results in more speed, but there are other factors involved. The heavier the keel, the more strongly the boat must be built, making the total weight of the boat higher. The heavier the boat, the more beating it takes from the seas, because it tends to go through them more than over them. So a heavy boat has to be built stronger if only because it's heavy in the first place. It sinks deeper in the water, so when sailing it has to push aside a greater volume of water than a lighter boat. The increase in sail-carrying capacity may be totally offset by the resistance of the hull moving through the water, brought about by the increased displacement (weight). A happy medium must be found between the ultralight-displacement boat and the sluggish, unmaneuverable, ultra-heavy-displacement boat.

Hull form also has a great effect on the stability of a sailboat. A wide boat has more stability than a narrow one. Photo 24 shows a daggerboard sailboat (the board goes straight through a slot, rather than pivoting) that is quite wide in comparison to its length. The crew would normally sit on the upper edge, but then we wouldn't have this photo on heeling. Note how much rudder comes out of the water, reducing its effectiveness. As it heels, a small amount of the boat submerges on the leeward side, whereas a large amount of the boat lifts out of the water on the windward side. The weight of the hull that lifts out, plus the crew sitting on top of it, counteracts much of the heeling force. The wider the boat, the more effective the hull shape is in reducing heeling. Again, there's a trade-off. The wide hull has more "wetted surface" (square feet of area in contact with the water) and, therefore, more skin friction. This slows the boat down in light winds and offsets the increased efficiency from resistance to heeling.

24. A wide daggerboard boat's reaction to heeling.

There are at least three terms describing stability: "initial," "ultimate," and "positive." A flat raft (like a heavy centerboarder) may have excellent initial stability in that it may take quite a number of people standing on one edge to raise the other edge out of the water. However, once one edge is sunk and the raft is heeling at a steep angle, it takes very little additional weight to increase the angle until it finally flips over. This indicates that the raft has poor ultimate stability. A deep keelboat will have the opposite. It will heel the first few degrees very easily, yet will be practically impossible to capsize. Thus, it has poor initial stability and good ultimate stability. If it does capsize, which can only be due to a freak wave or a phenomenon of that sort, the deep keelboat will "turn turtle," in other words, spin 360° and come around right-side-up again. This self-righting ability is called "positive stability." Of course, the boat must not get water in the cabin as it flips or it may sink. Most cruising keelboats have self-draining cockpits, watertight hatches, and hatch boards to keep the water out.

Figure 53 diagrams the difference in stability between a keelboat and a centerboarder. Stability is obtained from the lever arm between the center of buoyancy (CB) of the boat pushing upward (resisting any tendency to push the hull deeper in the water) and the center of gravity (CG) of the boat pushing downward. The center of gravity is the center of the earth's gravitational effect on the boat. A boat suspended by a wire at its exact center of gravity could be rotated in any direction, yet remain motionless when released. The center of buoyancy is really the center of gravity of all the water that particular hull shape displaces. The CG remains in one position because the hull shape and weight position don't change (except for crew weight). The CB

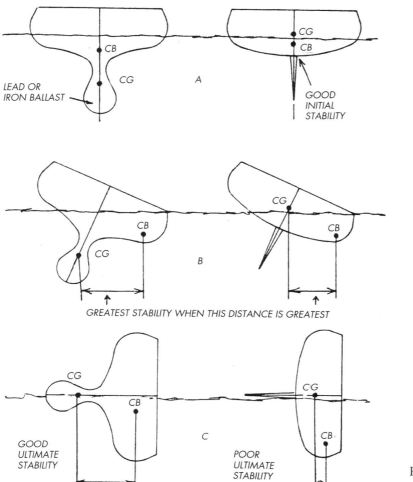

LEAD OR IRON BALLAST

CB

CG

GOOD INITIAL STABILITY

CG

CB

A

CB

CG

B

CB

GREATEST STABILITY WHEN THIS DISTANCE IS GREATEST

CG

CB

GOOD ULTIMATE STABILITY

C

POOR ULTIMATE STABILITY

CG

CB

Fig. 53. Stability.

moves in relation to the amount of hull that's submerged. As some of the boat lifts out of the water when heeled and the leeward side submerges deeper, the CB moves to leeward. Figure 53a shows that, at rest, the CB and CG are in vertical alignment in both the keel and centerboard boat. As they heel, Figure 53b, the CG of the keelboat has swung out to windward because it's so low, whereas the CG of the centerboard boat has remained in the same spot. They are both developing a lever arm to resist heeling based on the lateral distance between the CB pushing up and the CG pulling down, but are attaining the leverage in two diverse ways. Figure 53c shows both boats on their sides, an unusual situation. Note that the lever arm on the keelboat is now the greatest it has been, but on the centerboarder it is almost nonexistent. If the latter tips any further, the CG will get on the other side of the CB and turn the boat upside-down.

Since centerboard sailboats can capsize, they are designed to be small enough to be righted by the crew with a minimum of outside assistance. Some shallow-draft cruising boats have centerboards that reduce leeway (sideslipping) when sailing to windward, but they are really keelboats in that they have positive stability (are self-righting).

Balance

The hull and sails of a well-designed sailboat work together in harmony. On some cruising boats, one can set the sails for a closehauled course and leave the helm completely unattended. Such a boat is said to be perfectly balanced. If the boat tends to head into the wind when you release the helm, it has "weather helm." Conversely, if it veers to leeward, it has "lee helm."

When sailing to windward, a small amount of weather helm is desirable. It gives the boat more "feel." Instead of having to steer the boat in both directions, you only have to steer it away from the wind, since the boat wants to steer itself into the wind. The skipper only has to keep a slight constant pull on the tiller to windward in order to steer a straight course. Also, the boat will automatically head up in the puffs if there's a slight weather helm. This reduces heeling and maintains the angle that the wind originally made with the sails, because, as mentioned previously, the apparent wind comes aft in puffs.

Furthermore, the keel and rudder are "lifting" surfaces, just like the sails, and are subject to the same aerodynamic principles. If the water flow hits the symmetrical keel at an angle, it has to travel further on one side than on the other, velocity is increased, pressure is decreased and lift develops on the windward side of the keel. "Fine," you say, "but doesn't the water hit the leading edge of the keel straight on?" No! The fact is that the closehauled sailboat is sideslipping a little due to the side force in the sails. This creates a "leeway angle" between the direction the boat is heading and its track through the water (the angle of attack of the water). Figure 54a demonstrates this angle. The rudder is also a lifting surface, but the keel redirects the water flow so that it's hitting the rudder head-on. If the rudder has to be angled, as in Figure 54b, in order to steer straight because of weather helm, then it too will develop lift and reduce leeway more effectively. So a slight weather helm helps the feel of the boat and increases its efficiency to windward.

Lee helm is completely unacceptable (and, luckily, a rare occurrence) because it produces lift to leeward and makes steering awkward. And excessive weather helm is also unacceptable. Figure 55 shows the rudder positions for a balanced helm, slight weather helm, and excessive weather helm. The latter creates an inordinate amount of rudder drag and turbulence as the skipper holds the tiller at a large angle to windward in an attempt to keep the boat sailing a straight course.

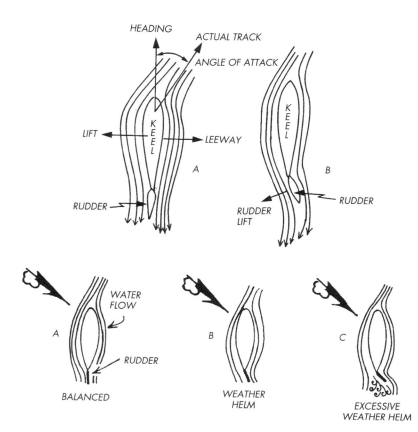

Fig. 54. Cross section of keel, looking down from above. A slight weather helm improves the total lift of the keel and rudder.

Fig. 55. Cross section of keel, looking down from above. Excessive weather helm creates rudder drag and slows down the boat.

One of the main causes of a strong weather helm is heeling. There are two reasons for this. First, the shape of the hull is such that the leeward curved side of the bow forces the bow to windward when heeled. If you throw a curved piece of wood in the water, it won't travel in a straight line; neither will the curved leeward side of a sailboat. Note the bow wave of the boat in Photo 25. It is larger to leeward, forcing the bow to weather. The greater the heel, the more pronounced this becomes.

Second, heeling places the sail area out over the water. If you draw a vertical straight line from the lee edge of the hull in Photo 25, you can see that a large portion of the sail is not over the boat. The forward pull of the sail is out of alignment with the drag of the hull in the water and causes a turning moment to windward.

Perhaps this is easier to understand when applied to reaching and running rather than to heeling. Figure 56 shows a boat on a run with the force of the sail out over the water. With the drag of the hull in the opposite direction, the boat wants to turn to windward. If there were no wind and you tried to tow the sailboat with a motorboat by a line attached to the end of the boom out over the water rather than to the bow, obviously the boat would turn rather than tow straight. It's the same idea.

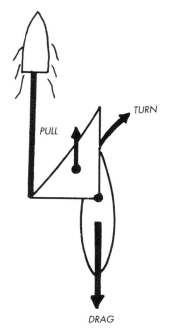

Fig. 56. If a powerboat pulls a sailboat by a line tied to the end of its boom, the sailboat will rotate. The same applies to the normal force of the wind on the mainsail.

25. The large bow wave on the leeward side pushes the bow to weather (toward the wind).

26. The water turbulence indicates a stalled rudder, resulting from excessive heeling.

When heeling becomes excessive, weather helm becomes quite strong. Photo 26 shows a keelboat heeled over. The rudder is being turned to counteract the resulting weather helm and is practically stalled. Note the turbulence from the water passing the rudder. There is so much rudder drag that boat speed is markedly slowed. Also, as the boat heels, the rudder comes further out of the water and loses more of its effectiveness.

One of the fundamental relationships to the proper balance of a sailboat is that between the center of effort (CE) of the sail plan and the center of

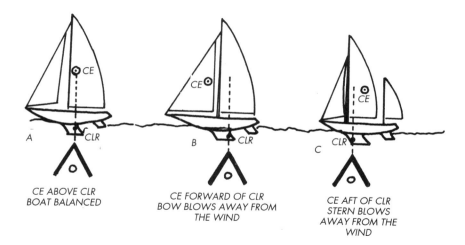

CE ABOVE CLR
BOAT BALANCED

CE FORWARD OF CLR
BOW BLOWS AWAY FROM
THE WIND

CE AFT OF CLR
STERN BLOWS
AWAY FROM THE
WIND

Fig. 57. Sailboat weather vane.

lateral resistance (CLR) of the hull shape. The center of effort is the geometrical center of all the sails set on the boat. The CE of each sail is obtained by drawing a line from each corner to the midpoint of the opposite side. The combined CE of all the sails on a boat is important in its balance. Half of the total sail area is behind the CE and half is forward of it.

The center of lateral resistance is the center of the underwater surfaces of the hull. If you draw the underwater portion of a sailboat and cut the profile out of cardboard, the CLR is the point where the piece of cardboard will balance level on the head of a pin.

The relationship between CE and CLR, and their effect on the balance of a sailboat, is best described in terms of a weather vane on top of a roof with the pivot point at the CLR. If the CE is directly above the pivot point the weather vane won't rotate, just as if the boat were perfectly balanced as in Figure 57a. Actually, this is an oversimplification since naval architects design a boat with the CE slightly forward of the CLR (a distance called "lead") in order to balance the boat. If we add a larger jib to our weather vane as in Figure 57b, we move the CE forward. When the wind blows, the bow rotates to leeward. Conversely, if we add sail area near the stern of the boat (Figure 57c), the CE will be moved aft of the CLR, the stern will be blown to leeward, and weather helm is simulated.

In theory, the most effective way to change the balance of the boat is to change the location of the whole rig. If you move the mast and sails aft, you increase weather helm; moving the mast forward reduces it. Since lee helm is highly unusual, we usually talk about adjusting to more or less weather helm. Anything in the latter direction, carried to extremes, will produce lee helm.

Though moving the whole rig forward or aft is possible on many small boats, it's time-consuming. On larger yachts it's an extremely expensive proposition. Another solution is to change the amount of sail area forward and aft, as on the weather vane. Adding a bowsprit to a yacht allows the headstay to be moved forward and a larger jib to be used. The center of effort will be moved forward and weather helm will be reduced.

To take the sail area idea to extremes, imagine sailing a sloop under jib alone. Since the total sail area is forward, a strong lee helm will be developed. If you sail the same boat under only the mainsail and no jib, there will be a strong weather helm. By luffing the sails and reducing their efficiency, the same results may be obtained. If the mainsail is luffed, the CE is moved forward toward the jib which is full of wind, and weather helm is reduced. Luffing the jib while the main is kept full increases weather helm. An excellent drill, discussed in Chapter 7, is steering without touching the tiller. Increasing or reducing weather helm is accomplished by luffing the sails judiciously. It's good practice, because one never knows when a rudder might be lost. I was on one Transatlantic Race when the rudder did indeed break loose and was lost. We sailed the last 1,000 miles steering only by the trim of the sails, and finished the race in fourth place overall out of seventeen boats.

There are a number of more subtle ways to move the center of effort of the sails. By raking the mast aft, the sail area is moved aft. To rake a mast is to lean it aft by lengthening the headstay and tightening the backstay. Do not confuse this with bending the mast, which is done by tightening the backstay without adjusting the length of the headstay.

The balance of the boat can also be affected by sail shape. If your mainsail is old and stretched out, it may bag in the middle. The leech of the sail points more to windward, and the airflow, instead of exiting straight off, will be curved to windward. This turning of the air will push the aft part of the sail to leeward and create weather helm.

We can increase or reduce weather helm in another way: by leaving the center of effort where it is and moving the center of lateral resistance (CLR) forward and aft. As mentioned before, the CLR is the center of the underwater surface of the boat (normally called the "underwater plane" of the boat). If we submerse the bow of the boat further by placing equipment or crew forward, some of the underwater plane of the boat near the stern lifts out. The CLR moves forward of the CE and weather helm is increased. If you sink the stern deeper, thereby lifting the bow out, weather helm is decreased. As a memory aid, imagine the bow being blown to leeward by the wind because more of it is out of the water. We know the real reason is that the CLR moves aft, but the above example may help you remember.

Sailboats with centerboards can adjust the fore and aft placement of the CLR easily. A centerboard pivots on a pin at the forward end. When it is halfway down, the surface exposed to the water is further aft than when it has been pivoted all the way down. Note in Figure 58 that the CLR in diagram A, with the board lowered halfway down, is further aft than in diagram B,

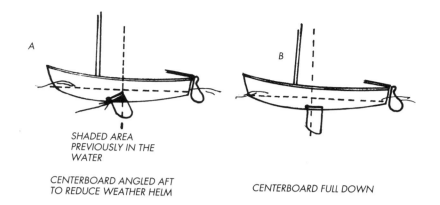

SHADED AREA
PREVIOUSLY IN THE
WATER

CENTERBOARD ANGLED AFT
TO REDUCE WEATHER HELM

CENTERBOARD FULL DOWN

Fig. 58. As the centerboard is raised or lowered, the major area is aft of its full-down position. This brings the CLR aft and reduces weather helm.

where the board has been lowered all the way. The centerboard is used mainly when closehauled to reduce leeway. On reaches, leeway isn't as much a problem, because the sail forces are directed more parallel to the boat's heading. But weather helm *is* a problem because the sail area is out over the water. By raising the centerboard to a midway position, the CLR moves aft to reduce weather helm, yet there is still enough board down to reduce leeway. As can be seen in Figure 58, only the small shaded area is lost, though the board has been raised considerably.

The following methods can be used to reduce weather helm: (1) increase sail area forward (larger jib); (2) reduce sail area or effectiveness aft (reef or luff the main); (3) reduce mast rake; (4) place the mast more forward; (5) move weight aft; (6) keep the boat flat (less heeling); or (7) raise or lower the centerboard halfway.

Boat Speed

Since the speed a sailboat can sail is uppermost in the beginner's mind, let's consider it for a moment.

If two boats are of the displacement type, meaning that they are heavy boats with deep, ballasted keels, the one with the longer waterline length will sail faster than the smaller one. The speed of both is restricted to their theoretical "hull speed" which is expressed as $1.34 \sqrt{LWL}$. In other words, a cruising/racing boat with a waterline length of 49 feet has a theoretical hull speed of about 9.4 knots (1.34×7—the square root of 49). Some people say "maximum hull speed," but that's redundant because "hull speed" is the maximum speed a particular hull can attain.

As a sailboat plows through the water, she creates a bow wave and a series of little transverse waves that move along the hull. The faster she goes, the more volume of water is pushed aside and the larger the bow wave becomes.

27. At hull speed, there is only a large bow wave and a large quarter wave.

The length of a wave is directly proportional to its height. As the bow wave gets higher, the distance from crest to crest lengthens. What begins as a series of small waves along the hull becomes a smaller number of larger waves until at last the distance between crests equals the waterline length of the boat. At this point a boat has an enormous bow wave followed by an equally large quarter wave near the stern, with a trough between the two.

Photo 27 shows a sailboat motoring at hull speed. The boat has reached her hull speed, because any greater speed causes the quarter wave to move even further aft. Without a wave to support the stern, it will drop into the trough. I've seen sailboats towed by larger powerboats at speeds exceeding the sailboat's hull speed. Their sterns tend to leave the quarter wave behind and drop into the trough between the crests. They end up almost under the water (Figure 59) as the boat angles upward to the bow. A sailboat would never have enough power in her sails to exceed her hull speed. The formula is derived from the speed that a wave travels through the water, which is 1.34 times the square root of the distance between crests. Since the distance between the crest of the bow wave and that of the quarter wave can't be greater than the waterline length of the boat, the theoretical maximum speed of the boat becomes equal to the speed of the bow and quarter waves.

Fig. 59. Boat towed faster than its hull speed.

28. Surfing.

This maximum speed varies a great deal with hull shape and the weight-to-length ratio of the boat. Actually, the theory only works well with heavy-displacement sailboats. Centerboard boats with flat hull configurations and many fin-keeled boats don't have a true hull speed. At slow speeds, such boats plow through the water just like a displacement boat. However, as their speed increases, they start skimming the surface of the water on their flat hulls, just as children "skip" flat stones on the water. This is called "planing," and such boats are called planing sailboats. Most powerboats act the same way. At slow speed, they plow the water aside. At greater speeds, the boat is shoved higher and higher up on its bow wave at a steep angle until the unsupported bow, with the bow wave well aft, levels off and the boat breaks onto a plane. The lighter the sailboat in relation to its length, the greater potential it has for planing.

Actually, planing is done in the absence of waves. When large waves are present and pushing the sailboat from behind, another type of propulsion takes place: surfing. Just like a surfer on a surfboard, a sailboat can catch the front side of a wave while running downwind and literally fall down the wave with a tremendous burst of speed. The sailboat in Photo 28 is surfing on a wave. It's a tricky, exhilarating test of helmsmanship. Though light sailboats surf more readily than heavy-displacement sailboats, the latter are perfectly capable of surfing and attaining speeds far in excess of their theoretical hull speed.

◆ 7 ◆

Gaining Sailing Proficiency

Sailing Board Boats

The category of "board" boats includes both centerboard boats (with pivoting centerboards) like the Lightning, Snipe, and 470, and daggerboard boats (with a board that lowers straight down like a dagger in a sheath) such as the Sunfish, Laser, Force Five, and Optimist dinghy. These are common examples but there are literally thousands. The basic sailing procedures hold true whether the sailboat is a board boat or a keelboat, with one notable exception: a board boat can capsize.

Most of the boats mentioned above are of the size that can be righted fairly easily by the crew if capsized. If the boat is large enough to need outside aid to get it right-side-up again, it's usually designed with a keel so it cannot capsize.

Since drownings have resulted from capsizing, there are a number of safety rules one should follow when sailing capsizable boats:

Life Vests

Wear a life vest. To be a good swimmer is not sufficient. The danger isn't in the first time you capsize on a warm, sunny day. It's after a series of multiple capsizes caused by a squall that has both caught you by surprise and cooled off the weather, making you not only exhausted but cold. Then, when you no longer have the strength to get the boat upright again, if you lose your grip on it and it's blown out of reach, you're in trouble. I have rescued people in this sort of trouble, have talked to others who have had like experiences, and know first-hand how tired one can get from righting a capsized boat a number of times.

29. A compact, flexible Coast Guard–approved sailing vest for flotation.

There are a number of makes of comfortable, flexible, soft Coast Guard-approved life vests, as in Photo 29. They do not inhibit movement and were designed for sailing. Not only will they float the wearer, but they help insulate against the cold. Remember to wear them, though. Just to have them aboard is not adequate, as they can float away during a capsize.

Capsize

Righting a capsized sailboat is fairly simple if done properly. Make sure that the mainsheet is completely loose so you won't be lifting a sail full of water as it comes up. Then rotate the boat so that the luff of the mainsail is headed somewhat into the wind, as in positions B, C, and D in Figure 60. Climb up on the centerboard, as in Photo 30, and lean out with your weight to break the mast free of the water. As soon as the wind gets under the sail and breaks it free of the water, the boat should come up easily. As it comes up, step from the centerboard over the side into the cockpit (Photo 31), trim the sails, and you're off.

One of the mistakes a novice often makes is trying to right a board boat in positions F and G. The mast is coming out of the water on the windward side instead of the leeward side. As it comes upright, it blows right over and recapsizes on top of the person righting it, who then has to swim around the boat and go through the whole procedure again. One helpful trick if you do right the boat with the mast to windward is to take a deep breath, hold onto the board as the boat rights, go under the boat, and come out the other side

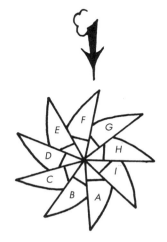

Fig. 60. A dinghy that capsizes in these different positions has to be righted in different ways.

30. To right a capsized center-boarder, stand on the board and lean out.

31. As the boat comes upright, step into the cockpit.

as it recapsizes. Only do this if you are experienced with the type of boat you are righting.

If the boat is in positions H and I of Figure 60, stand on the board and lean out just enough to raise the sail slightly out of the water. The wind will catch the sail and rotate the boat to position A or B. As the boat turns toward position B, lean out more to allow the wind to get under the sail. At this point the boat should come upright easily.

Sometimes a sailboat "turns turtle," as in Photo 32. This means that it has turned completely upside-down and the bottom looks like the shell of a sea turtle on the surface, hence the boat has "turtled." Just grab the end of the daggerboard and lean back until the sails and board get parallel to the water. Then

32. A "turtled" sailboat is one which has flipped completely upside-down.

follow the same procedures as above to right it the rest of the way. If the sailboat was running, the daggerboard may not have been down all the way and probably dropped out of the slot as the boat turtled. Instead of diving under the boat and trying to reinsert it up through the slot, climb onto the bottom of the turtled boat and insert a small amount of the board into the slot the wrong way (from the bottom-of-the-boat side) and lean out, using the board for leverage the normal way. As the boat starts to come upright, pull the board out of the bottom and bring it into the cockpit with you for insertion in the proper direction.

Stay Aboard

If all else fails, at the very least, stay with the boat. Most drownings occur because sailors think that shore is close enough to swim to, and that they can get help for the others aboard. Shore usually turns out to be much farther away than it looks (note the people on the beach in Photo 33). A sailboat can float for days upside-down, so wait for some one to spot your predicament and come to your rescue if you are unable to right it yourself.

Practice

Practice capsizing on purpose. There are two benefits to this—it prepares you for what to do when you capsize inadvertently, and it changes your attitude toward capsizing. The latter is most important. Many people are not only afraid to capsize, but consider it a disgrace—a graphic indication that they are lousy sailors. This just isn't so. To capsize a board boat is commonplace and only means that you have pushed the boat beyond your limit. The best board boat sailor in the world will capsize when planing at high speeds at a wind strength beyond what he can comfortably handle. A less experienced sailor will capsize in lesser conditions. It only means that he hasn't been timid or

33. Always hang onto the boat until help comes.

holding back to avoid capsizing. So remember—there is no stigma attached to capsizing. Practice it enough so that you can right the boat in a moment. Do not go sailing far from land until you know for sure that you and your crew, if any, are capable of righting the boat. In the case of lightweight people, children, and some older people, there may be insufficient weight and/or strength to right the boat. You don't want to discover this fact when you're out of sight of help.

Drills

To sail a boat well takes practice. Most people believe that if they have sailed every weekend all summer they have had a great deal of practice. I disagree. "All summer" may mean 12 weekends. Their practice, therefore, means picking up the mooring once a day for 24 days. True practice is picking up the mooring 24 times in two hours.

Tacking and Jibing

The practice of any sport is dull unless a game or goal is made of it. First, determine the specific area of your sailing that needs improvement, devise a test that emphasizes that area, and practice that test until it becomes second nature. For instance, you decide your tacking and jibing need work. One obvious solution is to go out sailing and practice tacking and jibing. But if you have no goal or yardstick to measure your improvement, you will very quickly tire of it. So design a test. Find two marks, one dead upwind of the other. Start at the leeward mark and beat to the weather mark, timing the interval needed to cover the distance with a certain number of tacks. On each beat to the weather mark, add one or two tacks, and on each run to the leeward mark, add one or two jibes. Try to do it without losing much time against what it took to cover the distance during the first beat and run.

If you are lucky enough to have a friend with an identical boat, you can have a good time practicing reach-to-reach tacking and jibing by developing

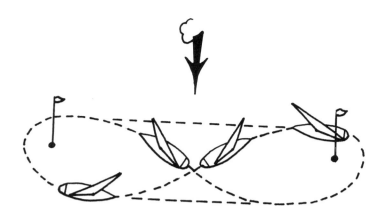

Fig. 61. Pursuit drill and figure-eight drill.

a pursuit test. Set two buoys perpendicular to the wind direction. Start one boat at one buoy and the other at the second buoy. Chase each other around the buoys and see who gains (Figure 61). This is much like the standard bicycle pursuit races where two cyclists start at opposite sides of a track and try to catch one another. It tends to make practice more fun. A variation is to make the course into a figure-eight, but be careful that you know the right-of-way rules at the cross in the middle.

Moorings

Picking up the mooring can be practiced by changing the approach to the mooring buoy and the number of crew members handling the boat. We mentioned before that the best approach is a reach, but there may be times under crowded mooring conditions when such an approach is impossible. So, also practice both a closehauled approach and a running one. After each set of approaches, reduce the number of crew members in the act by one until, in the end, one person is picking up the mooring single-handedly. This is a great confidence builder for those who are concerned about how to handle the boat if the skipper falls overboard.

Boat Control

Simple boat handling is an area not practiced enough by the beginning sailor. By this I mean boat control at slow speed, stopping and accelerating the boat. To practice stopping, come up to a mark sailing as fast as you can on various points of sail. Then put on the brakes when your bow comes abreast of the mark. See if you can't shorten the distance it takes you to stop each time you do it. By "putting on the brakes," I mean backing the main against the wind on the leeward side, as in Figure 62. Have a crew member push it out as far as possible and at the same time head up into the wind to counteract the strong lee helm that will develop and to expose more sail to the wind. (If

Fig. 62. To stop a sailboat quickly, back the mainsail.

you don't counteract the lee helm, the bow will fall off to leeward. The more it falls off, the further out the main has to be backed to be effective.) Violent rudder motions back and forth will also slow the boat, so experiment using them. When you are running, you can slow the boat by trimming the main and jib amidships (in the middle of the boat). This should be done only on a keelboat since this can capsize a centerboarder.

To hold a position almost motionless in the water, again use a buoy as your guide. Stay as close to it as possible by luffing and trimming your sails. Trim the main to scoot the bow into the wind or trim the jib to make the bow fall off. Your rudder is of little use to you in this exercise, so concentrate on making the sails do the work. A series of little scallops up, down, up, down on both tacks (but basically into the wind) will keep you within a very small radius of the mark and train you to keep complete control over your boat. Also, sculling the rudder can help you turn the boat or give you forward motion when there is no wind. Sculling is a series of strong rudder movements back and forth which makes the rudder act like a tail of a fish for propulsion.

Accelerating is the third boat control aspect not practiced enough by beginners. To steer a sailboat with a rudder, there must be water flow over that rudder. We often see novices try to pinch up to avoid an obstruction, before they have enough steerageway. Unable to turn, they end up hitting the object they wished to avoid. Try setting off from a standing start and reaching top speed in the shortest distance possible. You'll soon learn that there's a very delicate balance between trimming the sails and pointing. If you trim the sails too fast or point too high, the boat will drift sideways due to the lack of lift on the underwater surfaces. A good test is to time how long it takes to reach a mark a short distance upwind. From a position dead in the water, trim or back the jib to throw your bow off to a close-reach heading. At the same time, start trimming the main and hike out hard, a maneuver that will flatten the boat and swing the sails up toward the wind to give you more power. As you begin to pick up forward speed, trim the main harder, but not so hard as to create strong weather helm. Your goal should be to pick up speed using a minimal amount of helm. As you start moving faster, gradually head up to a close-hauled course so you achieve full speed and a closehauled attitude at the same time.

Mooring Pickup Drill

If you keep your boat on a mooring, it's probably in front of a marina or yacht club in plain view of curious spectators. Since you only pick up the mooring once a day or possibly twenty times a summer, it's a good idea to go off by yourself and practice. It could save you some embarrassment. Try it both under engine and under sail, because you never know when your engine might not be available. Pick a point downwind of the buoy, approach on a reach, and shoot into the wind when you have arrived at your downwind position. If you have judged correctly, you will come to a complete stop when your bow reaches the buoy. You might think that on windy days, when the boat is sailing fast, it will shoot farther before coming to a stop and that on light wind days, with the boat sailing slowly, you would need to pick a turning point closer to the buoy. Wrong. The reverse is true. Heavy winds stop the boat abruptly when you shoot, so turn quite close to the buoy and allow more distance to shoot in light winds. This same drill may be helpful when a crew member falls overboard, so make sure you practice.

Rudderless Drill

Another drill one hopes never to have to use is sailing without a rudder. Though you may sail 20 years without losing your rudder at sea, it could happen your first time out. We have already briefly mentioned that this is done by changing the efficiency of the sails fore and aft. By luffing the jib and trimming the main, we create weather helm and the boat turns into the wind. By luffing the main and flattening the jib, the wind pushes the bow to leeward—in other words, lee helm. To practice this, trim your jib reasonably flat and ease your mainsail until the boat is balanced and sails straight ahead when the helm is released. Then change your course by trimming the main to head up and pushing the boom out to fall off. When the bow starts swinging in one direction, you must immediately begin the opposite procedures to counteract the swing. In order to tack, free the jib sheets and trim in the mainsail hard and fast. As soon as the boat is past head-to-wind, trim the jib and ease the main to force the bow down. If necessary, back the jib. Jibing is much more difficult to do without the rudder because the mainsail causes the boat to turn toward the wind when running. To try it, ease the main completely, making sure the boom vang is also loose, and back the jib to windward. As you fall off to a run, move all the crew to the windward side of the boat and hike out. By heeling the boat to weather, lee helm should be created. Just as a bow wave on the lee side pushes a heeling boat to weather, a bow wave on the windward side (caused by heeling the boat to windward) pushes the bow to leeward. In this case, we are using crew weight to help a rudderless jibe, but at other times crew members hike out to weather, not only when closehauled, but on reaches and runs to reduce weather helm.

If the breeze is very light, we can make minor adjustments to the helm by moving the crew weight forward and aft. With the boat balanced as described above, move the crew well forward toward the bow. The boat will head into the wind as the curve of the bow bites more deeply into the water. By moving the crew to the stern, the bow will fall off to leeward.

Sailing Backward

Another drill that helps the novice learn how to steer and control a sailboat better is sailing backward. It may seem like a strange exercise, but there are many times when the boat is going backward and the skipper needs to

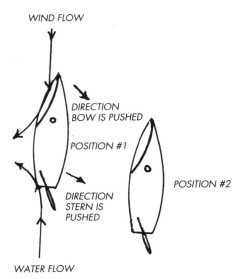

WIND FLOW

DIRECTION
BOW IS PUSHED

POSITION #1

POSITION #2

DIRECTION
STERN IS
PUSHED

WATER FLOW

Fig. 63. When a skipper puts the tiller the wrong way as the jib is backed, the two actions nullify each other.

steer the proper way instinctively. For instance, when a sailboat drops off from a mooring she is in irons and the jib has to be backed to throw her off onto one tack or the other. Nothing galls me more than hearing a sailor scream at his wife or crew to "Back the jib, back the jib!" only to notice that the reason he's falling off on the wrong tack toward another moored boat is that he's pushing the tiller the wrong way. If a skipper feels it necessary to yell at someone else, he should be sure he's doing his own job properly. In the case above, if the jib is backed to the port side of the boat but the helmsman has the tiller over to the same side, the rudder and jib are working against one another since the boat is moving backward. He believes he is turning the boat to starboard and he'd be correct if the boat were moving forward. Figure 63 shows the bow being pushed to starboard by the backed jib, but the rudder is also directing the stern to starboard as the boat goes backward. If the boat is drifting backward fast enough, the two can cancel each other out and the boat will stay in irons.

That's usually when the yelling starts. The frustrated novice skipper is convinced that his crew is doing something wrong when actually he is the one at fault for not understanding what he is supposed to do with the rudder. If he had looked over the side at the water, he would have noticed that the boat was going backward and steered accordingly.

Everyone should learn to sail backward. When you practice it, you'll find that the first problem is to get the boat moving astern in the first place. The easiest way is to do a slow tack into the wind, so that almost all headway is lost by the time the bow is slightly past head-to-wind. Now, push the mainsail way out over the same side of the boat it was originally on (see Figure 62).

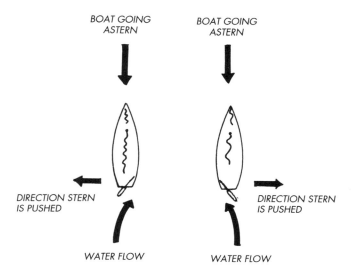

BOAT GOING
ASTERN

BOAT GOING
ASTERN

DIRECTION STERN
IS PUSHED

DIRECTION STERN
IS PUSHED

WATER FLOW

WATER FLOW

Fig. 64. A sailboat backing down.

Backing the main will stop the boat dead in the water and it will soon start moving backward. At this point, the helmsman will be able to steer with the rudder and the crew can cease backing the mainsail, allowing the sail to luff in the middle of the boat. The wind in the rigging should be sufficient to push the boat backward at a good clip. The key is to keep the boat sailing dead downwind. If it falls off one way or the other, the sails may fill and start the boat sailing forward. To make the stern go to port, put the tiller to starboard and vice versa, as in Figure 64. On most boats, the rudder post is near the leading edge of the rudder. When sailing backward, the trailing edge is forward and it takes a great deal of strength to hold the tiller straight if the rudder gets slightly sideways to the water flow. It's like a child pushing a little red wagon instead of pulling it. If it turns slightly off from a straight line, it spins out. At the end of the backward run, decide which tack you want to sail on forward. If you want to end up on the port tack, put your tiller to starboard and vice versa.

Right-of-Way

It's incredible how many sailboats on the water are skippered by sailors who know practically nothing about the navigation rules—the right-of-way rules. I've heard skippers say that the rules don't matter if one just gets out of the way of other boats. This works until two boats are approaching one another on a collision course and both "get out of the way" of each other in the same direction! It's much like an Alphonse and Gaston act, with less comical consequences.

You must first be constantly on the lookout for any other boat in the vicinity that could possibly collide with you. This may sound obvious, but sailors become accustomed to the wide open space of water around them and often succumb to a reduction of vigilance to a level they would never permit themselves while driving a car. When the helmsman and crew are sitting to windward, they are blind to boats approaching from leeward behind the sails. It is the ultimate responsibility of the helmsman to be sure that no boat collides with him, so he must occasionally look to leeward or assign one of his crew the job. Collisions often occur when two boats are closehauled, as in Figure 65, where each is sailing in the other's blind spot and no crew member has gone to leeward to take a look. This is inexcusable in the case of a port tack boat, since a closehauled boat on starboard tack has right-of-way. But even if you're on starboard tack, you should avoid the complacency that often comes with having the right-of-way and keep a watchful eye open.

A crew member may spot a boat first and, if a collision is imminent, must quickly and accurately describe its location to the skipper so he or she can make the necessary course corrections. Figure 66 indicates the words which are spoken by the crew member to describe the position of a boat in the direction of the solid arrows. The dotted arrows further define the position. Each

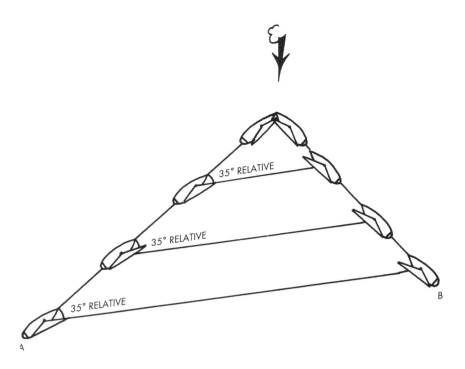

Fig. 65. If the bearing to another boat doesn't change, a collision is imminent.

dotted arrow is a "point." There are 32 points in the 360° of a compass, or 11.25° to a point, 8 points to a quadrant. A converging boat may be one, two, or three points "forward of abeam" or "abaft abeam" (aft of abeam). Or it may be one, two, or three points "on the starboard bow" starting from dead ahead, or one, two, or three points "on the starboard quarter" starting from dead astern. Though we are only covering the starboard side of the boat, the same applies for the port side.

When you do see a yacht on a converging course, there is one way of being sure whether or not it's a collision course (one that will result in a collision). Take a bearing on the other boat, either by using your compass or by lining it up with a shroud, stanchion, or other fixed item on your boat. If, a little while later, the bearing hasn't changed and you haven't altered your course or speed, then you are on a collision course. That the boats are traveling at different speeds makes no difference. Boat A in Figure 65 is obviously sailing faster because it is covering more distance in the same amount of time as boat B. Each time the skipper of A takes a bearing on B, it remains 35° relative, so the collision is inevitable unless A changes course.

A relative bearing is one which uses the bow or centerline of the boat as zero degrees and measures 360° in a clockwise direction, just like a compass with the bow as north. A magnetic bearing is one that reads directly off the compass. For instance, if boat A in Figure 65 is sailing due east (90°), the magnetic bearing to boat B will be 125° (90° + 35°) When taking bearings on a

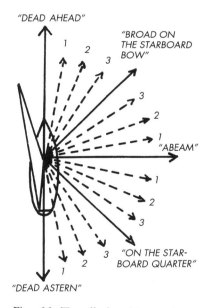

Fig. 66. To tell the skipper the location of another boat, the crew uses the terms "dead ahead," "broad on the starboard (port) bow," "abeam," "on the starboard (port) quarter," and "dead astern," and the number of "points" between them.

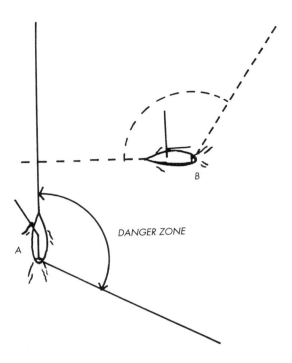

DANGER ZONE

Fig. 67. A motorboat in another's "danger zone" has the right-of-way.

converging boat, we are usually dealing with a magnetic bearing taken from the compass. Let's say the second bearing taken on boat B is 115°. This indicates that: (1) the bearing is changing so there won't be a collision; and (2) it's getting closer to A's heading of 90° so B will cross ahead of A. If the second bearing is larger than the original 125°, A will cross ahead of B.

So far, we have spotted a converging boat, the crew has correctly indicated its position to the skipper, bearings have been taken, and the determination made that a collision is a possibility. The next decision is which boat is the "stand-on vessel," the one with the right-of-way, and which is the "give-way vessel," the one that must keep clear of the other. This varies, depending on whether two motorboats are approaching each other, or two sailboats, or one of each.

The major rule governing two motorboats is shown in Figure 67. A boat's "danger zone" is an area from dead ahead to two points abaft of the starboard beam. Any boat in your danger zone has right-of-way over you. Note in Figure 67 that boat B is in A's danger zone. Also note that we have drawn two sailboats, and the reader may wonder at this. Why are two sailboats being included in the rules governing motorboats? Their sails are not raised in the diagram and they are powering under auxiliary engines, so they come under the motorboat rules of the road. Actually, it doesn't matter whether the sails are set or not. If they have an engine running and in gear, even a tiny outboard motor on a small day sailor, they are classified as a motorboat.

The other most common motorboat rule to remember is that if two vessels are approaching almost head-on, each will avoid the other by turning to starboard. It's most important to make your intentions very clear to the other skipper. A sharp turn to starboard followed by a gradual turn back to your original course will indicate that you plan to pass port to port (your port side passing their port side.) Motorboats use horn signals for passing and, legally, sailboats under power should too. As a practical matter, though, when a day sailor uses an outboard, it's such a rare occurrence that the horn is usually buried in a bucket or tool kit somewhere and not handy. Therefore, make sure your turns clearly indicate your course intentions. One other common motorboat rule is the overtaking rule. A boat catching up to another from any point aft of the danger zone is overtaking and must keep clear of the overtaken boat.

The rule covering sail versus power is quite simple. Almost every sailor knows that a sailboat has right-of-way over a motorboat. However, not many seem to know that there are a number of exceptions to this rule. If the motorboat is anchored, is disabled, or is being overtaken by a sailboat, the motorboat is the privileged vessel. A commercial vessel with limited maneuverability in a narrow channel and a commercial fishing boat trawling also have right-of-way over a sailboat.

A slightly more complicated set of rules governs two sailboats meeting one another. There are three basic possibilities covered by three rules: (1) if sailboats are converging on the same tack, the leeward boat has right-of-way; (2) if they are converging on opposite tacks, the starboard tack boat has right-of-way; and (3) as in motorboats, the overtaken boat (the boat ahead) has right-of-way over the overtaking boat.

TEST QUESTIONS ON PART I

1. What is LOA?
2. What is standing rigging? Running rigging?
3. What are stays? Shrouds?
4. What are halyards? Sheets?
5. What are the names of the three corners of a sail?
6. What are the edge areas between the corners called?
7. What is a beat?
8. What is hardening up?
9. What is a header? A lift?
10. What is a veering wind? A backing wind?
11. What happens to the apparent wind direction during a puff?
12. If the top windward wool streamer on the jib flutters before the lower ones, what does this indicate to you?
13. How do you steer without a rudder?
14. Describe planing.
15. Describe surfing.
16. What is the cardinal rule if you capsize?
17. How do you know if a boat is on a collision course with another?
18. What is the "danger zone"?
19. In the following situations, determine which boat has the right-of-way:

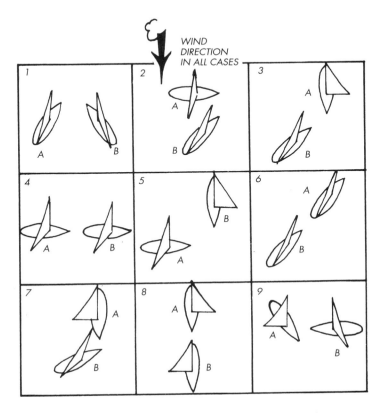

PART II

Fundamentals of Cruising

Introduction

I used to think cruising was for retired racing sailors. Why would anyone cruise when you were still young and strong enough to enjoy the excitement of racing? I've changed my tune since we started taking groups of our past students on sailing trips to the Bahamas, Tonga, Tahiti, New Zealand, the Grenadines, Virgin Islands, Greece, the French Mediterranean, and the Maine coast. Cruising is a great way to see the world and visit islands that one could never visit any other way—islands with no airports, few roads, and no cruise ship harbors—islands with delightful, sincere people in trades that haven't changed for hundreds of years.

The cruising bug has bitten many people and some of you reading this book will want to jump right into it without learning to sail a smaller boat first. Just about everything mentioned in the learn-to-sail portion in the beginning is usable on any size boat. We've had many students take our courses and immediately buy a $50,000 to $200,000 cruising boat. I see nothing really wrong with this if you can afford it, except that you won't have the background to know what size or style of boat will be best suited for your purposes.

The purpose of this section of the book is to help the person who is going cruising for the first time know what to expect and how to handle it. They say cruising is like flying—hours of boredom interspersed with moments of sheer terror. That may be a bit melodramatic on both ends. I don't believe cruising is boring. It's relaxing and is one of the few places in the world you won't be bothered by a telephone ringing. However, it is true that trouble seems to spawn more trouble. If you ever get your anchorline tangled in your propeller so you have neither anchor nor engine to keep you out of trouble, you're sure to be to windward of some reef you can't afford to end up on. So we hope the following can help you avoid such pitfalls.

A neighbor on my block told me his son sailed a 44' ketch frm the Great Lakes to Florida. When he called home along the way, my friend asked how he could be doing this, since he knew nothing about sailing. "Oh," the son said, "when I have any problem I look it up in this great book I have on board." "What book?" asked the father. "It's called *Fundamentals of Sailing, Cruising, and Racing.*" Well, he made it to Florida!

◆ I ◆

Basics

Engine Maneuvering

An engine aboard a cruising boat is an afterthought. It's called an "auxiliary" engine, and a boat so equipped will normally be called an "auxiliary cruising boat" or, more simply, an "auxiliary."

The engine is usually of low horsepower—a 35-foot cruising boat will have about a 30-horsepower engine. The reason for this is that after the boat reaches close to hull speed it would take tremendous horsepower to make it go any faster. Take the stock fiberglass 33-foot boat we used to own, for example. At 1800 or 1900 RPM we could make about 6 knots (depending on the seas). If we revved it up to 2700 RPM, we'd eat up our gas supply, strain the engine, and only go about a quarter knot faster. So, though the low horsepower may take longer to get the boat up to cruising speed, once there it doesn't take much force to keep the boat moving at that speed. There are a number of large schooners that have no engines at all. The Schooner *Bill of Rights* (sistership of the boat in Photo 2), for example, is 125 feet long and uses a little pushboat (like a long dinghy) with a small inboard to push her when becalmed. Even this small engine can push her at speeds of 5 knots, though it takes awhile to reach that speed.

The other peculiarity of an auxiliary is that while it takes a long time to get that mass of boat up to cruising speed, it takes even longer to get it to stop. The propeller is just not as effective in reverse. In fact, if you come into a dock downwind with a following sea under power alone and put it into reverse, you may never stop until something hard gets in the way or unless you're very handy with the lines.

The one most common mistake in docking is approaching too fast. A cruising boat often has a small two-bladed propeller hidden behind the keel, particularly if it's a boat used for racing also. Because of the inefficient propeller, you can put the engine in reverse, rev it up, and the boat still moves forward, gradually slowing down. I knew a man who had a beautiful 48-foot sailboat with a Mercedes diesel as auxiliary power. He always approached the dock too fast. About 100 yards away he'd be going 5 knots, put the engine in reverse, and hope that the boat would come to a stop by the time it was alongside. One day, when there was a 60-foot yacht on the far end of the dock, sticking out at right angles to the long side that my friend planned to approach, he misjudged the speed. Even though the engine was screaming in reverse, we were now alongside the dock with about 2 knots of headway and heading straight for the bow section of the other yacht extending past the edge of the dock end. My friend couldn't steer out because the stern would just bump if he tried to make such a sharp turn. Luckily I was able to toss a line from the bow to the other boat's owner, who ran aft and snubbed it around a piling. Our bow crunched into the dock as the boat's forward motion was checked just short of a collision.

The line tied aft from the bow described above is one of the common lines used in tying a boat up at a dock. It's called an "after spring" line, is tied to the forward part of the boat, and keeps the boat from drifting forward. These spring lines combine with the bow and stern lines to keep the boat parallel to the dock so it will rest on fenders and not rub its topsides on the dock or on pilings (see Figure 68 and Photo 34).

Actually, handling a cruising boat under power can be tricky. Many people think that once they've turned on the engine they can forget about the

34. Bow, stern, and spring lines.

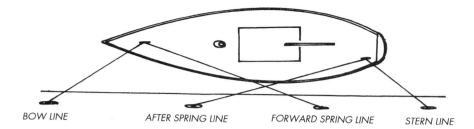

BOW LINE   AFTER SPRING LINE   FORWARD SPRING LINE   STERN LINE   Fig. 68. Spring lines.

things that concern them while sailing—wind direction and strength, current direction and strength, and wave force. On the contrary, these have to be considered more than ever because most of the time the engine is being used in close quarters for mooring or docking purposes.

Whenever possible, head into the wind when docking. If the wind is perpendicular to the dock it will cause you to drift sideways towards it. Imagine the dock to be a few feet to windward of where it actually is. Try to make your landing at this imaginary dock and by the time you stop, you'll find yourself laying gently alongside the real one. If the wind is blowing across the dock the other way, approach it at about a 45° angle. The stronger the wind, the more you have to approach directly into the wind; the lighter the wind, the more you can approach parallel to the dock (broadside to the wind; see Figure 69). Also, if the current is against the wind, the more parallel to the dock you can be; and if the current is with the wind, the more upwind and upcurrent your approach must be (note Figure 70). The reason is simple: the

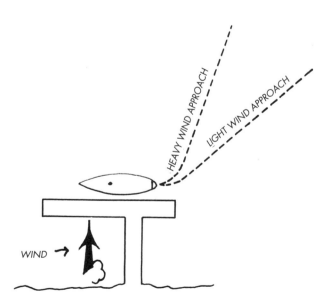

Fig. 69. Approaching a dock under power with a wind blowing boat away from it.

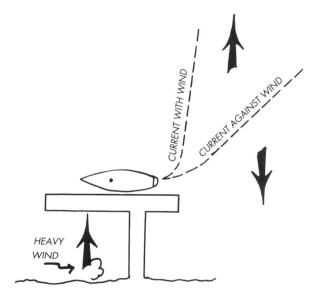

Fig. 70. Docking under power in a current.

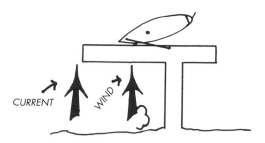

Fig. 71. Using a spring line to help bring the stern into the dock. Secure a bow line to the dock and run forward against it to bring the boat in parallel.

second you turn broadside to the dock, the wind and current push you away from it. When this condition is aggravated, you may have to get a bow line secured while the boat is headed into the wind and then turn the boat in forward gear, kicking the stern in and using the bow line as a spring line, as in Figure 71. Or, if it's blowing 35 MPH or so, you may have to forget the engine after the bow line is attached and just winch the stern into the dock with a stern line and a jib sheet winch.

Engine Operation

When operating a sailboat under engine, always shift into or out of gear with the throttle at idle. With the single lever Morse control, common to many sailboats, this is automatic. The handle is pulled out at the center and when pushed forward, will rev up in neutral. When pulled back to the vertical position, it should pop in automatically. Then when you push it forward from neutral, it first goes into forward gear and then accelerates more and more the further you push the handle. Pull the handle back to put it into reverse and the farther you pull it back the more it accelerates in reverse. Problems arise when people jam it forward fast, then pull it back, revving it in reverse without pausing when the handle is vertical. It's terribly rough on the transmission. So treat it gently. Put it forward just enough to hear it "clunk" into forward gear before revving it up and when you pull back, pause with the handle in neutral, then pull back just enough to hear the engine "clunk" into reverse before pulling it back for speed.

Some handles have a button in the middle that you press and push the handle forward to rev in neutral. When you pull the handle back to vertical, the button pops out automatically, allowing the handle to engage in forward or reverse.

It's a good idea to practice under power the first day, so you know how long it takes to stop, how well the boat tracks in reverse, how it pulls when you gun it in reverse, what sort of turning radius you have, and how much the wind will affect you when you make a circle under power. A good exercise is to try to make a perfect circle. Normally, the wind will cause the circle to be egg-

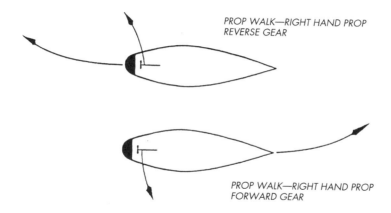

PROP WALK—RIGHT HAND PROP
REVERSE GEAR

PROP WALK—RIGHT HAND PROP
FORWARD GEAR

Fig. 72. Prop walk effect in forward and reverse gear.

shaped, but by advancing the throttle as you turn upwind and throttling back as you turn downwind, with practice you'll control the shape of the circle.

Now practice making a tight full circle in forward gear to port and then to starboard. The boat will normally turn in a smaller radius to port than to starboard. This is because of the direction of rotation of the propeller. A propeller that rotates clockwise in forward gear is correctly called a "right-hand wheel." Imagine it as a wheel that rests on the sea bottom. Clockwise rotation would "walk" the stern to starboard in forward gear and to port in reverse, as in Figure 72. For single-engined sailboats, a right-hand wheel is almost universally accepted.

I have talked to several architects, engine manufacturers, and propeller engineers, and read articles on why "prop walk" occurs, and am not satisfied with any answer. Among the answers are: (1) Unequal blade thrust between ascending and descending blades because of the downward angle of the shaft; (2) torque; (3) disturbed water near the hull on the upper half of the blade rotation isn't as effective as the lower half, and (4) more pressure at greater depths. Regardless of the true reason, think of the blades as having greater bite at the bottom of the rotation than at the top, so with a right-hand prop in forward the stern walks to starboard, and in reverse it walks to port.

Next, practice making a tight, full circle in reverse gear to port and then to starboard. Note how much tighter the turn is to port than to starboard for the same reason as above.

By using the knowledge we now have of the difference in forward and reverse in both directions, we can use forward and reverse gear to make the smallest possible circle in each direction. This can be very handy knowledge if you are powering into a small harbor to look for an open slip, find nothing, and need to do a 180° turn to exit from the harbor.

Try a turn to starboard as in Figure 73. Put the helm over to starboard to initiate the turn with the engine in neutral. Reverse the engine with short

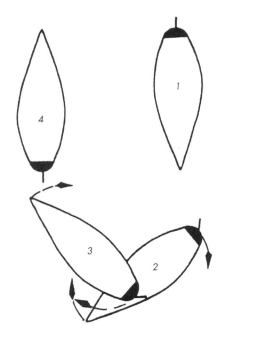
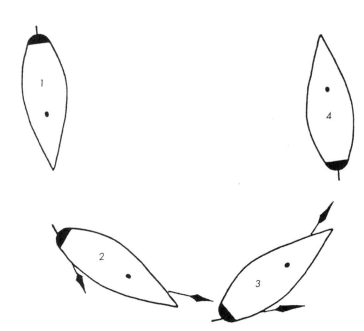
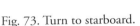

Fig. 73. Turn to starboard.
(1) Approaching the turn area, engine is in neutral to decrease speed.
(2) As turn is initiated with rudder hard to starboard, bursts of reverse are applied to (a) lose all forward way and (b) prop walk the stern to port.
(3) When boat has lost all way, a burst of forward with the wheel still hard over will complete the turn. In this instance, the normal prop walk turning the bow to port in forward is overcome by propeller wash against the rudder.
(4) The turn is completed.

Fig. 74. Turn to port.
(1) Approaching the turn, engine is in idle speed reverse to decrease speed more quickly.
(2) As turn is initiated with rudder hard to port, idle reverse is maintained to take all forward way off. Reverse speed may be increased if boat's way is going to carry it past the turn area.
(3) Helmsman watches the bow on the shoreline to note when the boat stops turning or forward momentum is lost. Then with rudder still hard over, bursts of forward are applied, returning the engine to neutral after each burst.
(4) The turn is completed.

bursts of power, leaving the helm hard over. You should be able to turn the boat completely around in little more than her boat length. If the boat starts going backward, you may need a few spurts in forward to complete the turn.

Next try a turn to port as in Figure 74. Put the engine in idle reverse and initiate the turn by putting the wheel to port as you coast to a stop. Then give the engine short bursts in forward gear alternating with slow reverse. This will kick the stern to starboard without creating much forward motion.

Once you have learned how the boat reacts in reverse, you can use it to your advantage. If the boat has a right-hand wheel, come alongside a dock at an angle, port side to. When you give it a slight burst in reverse to stop the forward movement, the stern kicks in to port and you end up parallel to the dock at the same time the boat stops.

When cruising under power, engine fuel consumption is greatly dependent upon engine RPM. For good fuel economy and to reduce engine wear, cruise at no higher than about 75% of maximum RPM. For instance, if you put the engine in forward gear after warming up, put maximum throttle to it for a moment, and register a top RPM of 2800, then you should cruise at no higher than 2100 RPM. For a displacement cruising sailboat, greater RPM results in only a modest amount of increased speed, yet greatly increased fuel consumption.

Current Effect on Engine Maneuvering

Current can be used to great advantage if used properly—or it can create disaster. As with wind and sea, avoid like the plague getting broadside to it. Approach any landing from the downcurrent side, heading into the current. If there's a 3-knot current running, your boat will have to be traveling 3 knots through the water into the current just to stay in the same place. This is where you can make current work for you.

Once I brought a 40-foot yawl from Charleston, S.C., to New York via the Intracoastal Waterway. We decided to stop overnight at a marina with docks laying parallel to the waterway. Only one berth was left open, a space about 45 feet long between another sailboat to the south and two Corps of Engineers tugs tied side by side to the north. A strong current was running north, so we went past the marina and made a U-turn into the current. When we got past the tugs and opposite the open space, I throttled down until the boat was just stemming the current. Then, I very gingerly pointed the bow a few degrees from directly into the current. The boat started to crab sideways. A little more throttle was needed to remain opposite the open berth. Although the boat was moving at a good clip through the water, over the bottom she was just moving sideways. A fairly large Sunday audience had gathered to watch the fun of some guy trying to put a 40-foot boat in a 45-foot space in a strong current in front of doubled-up tugs. We crabbed in sideways perfectly, and as we cut our engine after making fast to the dock, one of the spectators turned to his little boy and said, "Son, that's the way to park a boat!"

Once you learn how to maneuver your sailboat under power you will find moments of great satisfaction. Just remember to approach a berth very slowly and stay headed into the wind and current if possible. If not, be very aware of the wind's and current's potential effect on your boat, and avoid getting broadside to either.

Getting Underway Under Power

Now let's backtrack to the initial procedures of getting underway using the engine. On many boats there are two batteries aboard and a "battery switch." This switch points to a number of choices: Off, 1, All (or Both), and 2. The idea is to use one battery at a time, so if it dies the spare battery can start the engine to run the alternator which charges them back up. When the engine is not running, use either "1" or "2" for lights, instruments, or pressure water system. Alternate batteries over a period of a few days so they get equal usage. After a number of days of cruising it's sometimes hard to remember which of the two banks of batteries was used the previous day. A helpful memory aid is to use the even-numbered (#2) on even dates of the month and the #1 bank of batteries on odd dates. Before starting the engine, switch to "All" or "Both" so that the engine's alternator will be charging both batteries. *Do not turn the battery switch while the engine is running or you may damage the alternator!*

Many sailboats now have separate banks of batteries. One bank is exclusively for starting the engine, and the other batteries, called "House" batteries, are for everything else. The alternator charges both banks when the engine is running, but nothing can drain the engine batteries when the engine is off. This makes a foolproof system. You will always be able to start the engine to recharge even if the house batteries are totally discharged.

Before leaving, it's a good idea to make a last-minute check below the full length of the boat. If you're planning to sail and it's blowing fairly hard, all loose items have to be properly stowed so they can't fall when the boat heels. The bilge should be pumped dry so bilge water won't slosh up and get into the drawers on the lee side, as often happens on shallow-draft boats. This should be done while the boat is vertical, because if you think of it after the boat starts heeling most of the water may have already left the sump (hollow in the bilge where the bilge water collects for pumping) and you'll never get it dry. Even more serious is the chance you may drown out your batteries with salt water, if there's a great deal of bilge water. So make it a habit to pump the bilge dry every time before starting the engine.

Make sure opening ports (the windows in the side of the cabin) are closed if they can be submersed on the lee side or if a person can step through them on deck. The forward hatch should be closed and dogged down (secured by the thumbscrews that give it a tight seal), particularly if you expect to be beating and may be getting waves on the foredeck.

Also, close any seacocks (the valves that open and close the through-hull openings to the head, sinks, etc.) where necessary. A few boats have to have certain seacocks closed to avoid flooding when heeled way over. This is a design deficiency and depends upon the type of boat.

Open the necessary engine seacocks and valves. If the boat has been berthed for a long period of time, it's good practice to close all the seacocks in case the hose leading from one of them springs a leak or pops off, causing the boat to sink. It's also a good idea to close the valves leading from the fuel tanks lest a fuel line start leaking and some spark ignite the fuel. So, before getting underway, it may be necessary to open the salt water intake valve for the engine, the engine exhaust valve, and the fuel line valves.

If you don't already know it, check how much fuel you have in the tank. It could be dangerous to run out of fuel just as you are leaving a tricky berth. Also, if you have a diesel engine, air will get in the system when you run out of diesel fuel and you will have to "bleed" fresh fuel through the whole fuel system before you can start the engine again. This can take five minutes to an hour, depending on how often you've done it before.

Now, turn on the blower if you have a gasoline engine. This will exhaust any fumes that may be lying in the bilge. Diesels are less prone to fume fires because it's harder to ignite diesel fumes with a spark, so the blower is less important.

Next, advance the throttle, make sure the gearshift is in neutral, and start the engine. Starting procedures differ with engine types, so we won't get into this. The blower may be turned off after the engine starts.

Check the instruments after you have started the engine. The ammeter should be reading on the plus (+) side to show that the batteries are charging. Oil pressure should read the number of pounds designated in the engine manual, probably about 55–65 pounds. Water temperature should rise to 120°–150° F.

You probably are secured to the dock by bow and stern lines and two spring lines. By the way, before I am taken to task by old salts that we are normally using "piers" and "floats" and not "docks" for pleasure craft, common English usage has made the word "dock" (a basin with floodgates for receiving ships) include piers and floats.

Leaving the Dock

The objective in departing from the dock is to do it in a controlled and orderly fashion, leaving little or nothing to chance.

The following docking situations illustrate the techniques for leaving the dock in a controlled manner. In all cases the last two docklines to be brought onboard are doubled back to the boat. This allows all crew members to be aboard before the boat pulls away from the dock, eliminating potentially dangerous leaps to the departing boat.

Situation 1 (Figure 75)—Double bow and stern lines back to the boat so that the short end of the line is cleated on top of the long end.

The crew releases the bow line and pulls the slack back to the boat. When the bow has blown sufficiently away from the dock, retrieve the stern line in the same manner. Put the engine in forward and drive off. Note that the

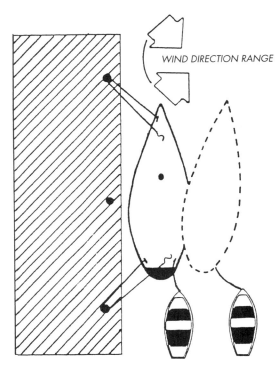

Fig. 75. Leaving the dock. Situation 1.

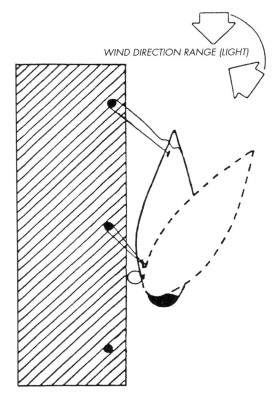

Fig. 76. Leaving the dock. Situation 2—springing the bow out.

dinghy is tied up short to prevent its painter from becoming tangled in the propeller.

Situation 2 (Figure 76)—Springing the bow out. Double bow and spring line as shown. Remove all other docklines and place a couple of fenders near the stern. A small amount of reverse will keep the stern against the dock if the wind is shifty.

Release the bow line and use reverse to back the boat against the spring line. This will draw the stern towards the dock and force the bow away from the dock.

When the bow is sufficiently off the dock, shift into forward and drive off slowly to allow time for the spring line to be retrieved.

Notice that because the propeller is forward of the rudder and prop wash in reverse is going away from it, turning the rudder will have no effect on the boat while springing the bow out.

Prop walk will be a consideration as the boat pulls away from the dock. When the boat in the diagram shifts into forward, the stern will "walk" to starboard. In this case prop walk is making life easy for the helmsman because

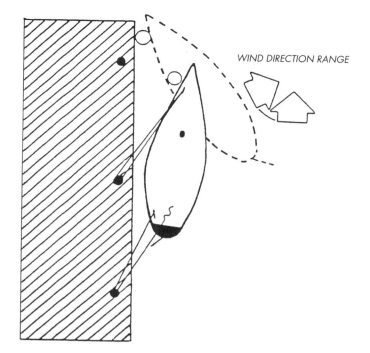

Fig. 77. Leaving the dock. Situation 3—springing the stern out.

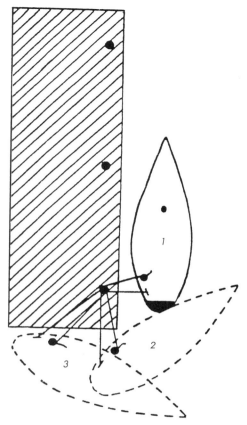

Fig. 78. Leaving the dock. Situation 4—pivoting the boat around the dock.

the stern walks away from the dock. Had the boat been tied starboard side to and executed the same maneuver, prop walk would be working against the helmsman. If this is the case, simply spring the bow a little further out than otherwise necessary and turn the wheel slightly toward the dock as you engage forward. Prop wash will be deflected to starboard by the rudder and this will mitigate the effect of the prop walk.

Situation 3 (Figure 77)—Springing the stern out. Again you can use the engine to hold the boat alongside the dock while all but spring line and stern line are removed. This time releasing the stern line with the engine in forward will force the bow in and the stern out. Again, fenders should be placed towards the bow. Turning the wheel hard to port (toward the dock) will cause the rudder to deflect prop wash to port and this will help kick the stern out. When the stern has moved sufficiently away from the dock, power out in reverse as the spring line is brought aboard. Prop walk will be a factor. In the diagram (Figure 77), as the boat reverses away from the dock, prop walk will bring the stern toward the dock, so it is important to account for this when deciding how far to spring the stern out.

If you want to turn the boat completely around in order to go out in forward gear, use this same system. Have someone on the dock walk the bow along the dock toward where the stern used to be.

Situation 4 (Figure 78)—Pivoting the boat around the end of a dock. (1) Reverse boat against doubled spring line. It is important to carefully place your fenders so that the hull won't be damaged against the corner of the dock. (2) Ease the spring line as shown. The boat will pivot more than 90° around the dock. (3) When the bow is pointed in the desired direction, the engine is shifted to neutral and the spring line is retrieved, allowing the boat to power off.

Another little trick comes into play if you are secured by docking lines that have spliced loops over dock bitts or pilings. Often other boats' docking lines are on top of yours. Just pull your loop up through inside the other loops, over the top of the bitt, down back through other loops and out, as in Figure 79. You don't have to take the others off to get yours.

Before we set sail, let's assume you have to go to the fuel dock to get fuel. Once secured to the fuel dock, make sure that no crew member is smoking, cut the engine (this is done by pulling the choke or turning the ignition key, depending upon the type of engine), and be sure that there is no open flame lit anywhere in the boat, such as a kerosene lamp or cooking stove. Close any openings into the boat's interior that are near the fill pipe. After the tank is full, tighten down the screw-cap and rinse off any spilled fuel with fresh or salt water. Then open the hatches, thoroughly air the boat out, and run the blower (if any) before starting the engine to leave the fuel dock.

After casting off the lines, make sure none are dangling over the side of the boat where they could tangle in the propeller. Remember how important that engine is to you when you're in a tight spot. It's best to keep the jib sheets in the cockpit rather than on the deck lest someone kick them overboard accidentally. Coil and stow the docking lines and don't forget to stow the fenders. There's nothing more land-lubberly-looking than fenders dangling over the side bouncing on waves.

Fig. 79. When your docking line is underneath a number of others, pass the desired loop up through the other loops, lift it off the top, and pass it back down through the other loops.

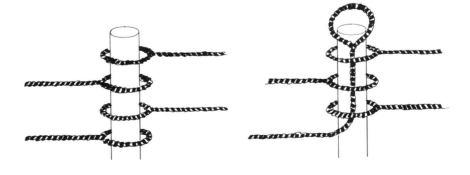

When the wind and/or current is from astern, it may be impossible to leave the dock in forward gear and make the turn away from the dock before running into trouble ahead. The safest departure is often to back away from the slip after springing the stern out as in Figure 77. In reverse the propeller is pulling the stern to windward or into the current and the bow just follows. The boat is under complete control. No surprises.

Setting Sail

When you're in an open area free of submerged dangers or moored boats, head into the wind to raise your sails. Remember as you are powering that your one salvation if the engine dies is the anchor. Have it ready to use immediately. You'll never raise sails fast enough if there's danger around, so anchor if the engine quits.

To raise sails, slow the engine down to idle speed and try to keep the boat stationary, headed right into the wind. If she starts to fall off, put her in forward gear and kick her into the wind again. Never change gears unless the engine is practically idling; certainly not if you're over 1000 RPM. Raise the aftermost sail first. If a yawl or ketch, the mizzen; or if a sloop, the main.

At this point let's define the different types of cruising boats so we know which sails we're talking about. Sailboats fall into categories based on the number of masts and their location.

Single-masted sailboats are either sloops, catboats, or cutters. The sloop has two sails, a jib forward of a mainsail. A catboat has no jib, is usually a fairly small sailboat, and the mast is near the bow. Actually, if the mast is more than two-fifths of the waterline length aft of the point where the bow emerges from the water, it's a cutter.

Double-masted sailboats are either yawls, ketches, or schooners. However, in the former two, the small mast is aft of the larger. The mizzenmast, as it is called, is near the stern of the boat. A good rule of thumb is if the steering apparatus (the tiller or steering wheel) is forward of the mizzen, it's a yawl (as in Photo 35), and if behind the mizzen it's a ketch. There are a few instances where this guideline doesn't work. Every boat has a rudderpost that turns the rudder for steering. Where this rudderpost intersects the waterline is the real point of demarcation. If the mizzen is forward of this point, it's a ketch; if aft, it's a yawl. Since many people don't like to steer a boat with a mast right in front of them, obstructing their vision, they have the designer arrange a steering mechanism that leads forward of the mizzen. Thus, though the wheel is forward of the mizzen, the rudderpost is aft and it's still a ketch.

If the boat has two masts and the forward mast or "foremast" is smaller or the same size as the after mast, it's a schooner. Schooners can have three, four, or even more masts.

35. A yawl with a genoa, mainsail, and mizzen.

By raising the aftermost sail first on any of these types of cruising boats, the boat is kept headed into the wind like a weathervane. Close any hatches you could fall through if hidden by an unfurled sail. A friend of mine was badly injured when he fell through a hatch that was covered by a loose sail and hidden from view. Take off and stow the sail stops that keep the mainsail furled. Raise the mainsail.

As the mainsail is raised, watch that the halyard isn't caught forward of a spreader and that the leech of the main doesn't foul in the shrouds on the way up. The mainsheet and the vang should be loose so the sail won't fill with wind before it's all the way up. The topping lift (the line that holds up the boom when the sails are down) should be eased when the mainsail is up so that the weight of the boom is on the leech of the sail, not on the topping lift, or the sail cannot be trimmed properly.

Having raised the main and mizzen, fall off on the desired tack and cut off engine *if there is no danger to leeward!* If there are reefs, moored boats, or any other potentially dangerous objects to leeward, keep the engine running until you are well clear. Also, it's good practice to run the engine at least 15 minutes to evaporate any condensation that develops in the first 5 minutes of running.

On a boat with a roller-furling jib, normally, the jib will already be on the headstay, the halyard tensioned and cleated properly, and the jib rolled up. However, if you have not sailed for a while, the jib may have been stuffed in a bag below deck to avoid ultraviolet deterioration from the the sun's rays. Or you may have ripped the genoa jib during the cruise and had a sailmaker repair it. In either case the sail needs to be put on the headstay and rolled. First remember how the system works. When the sail is unrolled, the furling line is rolled up on the drum. As you pull on the jib sheet, and the wind fills the jib, the furling line is wound up around the drum. So when you put a jib up the groove of a bare headstay, the furling drum must be full of line. After taking the genoa out of the bag, find the head of the sail. It's the narrowest corner. Insert the luff through the pre-feeder and into the groove of the headstay. If there are two grooves side by side and two halyards, use the port halyard with the port groove and the starboard halyard with the starboard groove. Don't cross them. Crossing them creates a chafing situation when you change sails.

Next, follow along the foot of the sail from the tack to the clew to untangle any twists that may have developed. This can be done from the head to the clew along the leech with the same results, but the leech is longer than the foot and checking it consumes more time. Each jib sheet should then be tied to the clew with a bowline, which is pronounced "bolin." Shackles aren't used much anymore on jib sheets because they can accidentally open, bang against the mast, dent and mar brightwork, chip paint, or bruise a crew member while the boat is tacking. The bowline has almost unlimited uses because no matter how hard the line is pulled, the knot can easily be untied, while many other knots tighten up when strain is applied. Moreover, bowlines are virtually "shake-free proof." Figure 80 shows how a bowline is tied. Make a loop in the standing part of the line (the part whose end is presumably made fast). Pass the free end (the loose end) around or through whatever you are tying it to—in this case, the clew of the jib. The free end goes through the loop you made before, around the standing part, and back down through the loop. Note that the two parts of the line pass through the loop in the same direction and lie parallel to each other. If they don't, you've made the knot wrong. Also, if you pass through the loop initially in the wrong direction, you'll soon discover you don't have a knot at all.

When it comes to tying the bowline for a specific purpose, rather than just for practice ashore, new sailors often get it messed up. The reason is perspective. In one situation, they'll tie it with the standing part leading toward them. In another, they have the standing part leading away. I recommend always making the knot with the standing part leading away from you. The following is a simpler method of tying the bowline than the common one described above.

Let's assume you are standing on the foredeck and have passed the jib sheet through the clew of the genoa. Lay the free end over the standing part. If you are right-handed, hold it with your right forefinger and second finger

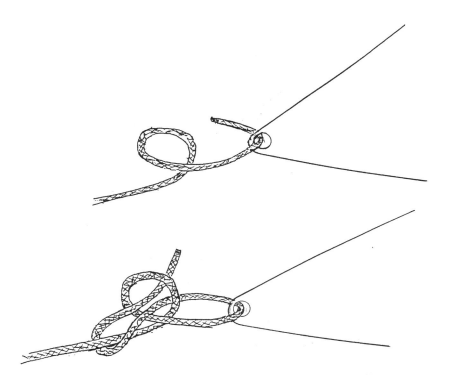

Fig. 80. Tying a bowline through the clew of a jib.

on top and your thumb underneath, as in Photo 36. Now, twist your hand as if you were pointing your forefinger at your knees, and with your left hand make a loop over the end of the line, as in Photos 37 and 38.

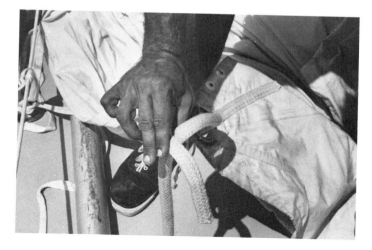

36. Pass the jib sheet through the clew and hold the line as shown.

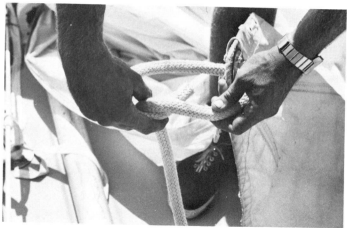

37. Twist the end inward.

38. A loop is formed with the end coming out.

Now the difficult part of making a bowline is over. The free end of the line is poking through a loop in the standing part and is headed in the proper direction. Just finish the knot by passing the end around the standing part and back through the loop the same way it came out, as shown in Photos 39 and 40. Pull the knot tight, holding the line as in Photo 41.

39. Pass the end behind the standing part of the line.

40. Pass the end back down though the loop the same way it came out.

41. Pull the bowline tight, as shown.

Make sure the knot is very close to the clew, so the genoa can be trimmed in tight before the knot hits the block on the deck. Since the knot won't go through the block, if the knot is not tied near the clew the sail won't be trimmed in very tight when closehauled. After tying the genoa sheets to the clew, they are generally led aft, outboard of all the shrouds, through the jib lead blocks and turning blocks (if any), to the winches. In some cases the sheets are led inside the shrouds, so check with the owner or skipper first.

Then, while on a reach, unfurl the genoa. If you unfurl it when headed into the wind, the flailing sail will not only slap at the crew working on the halyard, it will also tend to self-destruct as it beats against the mast and shrouds. Of course, this happens when tacking, but only momentarily. If instead of unfurling the jib you are raising one that has hanks on the headstay, get your turns around the winch, as in Photo 42, and pull from the winch. Don't pull the halyard above the winch or you will get overrides on the winch. An override occurs when the halyard going onto the winch crosses over and pinches the halyard leading off the winch, so you can't pull on it anymore. If this happens, you will have to take all the turns off the winch and start again.

Some halyards are wire with a rope tail. If so, hold onto the rope just where it's spliced to the wire and pull on the halyard until a foot or so of wire comes off the winch; then wrap that wire around the winch and pull again, Repeat the process until you can no longer pull any wire off the winch drum.

42. When the rope becomes wire, get wraps around the halyard winch.

Then, and only then, a second crew member inserts the winch handle into the winch. If the handle is already inserted, you will have to go around the whole winch handle to get extra turns of wire on the winch. As you "tail" (pull on) the halyard to keep it from slipping, the other crew member cranks on the winch (see Photo 43). The best and safest position is to stand with your back to the bow and pull the winch handle toward you from under the winch (if the winch is on the port side of the mast). The tailer is standing aft of the mast, facing forward. If the person winching pushes the handle instead of pulling it, the handle could pop out and hit the tailer in the face.

Make sure that the halyard is winched tightly enough that the "scallops" (little wrinkles at each jib hank that resemble scallop shells) disappear. Photo 44 shows scallops resulting from inadequate luff tension. When the halyard is tight, cleat it, coil it, and put the winch handle away. Never leave the handle in the winch as it can fall out and be lost overboard—it is expensive to replace. When cleating, make one turn around the base of the cleat before starting the standard back-and-forth crosses. The last loop should be under itself. This is called a "half-hitch," and keeps the line from uncleating itself.

All lines, and particularly halyards, should be neatly coiled. If a sudden squall hits the boat, you want to be able to release the halyards quickly and without the fear that they will get tangled up. Also, the bitter end of each halyard should be secured so that you can just let the halyard go, get on to the next emergency, and know that the halyard won't be lost up the mast. As you coil the line, make the coils clockwise. This will minimize kinking. For a right-handed person, hold the line in your left hand leading away from you, run the line through your hand as you stretch out your right arm (the same distance

43. Proper use of the jib halyard winch.

each coil), and then bring it in to your left hand in a loop, as in Photos 45–47. If there is a tendency to kink, twist the line clockwise in your fingers as you form the coils. Always coil starting at the fast end of the line and work toward the free end. That way, kinks disappear off the free end. If the line is long and

44. "Scallops" are caused by inadequate luff tension.

45. Start coiling with the line leading away from you.

46. Stretch your right arm to make loops of equal size.

47. Grab the loops with your left hand.

is terribly kinked, tow it behind the boat and the kinks will disappear. After a halyard is coiled, the line may be hung by pulling a section of the half-hitch through the center of the coil and over the top of the cleat, as in Photos 48–50. If you are coiling a loose line, finish the coil off as depicted in Photos 51–54.

48. Reach through the middle of the coil and grab part of the half-hitch.

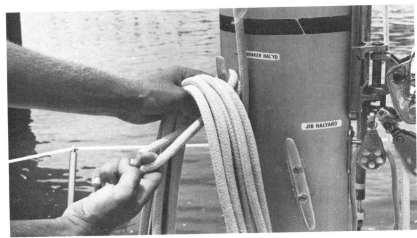

49. Pull the half-hitch through the coil.

50. Loop the half-hitch over the top of the cleat.

51. After coiling, wrap around the coils.

52. Make each wrap higher than the preceding one.

53. Pass a loop through the middle of the coil.

54. Pass a loop over the top of all the coils and pull tight.

If your boat doesn't have halyard winches for some reason or other, you will have to "sweat" up the halyard tight. It's easier with two people, though one can do it. After you have taken in all the halyard you can, wrap one turn around the base of a cleat and hold onto it. Then grasp the line a few feet above the cleat and pull straight out as if you were drawing back a bowstring to shoot an arrow, as in Photo 55. This will pull up the sail a little more, and

55. "Sweating" a halyard.

56. Snap the halyard shackle into a loop from the cleat . . .

57. . . . Then pull tightly and secure (cleat) the halyard.

friction will help hold it there as you take in the slack around the cleat. Keep pulling down on the halyard as you take in the slack, doing this a number of times until you get the halyard to its desired tension.

For a halyard that you are finished using but have no spot on the mast to secure the shackle, snap it to itself after making an initial loop around the base of a cleat, as in Photo 56. Then go back down and cleat it, as in Photo 57.

Operation of the genoa sheet winches is timed to that of the halyard winch. As the halyard is being winched tight, the jib sheets should be completely free. There should be a stop knot in the end of each sheet. When the halyard is tight, put two wraps around the sheet winch. More wraps are added as you pull in the sheet. Overrides are a problem if you put more than two wraps on the winch before the pressure makes it difficult to pull by hand (note Photo 58).

58. An override.

Such an override, with wind pressure in the jib, can get extremely tight. You can't crank the sheet in any further and you can't get the turns off to start afresh. The only solution is to take the strain completely off the jib sheet so the wraps can be loosened. This can be done by tying another line to the jib sheet forward of the winch and taking the strain on a second winch. The knot for this purpose is a specialized one that will not slip on the fouled line, as shown in Photo 59. Called a rolling hitch, it is tied as in Photo 60.

The more wraps you have on the winch, the easier it will be to tail with less chance of slipping. Remember—the line goes around the winch clockwise as you look down on the winch from above. The jib sheets should also be

59. A rolling hitch to another winch takes the load off the override.

60. A rolling hitch doesn't slip on another line.

coiled and laid down in the cockpit so that the coils run off the top of the coil. If laid down upside down (the coils running off the bottom), the sheet can get tangled. This can be very serious if you have to do a panic tack to avoid a collision and the jib sheet tangles when thrown off the winch, making it impossible to run through the sheet block. As you winch in the jib, watch it to make sure you don't winch too far. I've seen too many people concentrate on the winch, rather than on the sail and pull the clew right into the block or poke the spreader into the leech of the sail.

When the genoa sheet is eased to adjust to a slight course or wind change, place one hand over the coils on the drum (with your thumb next to your index finger, not sticking out where it can get caught in a loop). Ease the end of the line with the other hand, as in Photo 61. The hand on the coils acts like a brake controlling the speed with which the sheet is eased.

61. The correct method of easing a jib sheet.

Without it, the coils can stick on the drum while the sheet is being eased at the free end and suddenly jerk out, catching you by surprise and possibly pulling your hand into the coils around the winch. I've heard of people breaking fingers this way.

Tacking

As in smaller sailboats, there are two basic maneuvers while sailing: tacking and jibing. Since it is a longer process to tack a cruising boat and drains more energy from the crew than on small boats, one tends to be more conservative with tacks. There is a tendency to stay on one tack for a longer period of time and only tack when necessary. Therefore, it is worthwhile to plan the next tack beforehand, not to tack indiscriminately only to discover that you then have to tack again to avoid a right-of-way boat, an obstruction such as a moored boat, or to clear a point of land. Assuming that you are closehauled and sailing 45° from the wind, you will tack in about 90°. This means you can sight abeam from the high side of the boat and have a good idea of your heading for the next tack. Make sure that there is no danger in that direction, and also look aft to windward for boats that might have right of way on you after you tack.

One of the most common errors when tacking a cruising boat is to turn the boat too far. A helmsman usually watches the luff of the jib to determine if sailing too high or too low. On a small boat, the jib is trimmed in immediately after a tack so the helmsman can tell almost instantly whether the boat has been turned too far or not. On a cruising boat, however, it may take quite awhile to winch in the genoa all the way, so it luffs much longer. Inexperienced helmsmen tend to fall off to fill the genoa before it is all the way in. Thus, they not only have turned the boat well past 90°, but also have made it very hard on the crew winching in the genoa, which is now full of air.

The way to cure this problem is to note your compass heading on the original tack. Then add or subtract 90°, depending on which way you're turning the boat. This may sound a bit complicated, but most compasses have 90° lubberlines which make it considerably easier. Let's say you are sailing on starboard tack and heading 100°. Look on the windward side of the compass and note that the starboard lubberline is at 190° (if there's no lubberline, there's usually a screw or some other indication that will suffice). This will be your heading on port after tacking. Remember, this only works if you are closehauled on the original tack. To illustrate by exaggeration, if you were sailing on a beam reach and your heading were 100°, you would end up headed directly into the wind by turning the boat to the 190° in the previous example. So you must test that you are as close to the wind as possible on the original tack before you take your reading. The other caveat to this system is that the wind may shift as you turn. The compass course is only a temporary crutch and must be recognized as such. As soon as the jib is trimmed in, sail by the jib, not by the compass.

As for the actual mechanics of tacking, the process is a little different with a cruising boat as compared to a smaller sailboat because of the large overlapping genoa. As the boat turns into the wind to tack, the jib sheet has to be released the moment a good luff is seen in the jib. If not released early enough, the sail will "back" and fill with wind on the other side, forcing it into the spreader and swing the bow hard over. Though there is usually no danger involved in this instance, the sail will rub against the top of the spreader, causing undue wear, and the force of the full sail will put excessive strain on the spreaders. Also, when the sheet is finally released, it takes off with a vengeance, causing potential harm to a crew member who gets tangled in the sheet as it flies out.

As the sail starts to luff, the jib sheet is eased a few feet and then the turns thrown off the winch by lifting straight up and flicking them off at the same time as in Photo 62. A common mistake is to release at the command "Hard alee" from the helmsman. Usually, the helmsman gives this command as he starts to turn the boat, which is a bit early for releasing the jib. If the helmsman is late on his command, the jib sheet must be released before the jib backs. The crew had better be sure the helmsman was really intending to tack, though, or he may be in for some grief. There is one saving factor here; once the jib backs, the helmsman probably can't get the boat back onto the original tack without releasing the jib which is pushing his bow across. So if you aren't positive of the helmsman's intentions, but the boat is turning into the wind, you can't go wrong to release the jib when it's aback.

As the genoa comes across during a tack on a cruising boat, quite often the flailing jib sheet catches on a halyard, on the mast, the winch, the edge of a hatch, ventilator cowls, or other protuberances on the foredeck. This varies from boat to boat and some have no trouble at all, particularly if the

62. To release the jib sheet for a tack, lift straight up and flip the wraps off.

crew member takes up on the new sheet fast enough. If the sheet does tend to hang up on your boat, though, someone should be stationed forward of the mast to help get the sail and jib sheets across the foredeck. Stand in the middle of the foredeck so you can't get hit by the clew of the sail, pull the sail forward along its foot and pass it over your head. If you stand near the mast, you are more apt to get hit unless you just hang back and unhook the sheet after it gets caught, which isn't very effective.

As soon as there is some pressure on the sheet, the trimmer needs to add wraps to avoid losing what has been taken in. There is one fast and safe way of doing this. Take the line in one hand and pass it around the winch two or three times, allowing the line to ease through your hand as it goes. Don't ease enough to let the line slip on the drum—just enough to accommodate the extra wraps around the winch. The other hand is used only to feed line to the hand putting the wraps around the winch (see Photo 63).

I've seen sailors hold onto the line leading from the winch with one hand and make an extra wrap with the other. The result is that they are wrapping one hand into the winch coils, and if they don't get it out fast or if the sheet slips out on the drum, that hand can get caught (note Photo 64).

After sufficient wraps have been taken and the crew member can no longer take in any slack by hand due to the force of the wind in the sail, another crew member inserts a winch handle and cranks the sheet in. If you

63. One hand wraps the line while the other feeds.

64. An improper way to get extra wraps on a winch. Your hand may get caught if the jib fills and pulls on the jib sheet

stand with your shoulders over the winch and your feet spread for balance, you should be able to turn the handle continuously in one direction. Most winches have "high" gear in one direction and "low" gear in the other direction. When you no longer can turn the winch by turning the handle one way, you just change direction of rotation. Some have a gearshift lever in the handle and many also have a locking lever in the handle so it can't pop out and be lost. Lock-in handles are usually used on vertical halyard winches.

Watch the genoa as it is being cranked in. If it touches the spreader or the clew hits the jib sheet block, you have usually gone too far. Normally, the faster you can trim the better. It's also much easier to finish trimming the sheet in before the boat has completed its turn and the genoa fills with wind, but it's not as efficient if you are racing. After a tack the boat is going slowly and needs to pick up speed. Full sails (versus flat sails) will help the boat accelerate quickly and a little jib sheet ease makes the sail fuller. So, when racing, we crank in the last few inches as the boat accelerates. Now, cleat the sheet and be sure to take out the winch handle and stow it so it isn't lost overboard.

Half-Hitches

Many years ago, before the advent of Nylon and Dacron, manila lines that became wet shrank as they dried. A half-hitch put on a cleat with a wet line could tighten up and be very difficult to get off later. That shrinking problem resulted in a basic rule: don't use half-hitches to cleat any line that must be released in a hurry. A jib sheet was the typical line that fell into that category. If you were on a cruising boat on port tack and had to tack suddenly to avoid a starboard tacker, it could be embarrassing, or even dangerous, not to be able to release the jib quickly.

When nonshrinking synthetic lines were invented, the major cause of binding problems was eliminated. Yet, even today, parents still tell their children not to use half-hitches. They have it stuck in their minds that half-hitches are bad. All of us should rethink the whole thing. There are two good reasons to use half-hitches. First, fewer wraps are needed around the cleat to secure the line, so the process of cleating is faster. Second, a half-hitch ensures that the line does not slip or come uncleated.

There are one or two arguments against half-hitches. They are a little slower to release (though that's debatable) and they can tighten up if there's a great deal of pull on the line. However, if you put an adequate number of wraps around a winch before going to a cleat there should be very little pull between the winch and the cleat. The friction of the line around the winch absorbs most of the pull by the sail. In fact, if there is so little pull on the line that you can tie the half-hitch in the first place, there should be no problem freeing it later on. One Canada's Cup contender, an ocean racing boat, used only a single wrap around the base of the cleat followed by a single half-hitch to cleat the jib sheets (Photo 65). They had no trouble all during their racing campaign with this system. Again, the prerequisite here is that the winch drum take almost all the load.

A more common cleating arrangement is the one shown in Photo 66. It consists of a number of turns that end in a half-hitch. Note that the free end of the line should lie in the same direction as the previous wraps. Photo 67 shows a cleating arrangement which ends in a wrap around the base of the

65. This is adequate cleating only if there are enough wraps around the winch.

66. Proper cleating with a half-hitch.

67. Proper cleating without a half-hitch.

cleat. This wrap jams against the previous loops and keeps them from coming off, which means you don't have to use a half-hitch.

The controversy usually revolves around whether to cleat by the method shown in Photo 66 or that in Photo 67. Personally, I use both interchangeably. However, the more strain there is on a winch, the more likely I am to use a half-hitch and I've never had any problem freeing a jib sheet quickly when using a half-hitch.

Jibing

Without a spinnaker set, jibing is a fairly simple procedure. Whereas the main is pretty much forgotten when tacking, when jibing careful control of the main is very important. On a small boat we're concerned with the boom swinging over and beaning somebody, but on a cruising boat, where the forces are so much greater, the mainsheet is just as much a threat. A crew member who gets tangled in the mainsheet as the boom swings across the boat can get hurt quite badly. For this reason, we overhaul the mainsheet as we jibe, trimming it in as the boat turns. As soon as the boom crosses the centerline of the boat, we let the mainsheet out fast.

To jibe, we first have to release the boom vang if it's attached to the rail. Then we start trimming on the command "Prepare to jibe," and when the

68. Easing the jib sheet too far when jibing allows the sail to wrap on the headstay.

skipper sees the trimming well underway he or she turns the boat. The turn to jibe is delayed, because there is no way a crew member can trim in the main as fast as the skipper can turn the boat, except in very light air conditions. In extremely heavy air, the skipper often has to sail the boat slightly by the lee to relieve the force on the sail to allow the crew to bring in the main. There should never be a winch handle involved with this type of trimming. Just bring in the sheet hand-over-hand (with one or two turns around the winch so when you ease it out after the jibe you won't get a rope burn on your hands).

The jib takes very little effort when jibing. Just ease the old jib sheet out and pull in the new one. There is only one potential problem: if you ease the old sheet too far, the jib will fly out beyond the bow of the boat and when you try to pull it in on the new side, the whole sail has to be pulled across the headstay (note Photo 68). The accompanying friction and the flogging of the jib can make this very difficult. The new sheet should be trimmed as the old one is eased under control so that the clew of the sail is kept from going too far forward of the mast as the boat jibes.

Head Operation

If we consider that all the foregoing has been taught to you on your first time out in a cruising boat, and that you've had a few sodas to quench your thirst after all that tacking and jibing, it's just about time for someone to need to go below to use the head (the bathroom). So let's review the procedures to avoid embarrassment. One simple rule to make on a cruising boat is that the head door will be hooked open unless in use. This has two benefits: (1) it allows fresh air to circulate through the head, and (2) one knows just by looking below whether or not the head is in use.

Another rule to impress on the crew is that only two things are ever flushed: (1) toilet paper, and (2) that which has already been eaten. Anything else can clog it up, including paper towels and sanitary napkins. He who clogs it, cleans it! You only need to go through the messy job of taking a toilet apart once and you'll be a believer for life.

Before using, depress the foot pedal or (if it's a lever-type) pull the lever upright and pump clean water into the bowl. After using, do the same as above and pump until the bowl is flushed clean, then keep on pumping the handle for at least 10 to 15 strokes. This flushes any sewage right through the system and out the hull.

Now take your foot off the pedal (or push the valve lever forward) and pump the bowl dry, so the water won't spill over the lip of the bowl as the boat heels. If there is any urine splatter or fecal residue on the bowl, it should be cleaned up right away with toilet paper and reflushed. A boat's head is small and has very poor ventilation. Any uncleaned residue around the bowl or in the system will soon start to smell very badly. Plus, it's a courtesy to the next person who uses it that he receive it clean and leave it clean. Flushing a little Joy or other liquid detergent through the toilet can help keep odors away. Lighting a couple of kitchen safety matches kills odors. Wet the matches in the sink after use. There are other types of toilets that treat the sewage before expelling it through the hull, and still others that use holding tanks. Just read the operating instructions carefully before using them.

Roller-Furling Genoa

Most cruising sailboats use roller-furling headsails. In this system, the jib is hoisted in a groove, but when not in use is furled around the headstay, rather than lowered. To furl the sail you simply pull on a line that leads from a drum at the base of the jib aft to a winch near the cockpit, which rotates the whole headstay, rolling up the jib. If you want to reduce sail area just roll it up halfway. The end result is not perfect because the middle of the stay lags behind the ends in rolling, and the middle of the sail becomes very full. Also, the clew rises higher in the air the more the jib is rolled up. This is fine when reaching in heavy air because there is less chance to scoop water, but it puts the center of effort high off the water and increases heeling. The jib sheet leads will have to be moved to accommodate the new angle made by the jib sheet when the jib is half rolled.

The sail, when rolled up, is still exposed to sunlight and subject to UV deterioration, so sailmakers add a panel of UV-resistant material along the leech. This panel is on the outside of the rolls as the jib is rolled up and protects the rest of the furled sail.

When using a roller-furling system, you generally sail on a reach to unroll the jib. This allows the sail to unroll without flailing against the mast and shrouds. As mentioned before, it's best to control the line from a winch rather than let it fly. If you don't use a winch, when the jib is about half unrolled in a fresh breeze you won't be able to hold the line, and if you just let it fly, the line can become tangled in a turning block or twist and become jammed around the furling drum, making it very difficult to rewind.

To furl the jib, it's necessary to luff it completely. Free the sheet and head the boat up to reduce speed and heel angle, but don't flog the sail against the shrouds. This hurts the sail and increases friction, making the sail more difficult to furl.

If the genoa furling line is hard to pull, *do not* put it on a winch. First check that the genoa halyard is really tight. To furl well, the luff of the jib needs to be stretched taut, or the furling mechanism won't work well. Excessive headstay sag creates the same problem. Obviously, turning a rod that's curved takes more force than turning a straight one. Extra backstay tension

69. A roller-furling jib in the process of being furled up. The dark strip along the foot and leech protects the furled sail from sunlight deterioration.

may help. If there's still resistance, check that the upper furling fitting turns freely. Sometimes another halyard gets wound up in it. Winching can break something. If everything seems clear, but it's still hard to pull the furling line, head downwind and blanket the jib behind the main. Only after you've exhausted other options should you use the winch to furl the genoa. If the jib won't furl at all, something must be broken and the headsail should be lowered to the deck.

After the sail is completely rolled up, roll a couple of extra turns for good measure. Wrapping the jib sheets around the outside of the sail locks the furl in place. There's less chance for the wind to catch some of the sail and unfurl it.

Returning to Port

If the jib has hanks on it, the procedures for returning home are pretty much the reverse of setting out. The jib is lowered first (as it was raised last). This can be done on any point of sailing, but is easiest on a run. When closehauled or reaching, the angle of heel can make it difficult to pull the jib aboard as it's lowered. If you have a large crew, you can assign someone to release the jib sheet, another to release the halyard, and the others to gather the jib in. If the boat is heeling, the crew on the foredeck should sit down while gathering in the sail. This way they can brace themselves and use both hands. They are also less apt to lose their balance and have the sail pull them overboard.

If you are shorthanded, leave the jib trimmed in for a closehauled course, but fall off to a run. When the wind is dead aft, the jib will be blanketed by the main and will fall right onto the foredeck when lowered, so all you need is one crew member on the halyard to douse the jib.

When the jib is down, clean it off the foredeck so it won't be in the way for docking or get dirty from the mooring line if you are picking up a mooring. Unsnap the hanks from the headstay. Then, or at the same time if you have enough crew, untie the jib sheets. By this time the engine should be started, though probably not put in gear, so be sure to tie the end of each jib sheet to the lifelines to avoid washing them overboard and getting them tangled in the propeller! Bag the jib, feeding the head and clew into the sailbag first. The tack should be the last corner to go into the bag, and should lay right on top since it's the first corner to attach when you want to use the sail again.

With the genoa out of the way, put the engine in gear, turn directly into the wind, and hold the boat in position with the engine as the mainsail is lowered. Trim in the mainsheet as the boat turns so that the boom won't be swinging back and forth too far. Be sure all hatches are closed lest a crew member fall through an opening hidden by the sail. Check that the topping lift is secure so the boom won't come crashing down on the deck (or someone's head) when the sail is lowered. Then release the main halyard.

The mainsail is left on the boom from one day to the next. It's difficult to remove it after each sailing session and if the sail is properly flaked down, secured, and a sail cover is used, removal is not necessary.

When lowering a main with slides attached to the luff, the slides remain on the mast, piling one on top of the other at the boom as the sail comes down. You flake the sail by starting at the clew and following up the leech, folding the sail over the boom as you go and securing the flaked sail with ties.

An alternative is to make a pocket along the foot of the sail by grabbing the leech 4–5' from the clew, folding the rest of the sail in the pocket (or hammock) formed by this portion of the sail, and rolling it up on top of the boom. Secure it with sail ties, and the sail is furled. This is neater looking if there's no sail cover.

After the sail is flaked or furled and stopped on top of the boom, we protect it with an ultraviolet (UV)-resistant sail cover. First, the cover should be secured around the mast and then stretched aft over the sail along the boom, with the clew end tied tightly. Then fasten the grommet snaps—or shock cord threaded through hooks and eyes—along the edges of the sail cover under the boom, starting at the gooseneck and working aft as in Photos 74 and 75.

Sail fabric is highly susceptible to the deteriorating effects of the ultraviolet rays of the sun. There is sailcloth and thread available that resist UV rays,

70. Pass the sailstop between the foot of the sail and the boom.

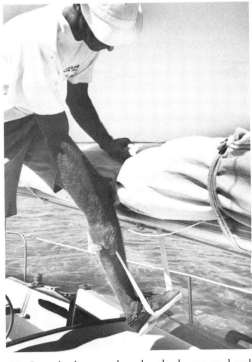

71. Pass the long end under the boom and pull tight. A foot sometimes helps.

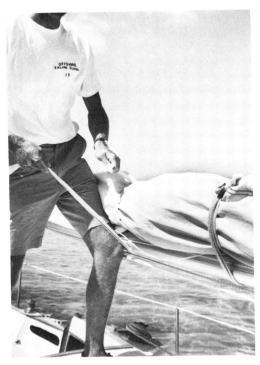

72. Bring the sailstop back up to the top on the sail . . .

73. . . . And tie a square knot with a loop in it (a reef knot).

74. Lace the sail cover around the mast first . . .

75. . . . Then pull tight and lash to the boom end and lastly, lace underneath the boom.

but they have not proved totally satisfactory. The only lasting solution so far has been to protect the sails with sail covers made out of "sunbrella" cloth that filters out almost all such rays, or to remove the sails completely and store them out of the sun, which is often the practice on smaller boats.

One other solution is to roll the mainsail vertically inside the mast, as in Photo 76.

Now it's time to get your fenders and docking lines out in preparation for docking, as in Photo 77. Do this early enough so there's no last-minute rush to get them ready. Plan which side of the boat will lay alongside the dock and make sure every crew member understands. The fenders are usually tied to the lifelines on the "dock side" of the boat at the boat's widest part. The knot used to tie the fender is a clove hitch, as shown in Photo 78, or two half-hitches, as in Photo 79. The latter is like a clove hitch on the line itself. These are common knots used for a multitude of purposes aboard sailboats, even for docking lines. The best way to secure a fender is a combination of these two knots. Use a clove hitch on the lifeline and lock it off with a half-hitch or two underneath. If there's enough crew, one person will carry a loose fender

76. This mainsail is being rolled *inside* the mast.

77. Prepare fenders early.

to use at any unprotected point of contact between the hull and dock or piling.

The approach to the dock should be very slow because, as we have said before, the reverse on a cruising sailboat is not very effective. Once lines are ashore to persons who are helping secure the boat, cut the engine. I've seen many landings messed up by a skipper trying to jockey a boat alongside a dock

78. Clove hitch.

79. Two half-hitches.

with the engine when the persons ashore could easily have pulled the boat safely into position without the help of the engine.

We described the docking procedures earlier, but not mooring pickup. Approach a mooring buoy slowly from the downwind side so that you are heading directly into the wind toward it. Once the pickup buoy or the mooring line has been retrieved, the skipper must hold the boat in position until the line is secured to the cleat. Put the engine in neutral unless you see the crew struggling to pull enough mooring line aboard to secure, in which case kick the boat forward for a short time to gain some slack in the line. If the mooring line has a loop in the end, this is placed over the cleat. The pickup buoy line is then cleated on top of the loop to ensure that the loop doesn't slip off the cleat. The latter could happen if the mooring line were stiff, the loop large,

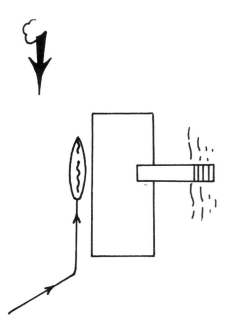

Fig. 81. When the wind is parallel to the shore, shoot into the wind alongside the dock.

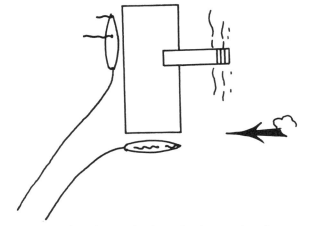

Fig. 82. When the wind is from the shore, either shoot into the wind at the end of the dock, or approach slowly and luff parallel to the dock.

and the bow of the boat pitched down off a wave thereby creating slack in the line.

There are times when you must dock under sail, either because your boat doesn't have an engine or because the engine is inoperable for some reason or other. The process isn't much different from sailing up to a mooring as described earlier in the drills. The boat must be headed into the wind to stop. Each approach depends on the wind direction. If the wind is blowing parallel to the dock (as in Figure 81), just shoot the boat into the wind and come to a stop alongside the dock. If the wind is blowing away from the dock toward the open water (as in Figure 82), there are two options: (1) use the end of the dock and shoot straight into the wind, or (2) shoot at an angle into the wind and luff the sails to slow the boat down. Then come parallel to the dock at the last minute.

Remember that if the boat is sailing slowly, as soon as you turn the boat broadside to the wind it will start going sideways (making leeway), so get bow and stern lines to the dock as fast as possible and walk the boat along the dock as it slows down.

When the wind is blowing toward the dock from the open water, docking is more difficult. The best approach is without any sails raised if the wind is heavy, or with only the jib if the wind is light. Round into the wind as in

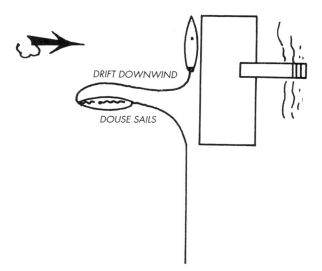

DRIFT DOWNWIND

DOUSE SAILS

Fig. 83. When the wind is toward the shore, douse sails to windward of the dock and drift in.

Figure 83 and lower the sails. Then drift into the dock. You'll be surprised how well many boats can sail without any sail up. Many can sail practically on a beam reach without any sail once they have picked up some speed.

Not all landings are perfect and a crew member may have to toss a docking line quite a distance to someone ashore. The line he intends to toss should have one end previously attached to the boat so that the whole line doesn't accidentally get thrown to the dock. Then the line must be neatly coiled and separated into two coils, one for each hand. One hand throws one coil and the second coil slides off the other hand as it goes out. Photo 80 shows the line ready for tossing. Photo 81 indicates the tangled mess you can create when you try to separate one coil of the whole line into two equal coils. The best way to avoid such difficulties is to coil the line halfway and grasp those coils firmly in your hand. Then continue coiling over your index finger the coils you're intending to toss, as in Photo 82. It often helps to make the throwing coils smaller than the others so they're more compact. An underhand toss to the person on the dock completes the job.

In many cases there's no one on the dock to help by taking your lines. A crew member has to jump "ashore" with the end of the line in hand and quickly tie it to a post (if there's no cleat available). The best knot is the ubiquitous bowline, and the following is the fastest way I know of tying it. The photos show it being tied to a jib, but it can be used anywhere. First, make a loose slip knot, as in Photos 83–85. This preliminary part can be done before you even jump to the dock. Make sure the knot slips on the standing part of the line, as shown, not on the free end.

Now pass the end of the line around the post. Reach through the loop of the slip knot and pull the end of the line back through it (Photo 86). Hold

80. Line coiled properly for tossing.

81. The difficulty in separating one coil into two.

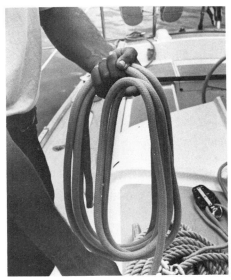

82. Solution—separate the coils as you make them initially.

the free end lightly and pull on the slip knot, as in Photo 87. The result (Photo 88) is a bowline that can be tied in less than a second after the initial slip knot has been made. A word of caution: if the docking line tightens up while your hand is still through the slip knot, you could be badly hurt. When a boat is

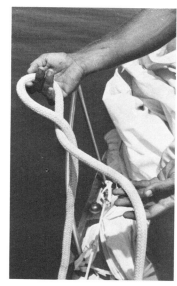  

83. To make a fast bowline: a loop is formed by laying the free end over the standing part of the line.

84. Reach through the loop and grasp the standing part . . .

85. . . . And a slip knot is formed that slips on the standing part of the line.

traveling fast, it is better to check its forward momentum first by putting a number of wraps around the post and letting friction do the job. It's much safer than jerking the boat to a stop, as would happen with a knot.

After docking or mooring, as a courtesy to other people living aboard their boats in a crowded marina or anchorage, you should always tie off your halyards so they don't slap the mast in the wind at night and keep people awake. Photo 89 shows the main halyard pulled away from the mast by a line tied to the shrouds.

Those halyards that can be tied totally away from the mast, should be. Snap the shackle end to the base of a stanchion, the bow pulpit as in the case of the jib halyard in Photo 90, or some other location away from the mast. Then pass the other end under another convenient fitting, such as the grab rail in the same photo, tie a rolling hitch, and slide it up the line until snug. If the halyard is not long enough, an alternative method is to pass the end under the rail, then through its own shackle, tie a rolling hitch underneath, and slide it down tight, as in Photo 91.

Before leaving the boat, make sure it's in a neat, orderly condition. The mainsheet should not be left on deck where it can collect dirt and moisture, but rather should be hung up to dry. Often the mainsheet is too long and heavy to coil in the normal way. One good method is to start at the fixed end of the mainsheet and loop it over the boom in long loops that hang on both

86. Pass the free end through the clew of the jib (or around a piling) and then through the slip knot.

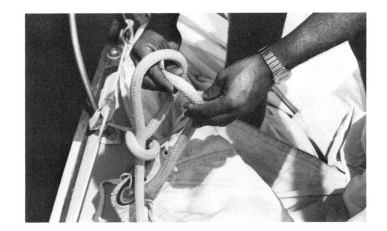

87. Hold the free end lightly and pull on the slip knot. This will pull the free end through the middle of the slip knot . . .

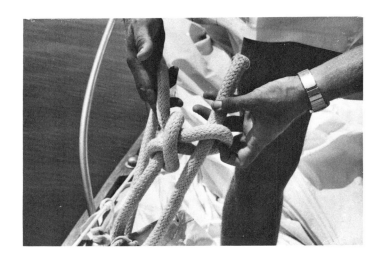

88. . . . And a bowline will be formed.

89. The main halyard is tied off to a shroud to prevent annoying slapping.

90. Halyard tied to handrail away from the most.

91. Halyard tied to its own shackle.

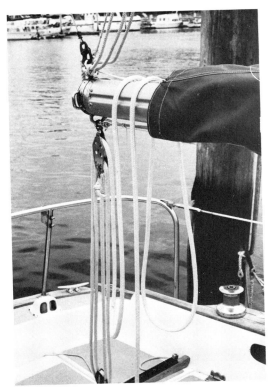

92. "Coiling" a long mainsheet over the boom.

93. Finish off the "coil" by wrapping and tying the middle.

sides of the boom (Photo 92). Continue looping back and forth over the top of the boom until you get near the end of the line. Then wrap the end a number of times around the middle of the line and finish with a half-hitch (Photo 93). The result will look as though you had coiled the line in the normal fashion and had hung it on the end of the boom, which is far from the truth of the matter.

Special Equipment and Procedures

Having covered the basic maneuvers, setting and dousing sails, and docking/mooring procedures, let's take a closer look at some of the more specialized equipment and procedures aboard a cruising yacht.

The Boom Vang

The purpose of a boom vang on a cruising boat is the same as for a smaller boat. It pulls the boom down when reaching or running, and in doing so keeps the leech from falling off to leeward. This reduces twist in the mainsail

94. "Cleat" a tackle by jamming one line under another leading into a sheave.

and makes it a more efficient airfoil because the angle of attack of the apparent wind will be maintained for the full length of the luff of the sail. However, the main of a cruising boat is so large that a much more powerful boom vang is needed to hold the boom down. This type of boom vang has to be taken off every time the boat is jibed and set up on the other side of the boat once the boom is across. When the wind fills the other side of the mainsail and tries to force the boom across against the restraining boom vang, something has to give if the wind is strong. The boom vang may break or the boat may broach (go out of control).

Sometimes there is no cleat handy for the boom vang tackle. In that case, just pass the free end (the end you pull) behind the line that passes into the sheave below it, or beside it for those pulleys with side-by-side sheaves. Now jam the line up. It is squeezed by the line leading into the sheave and it won't budge an inch until you pull it down again (Photo 94).

Modern cruising boats have short booms, so the chance of dipping them in the water on the lee side is slight. Hydraulic vangs with great power are attached to the underside of the boom down to the base of the mast, as in Photo 95. The advantage of this type of vang is that it doesn't have to be removed in order to jibe. Further, it keeps the boom down during the jibe and avoids the chance of the mainsail's hooking on a spreader or the boom on the backstay. With a solid vang you don't need a topping lift to hold the boom up when reefing or when the mainsail is lowered and furled.

95. Hall Spars "Quik Vang" in use on a maxi.

The Boom Preventer

This is the name given to a line leading from the end of the main boom forward to a cleat near the bow. If you are running dead downwind in rough seas on a cruising boat for a long period of time, there is always the chance of an accidental jibe, which could wipe out some unsuspecting crew member. The line to the bow is long enough so that if the wind fills the other side of the main, the line will just stretch rather than break, allowing the helmsman the opportunity to get back on course. The boom preventer is often used at night and on long downwind passages, but is too much trouble to set up for the short run. On short runs, it is up to the helmsman to keep the boat from sailing by the lee and for the crew always to be aware that at any time during a run the boom could come swinging across due to helmsman error.

Sailing Wing and Wing

Since a cruising boat has a very large jib in comparison to most smaller boats, it behooves us to make use of it at all times. When sailing downwind, it is blanketed by the mainsail. In other words, the mainsail is catching all the wind and none is getting to the genoa. The only way we can make the genoa "draw" (fill with wind) is to cross it over to the other side of the boat, the windward side, where the wind is passing unobstructed. This is called sailing "wing and wing," and as mentioned in the previous chapter on sail trim, is done on

96. Though the masthead fly indicates wind directly aft, flags show the flow off the main, which helps when sailing wing and wing.

small boats all the time. The mainsail does help, because it changes the direction of the wind that hits it. Notice in Photo 96 that the masthead fly (the wind indicator at the top of the mast) shows the wind almost directly behind the boat—that's the backstay you see in the photograph. However, the flags on the port spreader clearly show the wind coming from the starboard side. So the wind is hitting the mainsail and spilling around the mast at an angle. It's obviously effective to wing a jib out to that side and catch the force from the wind off the main before it's lost.

On larger cruising boats, however, since the genoa is so long on the foot, it's hard to keep it out without help, particularly in light air. It keeps coming into the middle of the boat rather than staying out where it should. The weight of the clew folds the foot in and collapses the sail. By sailing quite far by the lee, the jib will stay full, but this can cause an unscheduled jibe. The solution is to wing out the genoa on the spinnaker pole. (Small boats use a spinnaker pole also, if they have one, or use a "whisker pole," a pole designed solely for winging the jib on a boat that doesn't carry a spinnaker.)

First, attach the topping lift to the pole. If one crew member lifts with the topping lift and another guides the pole, it is easier to handle. (Remember—we are talking about a boat the size of a 30- to 35-foot cruising boat. One much larger or smaller might use slightly different techniques.) Next, attach one end of the pole over the windward jib sheet. That's the sheet on the side of the boat opposite the side the main boom is being carried on, not the literal side the wind is on. If you're sailing by the lee, the wind is coming over the same side as the main boom, but that still is the leeward side of the boat. Then, keeping the pole level with the topping lift, push the pole straight forward toward the bow and place the other end of the pole in the eye or socket designed for it on the mast. Last, release the leeward jib sheet and pull on the weather one. The clew will first go forward to the pole as you take in the slack. When it hits the pole, it will start to pull the pole aft. In most cases you can pull the pole all the way aft until it touches the shrouds, particularly if the genoa is a large one and you're sailing well downwind. You'll be quite surprised at how much this increases your speed.

This technique is also used on racing boats when it is blowing too hard to carry a spinnaker. When cruising, some boats lower the main and set two genoas out on twin poles to either side of the boat. The two jibs have more sail area than main and jib together, and tend to pull the boat along downwind so that it barely has to be steered.

When sailing wing and wing, you must anticipate right-of-way situations very early. For instance, if you are on port tack with your jib winged, you have to keep clear of boats on starboard tack. If you are caught by surprise and have to fall off sharply, in heavy airs the mainsail will jibe and the boat will broach. The spinnaker pole will be digging deep into the water as the boat heels, and it is entirely possible that the pole will break as it is pressed back against the lee shrouds. If you turn the other way or harden up, the winged-out jib will back (the wind will get on the other side of it) and force your bow back down in the direction you were trying to avoid—right into the right-of-way boat. Try it in medium breezes. Wing out a jib on a pole downwind and then try to tack. It's very unlikely you'll be able to tack unless the jib is a tiny one. So anticipate the right-of-way boat early to negate the need for a sharp, last-minute maneuver to avoid it. Watch carefully as it approaches. If the bearing doesn't change, you will have to make some change of course to avoid a collision.

To take the pole down and get the jib over to the normal side, you must take all the pressure off the sail. Therefore, ease the windward jib sheet. This will allow the pole to come forward to the headstay and the genoa to fly out in front of the boat. Remember to keep the boat downwind. You don't want to change course until the pole is completely off and the jib is in its normal position. Next, unsnap the windward sheet from the jaws of the pole and lower the topping lift so that the end of the pole rests in the bow with both jib sheets over it. Then trim in the leeward jib sheet to get the jib back to its normal position preparatory to hardening up. Last, take the pole off, stow it, and unsnap and secure the topping lift. When the pole is stowed double, check that it's not on top of a jib sheet.

Crew Overboard

This is one area of sailing that most people learn from books and articles, not from experience. When and if it actually happens on your boat, it is hard to know what the reactions will be and whether you have learned enough to handle the situation. Each situation is different, depending on the type of boat, whether cruising or racing, the number and competency of the crew aboard and their condition (perhaps all tired and seasick), who went overboard (perhaps the only experienced sailor aboard), what sails were set, visibility conditions, whether day or night, sea conditions and wind strength, whether the sea water is warm or cold (thereby shortening survival time), and a myriad of other factors. It's like trying to tell someone what to do at sea when a 90-MPH hurricane hits your boat. Each boat and crew tackle the problem differently, and what's good for one is not necessarily good for another. However, there are certain standard practices that are sound, and in recent years almost everyone who has been lost overboard on a racing boat has been picked up because of safety devices.

It is obvious that the location of the victim has to be marked so that he or she can be seen when the boat returns. A head bobbing in heavy seas is very difficult to see unless you are nearby. "High-visibility" foul-weather gear is pretty useless unless the person is floating high enough on a life preserver that some of the foul-weather gear is visible when he or she waves. Of course, the first item thrown to the person is a flotation device, such as the horseshoe life preserver in Photo 97. If the water is warm a person can last for days with

97. Life preserver and strobe light for tossing to a person overboard.

98. "Man overboard" pole.

flotation. Then other devices to litter the water to make the person more visible are thrown. One of these that is good for large seas is called a "man overboard pole" (Photo 98). This is a fiberglass rod about eight feet long with a weight on the bottom to keep it vertical and a float a couple of feet above the weight. A high-visibility flag is usually attached to the upper end. Even when the pole is in the trough of a wave, the flag can be seen over the crest.

Tied to the life preserver so it won't get separated (and also shown in Photo 97) is a "waterlight," a high-intensity strobe light with a mercury switch. On the boat it is hung upside down. When thrown into the water, it floats right-side-up and the mercury switch is activated. The flashes are easily seen for quite a distance at night.

One of the problems in throwing these items to the person is that the wind and waves often cause them to drift away from the swimmer faster than he is able to catch up to them. For this reason, a miniature sea anchor or drogue is often attached to slow down their drift. Other assorted items are also tossed to the person: a whistle and dye marker, for example. The whistle is much easier to hear over the howl of the wind than a voice yelling "Help!" The dye marker is for daylight use when there's an aerial search. All the equipment should be within reach of the helmsman and thrown over the side at the first cry of "crew overboard."

With extensive research and trials on the water, US SAILING's Safety-at-Sea Committee, the U.S. Naval Academy Sailing Squadron, the Cruising Club of America Technical Committee, and the Sailing Foundation of Seattle, Washington, joined forces to find the most effective way to save a person who has fallen overboard.

The result is two methods: the "quick-stop" and the "life-sling" method. With full crews the fastest is the "quick-stop," but with shorthanded crews or in extreme weather conditions the surest and safest is the life sling. In small boats and protected waters, use the third method described, the Quick Turn.

Quick-Stop Method

1. As soon as a crew member falls overboard, throw buoyant objects, such as cushions, PFDs, or life rings to the victim and shout "Crew overboard!" These objects may not only come to the aid of the victim, but will "litter the water" where he or she went overboard and help the spotter to keep him or her in view. It has been determined that the deployment of the standard overboard pole rig requires too much time. The pole rig is saved to "put on top" over the person in case the initial maneuver is unsuccessful.

2. Designate someone to spot and point at the person in the water. The spotter should *never* take his or her eyes off the victim.

3. Bring the boat into the wind, trimming the mainsail to closehauled.

4. Continue to turn through the wind without releasing the headsail until the wind is almost astern. Do not ease the sails.

5. Hold this course until the victim is aft of the beam, and drop or furl the headsail if possible. If the headsail is lowered, its sheets should not be slacked.

6. Jibe the boat.

7. Steer toward the victim as if you were going to pick up a mooring.

8. Stop the boat alongside the victim by easing or backing sails.

9. Establish contact with the victim with a heaving line or other device. A "throwing sock" containing 75 feet of light floating line and a kapok bag can be thrown into the wind because the line is kept inside the bag and trails out as it sails to the victim.

10. Recover the victim on board.

Spinnakers

The same procedure is used to accommodate a boat sailing under spinnaker. Follow the preceding instructions. As the boat comes head-to-wind and

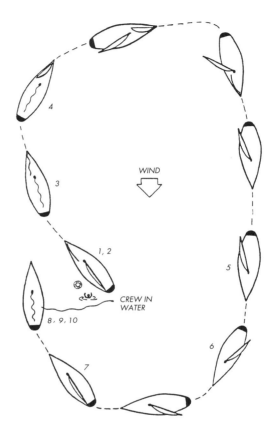

WIND

CREW IN
WATER

Fig. 84. Ten steps to a quick crew-overboard recovery.

the pole is eased quickly to the headstay, the spinnaker halyard is quickly lowered and the sail is gathered on the foredeck. The turn is continued through the tack and the approach phase commences.

Yawls and Ketches

Experiment with your mizzensail. During sea trials it was determined that the best procedure was to drop the mizzen as soon as it is convenient to do so during the early phases of quick-stop.

Use of the Engine

The use of the engine is not required although it is advisable to start the diesel but to keep it in neutral during the quick-stop phase unless it is needed in the final approach.

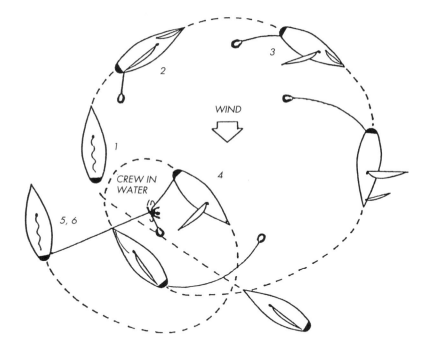

Life-Sling Method

The life-sling is a specialized piece of equipment. It consists of a floating horsecollar device that doubles as a hoisting sling. The life sling is attached to the boat by a length of floating line three or four times the boat's length. When a crew member falls overboard the scenario should proceed as follows:

1. A cushion or other flotation is thrown while the boat is brought *immediately* head-to-wind, slowed, and stopped (Figure 85).
2. The life sling is deployed by opening the bag that is hung on the stern pulpit and dropping the sling into the water. It will trail out astern and draw out the remaining line.
3. Once the sling is deployed, the boat is sailed in a wide circle around the victim with the line and sling trailing astern. The jib is not tended but allowed to back from the head-to-wind position, which increases the rate of turn.
4. Contact is established with the victim by drawing the line and sling inward by the boat's circling motion. The victim then places the sling over the head and under the arms.
5. Upon contact, the boat is put head-to-wind again, the headsail is dropped to the deck, and the main is doused.
6. As the boat drifts slowly backward, the crew begins pulling the sling and the victim to the boat. If necessary, a cockpit winch can be used to assist

in this phase, which should continue until the victim is alongside and pulled up tightly until suspended in the sling and cannot drop out. Then a block and tackle arrangement is attached to a halyard and the sling to lift the victim aboard.

Both these methods should be practiced, so your crew will automatically make the proper response if someone falls overboard. Otherwise the crew will be paralyzed when the incident happens.

Quick-Turn Method

For small inshore keelboats whose stability characteristics may result in loss of control during a jibe in heavy weather, the Quick-Turn (or Figure-8) recovery allows for a return to the victim without jibing. Take the following steps in a Quick-Turn recovery:

1. As soon as a crew member falls overboard, throw buoyant objects, such as cushions, PFDs, or life rings to the victim and shout "Crew overboard!"
2. Designate someone to spot and point at the person in the water. The spotter should *never* take his or her eyes off the victim.
3. Sail the boat on a beam reach for a maximum of four boat lengths.
4. Tack into the wind and fall off onto a very broad reach, crossing the boat's original course.
5. When downwind of the victim, turn into the wind as if you were going to pick up a mooring.
6. Stop the boat alongside the victim by easing or backing sails.
7. Establish contact with the victim with a heaving line or other device.
8. Recover the victim on board.

Shortening Sail

It's common practice on cruising boats to reduce the sail area when the wind velocity increases to the point where the boat is "overpowered." This means that the boat is heeling so much that its speed is decreased. As soon as the lee deck is awash, the boat slows down considerably. This is caused by the resistance of the shrouds, stanchions, and fittings to the water, the very strong weather helm (and therefore rudder drag) that develops when the boat heels excessively, the fact that less sail area is exposed to the wind the more the boat heels, and that less keel is exposed to the water to keep the boat from making leeway (sideslipping).

The normal progression for shortening sail is to change to a smaller jib first; then, if the wind increases, to reef the main. With still more wind, change to an even smaller jib and, if that isn't enough, take a second reef in the main.

The object is to reduce sail equally between the main and jib to keep the boat well balanced. You can take the main down completely and sail under a small jib alone if you are reaching or running. If beating to windward, however, dousing the main completely is a good way to lose a mast. The mainsail absorbs a great deal of the shock when the boat pounds through a wave. As it hits a wave, the mast whips forward and then aft. The presence of a mainsail, even reefed, reduces this whipping.

I remember sailing a particularly windy Block Island Race (a weekend race in Long Island Sound) a number of years ago on a 53-foot yawl. The owner claimed that the boat was unbeatable to windward in a blow with a #2 jib and no mainsail. He was proving his point as we were nearing the finish in the lead that night when the headstay parted from the strain and we had to retire from the race.

A number of dismastings in recent years have been attributed to sailing without a mainsail. In one St. Petersburg to Ft. Lauderdale race, the wind was a steady 35 knots on the nose. The Gulf Stream was against the wind, causing quite a steep chop 10 to 12 feet high. We were down to a small genoa staysail and the main was reefed as far as we reasonably could. The professional hand on the boat insisted we douse the main and I strongly insisted we not douse the main. I won out and when we arrived at Ft. Lauderdale and looked over the boat in daylight the next day, we found two strands of wire had pulled out of the swagged fitting that forms the eye for the turnbuckle jaw on the starboard after lower shroud. We were on starboard tack and, as the middle of the mast bowed forward after the boat "fell" off the top of one wave after another and hit the bottom of the trough, the after lower shroud and the mainsail were the only two things keeping the mast from bowing further forward. If we had lowered the main, we would have certainly lost that lower shroud and on the next wave would have lost the mast. These are just examples of the reason for an equal distribution of sail area.

Reefing the Mainsail

The standard method of reefing a mainsail is called "jiffy reefing" or "slab reefing"—take your pick. Though boats are rigged in various ways, a common rig is as follows: A line runs from an eye on the boom up through a grommet hole in the leech of the sail a few feet up, back down around a pulley at the end of the boom and forward to a winch near the gooseneck (Photo 99).

A similar grommet hole is located a few feet up the luff of the sail above a hook welded to the gooseneck. To reef:

1. Ease the mainsheet.
2. Lower the halyard (Photo 100).
3. Hook the luff grommet on the hook. You may have to take the lower slides out of the groove of the mast.

99. Reefing hooks at the goose-neck. Note reefing lines exiting over toggle clamps so the line can be taken off the winch (out of photo, just under the "Danger" sign).

100. Lower halyard far enough to hook the luff grommet on the reefing hook.

101. After hooking, tighten the halyard so the luff is very tight.

102. The leech and reefing lines before reefing.

103. Winch the leech reefing line very tight so horizontal wrinkles show along the foot. Mainsheet and vang must be loose. This is done after the reef of the luff is finished and the halyard is tight.

4. Tighten the halyard (Photo 101).
5. Winch the leech line in tight (Photos 102 and 103). You may have to ease the boom vang to get it tight.
6. Trim in the mainsheet and the reef is finished. The excess material along the foot is just disregarded or tied in with reef points. This is an extremely fast reef to make and is very popular on modern cruising boats. The order is extremely important. Complete the forward part of the sail first, before touching the leech reef line. If you start winching in the leech reef line before the new tack is hooked or the halyard is tight, you will cause yourself all sorts of problems. To shake out the reef, do all the foregoing steps in reverse order. If you don't untie the reef points before easing the leech reefing line, you will rip the sail at the reef points.

104. For neatness, the excess material from the reefed mainsail is laced around the boom.

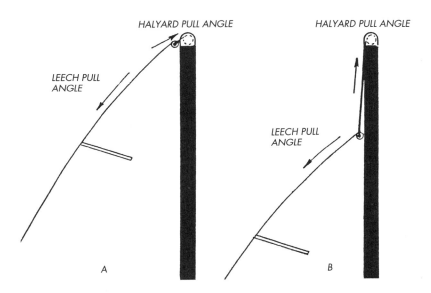

Fig. 86. (A) Unreefed, leech pull is opposite the main halyard. (B) Reefed, leech pulls luff away from mast and halyard has to be highly tensioned to counteract it.

When reefing, tighten up the main halyard extremely tight. There is a tremendous amount of pull on the head of the sail transmitted along the leech from the mainsheet tension. When the head is near the top of the mast, the halyard pull angle is almost opposite the leech pull angle (Figure 86), but when reefed, most of the leech pull is against the upper slides. That's why the slides near the head of the mainsail on a cruising boat are usually doubled up and sewn on with special care. The strain on them can be eased by very tight halyard tension. If you don't tighten the halyard you may very well rip off the upper slides, particularly if you are beating, which is the point of sailing that produces the most mainsheet pull on the leech of the sail.

The other half of shortening sail is to roll up the roller furling jib. Roll it far enough to keep the boat well balanced. Gusts of wind shouldn't blow the bow off to leeward. If there's a second jib, a fore staysail, to the middle of the foredeck, use it instead of the genoa when the wind gets over 30 knots. It's an excellent heavy weather sail.

Changing Jibs

When you ease off from closehauled to a reach, it is sometimes necessary to change jibs. When beating you may have had a large genoa set whose foot lays right along the deck. On a reach, the sheet is eased and the foot is out over the water. If the boat is heeling and there's a heavy sea, the bow plunges into heavy seas and tosses a few hundred pounds of water into the sail with each plunge, causing the stitching to give way. The solution is to change to a smaller sail with a high clew and a foot that's well up in the air clear of the waves. A #3 genoa often has this configuration, though most racing boats have a larger sail with a high clew, called a "reacher," which is set, obviously, when the boat is on a reach. Many boat owners place a grommet hole midway along the foot of the low-cut genoa. Then, with a halyard or spinnaker pole topping lift snapped into the grommet hole, the foot of the sail is lifted clear of the waves to keep it from scooping. This saves them the time and effort of changing jibs (note Photo 105). Other boat owners have reef points in a line from the

105. Hoisting the foot of a genoa to keep it from "scooping" the bow wave.

tack of the genoa to a higher clew cringle (a second one further up the leech of the sail). They change the jib sheets to the second cringle and tie up the foot of the sail so it can't scoop on a reach.

◆ 2 ◆

Distance Cruising

Sailing is one of the safest sports there is, but as the wind and sea build up, visibility decreases, navigation problems develop, and parts of the boat start to fall apart (like a short in the electrical system, a broken boom, ripped sails, or a leak), one begins to wonder just how safe it is. The problem is that you can't just cry "Uncle . . . I've had enough, let me off." You have to cope and often have to head further offshore until the wind subsides because of dangers near shore that you're unable to see. It's doubly hard when you know there's a nice snug harbor back there you'd love to be in, but don't dare approach.

If you are planning a cruise that entails some ocean going and encompasses a night or two at sea, here are some basic tips that might make your life easier if caught in a storm. Be sure to have enough crew members aboard. There should be at least two people on deck at all times. When the going is very bad, I've found, even on boats with experienced crews, that often 50% of the crew will be seasick and essentially helpless. With an inexperienced crew, there may be only one or two out of six or seven crew members who are not sick. This is a disaster for the healthy ones if the storm lasts a couple of days. So, not only must you have adequate numbers of crew, you must be sure of a nucleus of crew members you can depend on in any sort of blow.

Medical Problems

Seasickness

In order to ensure a greater percentage of your crew on deck at crucial times, have a good supply of seasick pills aboard. Make sure that anyone with a propensity to seasickness takes a pill before the weather gets rough. As for seasickness drugs, Scopolamine behind-the-ear patches, which can be obtained only with a prescription, worked well for many people but are no longer on the market. There were side effects such as drowsiness, dry mouth, and in some cases double vision. The instructions indicated those who should not use them. The patches allowed a slow release of the drug into the bloodstream, which minimized side effects, but side effects were still there.

The wrist bands with a button which applies acupressure at a point between tendons on the wrist work well for many people and are not drugs. Medical doctors claim there's no proof of their effectiveness, and they're right. If you don't get seasick when wearing them, who's to say you would have gotten seasick without them? However, when two of our employees were suffering with acute morning sickness from pregnancy, we suggested they try the wrist bands and both got instant relief. Is the nausea of morning sickness the same as that of seasickness? Who knows, but even if the results are only psychological, all sailors care about is whether they get sick. Since the wrist bands seem to work for many people, they are worth trying.

There is no one I know of who can't get seasick if the conditions are right, but there are some things that can be done to reduce the possibility.

1. Don't drink liquor excessively the night before departing. The slight morning-after feeling can be many times compounded on a boat.

2. Be careful to avoid greasy foods. The first sign of seasickness is indigestion and it often never gets past that point.

3. Drink Coke or Pepsi. These two drinks help reduce the chances of getting sick because they contain phosphoric acid, which is an ingredient in Emetrol, a drug to control vomiting. That's the medical explanation I received from a doctor when I asked why a Coke seems to settle the stomach. Eat Saltine crackers. They absorb the excess acidity very well. If the indigestion is really bad, take an antacid.

4. Stay up on deck where the air is fresh and you can see the horizon. The worst thing is to focus on a near object that is moving around in relation to the background like making an intricate repair belowdecks in the forepeak of the boat. There's a little experiment you can try to see what effect focusing has on balance, a prime factor in seasickness. First, spin around (like a figure skater), looking up at the sky at an angle not directly over your head. You'll find yourself getting a little dizzy after a few spins. Next, hold a broomstick handle up in the air at arm's length and focus on the tip of it at about the same angle as before. Now spin again. The effect is far greater and you may be close to falling down from dizziness. When you stay on deck, you can see the horizon and it greatly helps maintain your equilibrium and orientation. Also, since the smell of diesel fuel can aggravate seasickness, fresh air helps.

5. If you have a choice of berths, don't choose one in the forward cabin. There is less pitching motion in the center of the boat and the quietest berth

from the point of view of movement is often the quarter-berth, if there is one.

6. Sleep on your back. This seems to support the stomach better from bouncing around, though, not being a doctor, I couldn't tell you why.

7. Keep busy on deck. Some say seasickness is completely psychological. I know of people who have gone asleep feeling well, only to wake up seasick, so I doubt it's all psychological. However, if you sit around worrying that you might get seasick, it's apt to happen. Seeing and smelling others seasick doesn't seem to have an effect on me, but it may cause others to feel sick. If you're very busy on deck steering, or trimming and changing sails, you are less apt to feel bad, but once you do feel sick, activity tends to make it worse. You'll feel much better if you tickle your throat over the side and get rid of it. Obviously, this has to be done on the leeward side of the boat and it's best to have someone hold onto your belt in back, because you don't have much control while vomiting.

8. Have your ears cleaned before a long race or cruise. This has helped many people reduce their proneness to seasickness by allowing the balance mechanism in the ears to work better. I've never had it done myself, but I've heard it helps.

9. Be in good physical condition. It reduces your chances of becoming seasick and also reduces its debilitating effect on you if you do.

10. Steer. This even helps the crew member who has already started to feel queasy. Steering necessitates looking at the horizon (#4) and keeping busy (#7), and provides anticipation of what the next movement of the boat will be.

When you encounter very rough weather early in a distance race or long cruise, particularly early in the season or before you have had a chance to get much sailing in, your chances are higher you'll get sick. If you have a couple of days to get your "sea legs" (this term applies to maintaining your balance and insofar as balance affects your tendency toward seasickness it has come to apply to that also), you should have no trouble.

Other Medical Problems

There are only a couple of other maladies that seem common on sailboats. One is *constipation,* a problem usually occurring only on very long sails, because on shorter trips you get into port before the problem becomes acute. I've been on boats where a crew member hasn't gone in four or five days. For that reason a Fleet's enema is a good item to carry in the medical chest. It may be that unfamiliar sleeping habits caused by watch systems throw off other body functions in some people. Often the weather is so bad that using the head is a very uncomfortable process so you forgo it for a day. That day is enough to plug most people up for the day after, and so on. My only advice is to give it a try every day, particularly the first few days, no matter how uncomfortable the conditions.

The other common problem is *sunburn* on southern cruises. It's probably more of a problem on a boat than ashore because of the glare on the water. The cooling breeze makes you feel that the sun isn't as hot as it really is. Not much can be said that isn't obvious: cover up the first few days, use a sun lotion with a good sunscreen, and wear a hat. I have found the tennis-visor cap just great for this purpose. You can wear it low over the eyes; it doesn't come off easily and is compact enough when folded to put in any pocket. If you wear sunglasses, be sure they're tied on and preferably not breakable.

Accidents

Equipment Weaknesses

Equipment breaks on a sailboat when the forces become great enough. One way of minimizing your chances of being hurt is anticipating what might break. One of the most common failures occurs with turning blocks. Often a spinnaker or genoa sheet leads aft through a block and then forward to a winch. If the shackle holding the block lets go or breaks, the rig becomes a big slingshot with the block as the missile. A few summers ago, a teenager aboard a cruising boat was killed when a turning block was flung into his head. So don't stand forward of a turning block or in the bight of the line (the loop where both parts of the line go forward). Even if the sheet only pops out of the block, it can trip you up and flip you overboard if you're standing in the bight.

Chafing can be a major problem. A line that rubs on anything can eventually wear through and when the line breaks someone can get hurt. Watch for chafe and cover the line where it's rubbing with chafing gear, as shown in Photo 106.

Wire halyards are constructed with many small strands of wire for flexibility and strength. Often a few strands break, as in Photo 107. This doesn't greatly impair the strength of the halyard, but the strands are sharp and can make nasty cuts in unwary hands. Such broken strands, called "burrs" or "meathooks," can be cleaned off the wire by running the sharp blade of a knife rapidly up and down across them, as in Photo 108. They are not being cut by the knife, but are being bent back and forth until they break off under the surface.

Another area of weakness is the main boom gooseneck, the universal joint that connects the boom to the mast. There is a tremendous strain there and in a heavy blow closehauled, goosenecks have been known to rip off the mast and fly to leeward. I know of another man who was killed when the gooseneck failed and the boom hit him in the head. If there's a choice, therefore, walk forward or aft along the windward side of the boat in heavy winds.

The spinnaker pole is another weak point. Avoid standing near or under it. One fell from its mast fitting about eight feet up as I was raising it, grazed

106. Chafing gear of cloth, rubber, leather, and other materials is put over lines to keep them from rubbing through.

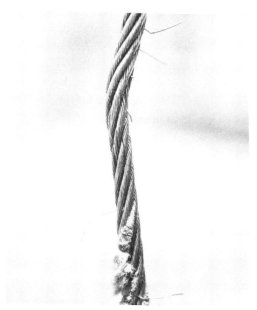

107. "Burrs"—sharp, broken strands of wire that are deadly on the hands.

108. A knife, properly used, can clean off burrs.

my head, and was stopped by a winch on the mast just before it would have landed on my shoulder. There is a tremendous compression load on a spinnaker pole when the sailboat is on a reach. I've seen a wooden pole splinter into smithereens from the load. A pole on a 12-meter sailboat I was crewing on broke away from the mast and shot like an arrow into the deck by the compression, denting the deck not a foot away from where a crew member was lying on the weather rail.

Wherever there's a strain, there's a chance of a failure. In heavy seas or at night when crew have to go up on the foredeck to change sails, they usually wear a safety harness, a line with a snaphook which can be snapped onto a lifeline or a jackline. If a crew member is washed overboard, he or she will be attached to the boat and can be pulled aboard. Care should be taken not to snap into anything that has a strain on it. One crew member snapped into the headstay while hanking on a smaller sail in preparation for a jib change. He then had second thoughts and snapped onto the lifeline instead. A few seconds later the whole headstay carried away over the side, jib and all, and he would have gone with it.

Spinnaker Accidents

On some cruising boats the method of dousing the spinnaker is to let the pole forward to the headstay where the foredeck crew pulls open the snapshackle holding the spinnaker at the pole. If you are reaching, the pole is at the headstay anyway, so it doesn't have to be let forward. It also means it's under a great load and the afterguy holding it is stretched out. When the snapshackle is opened and the spinnaker released, the pole jerks aft as the line recoils. I saw a classic example of this. The foredeck man was reaching over the pole to pull the snapshackle release pin and the side of his head was even with the pole on the windward side. I only had time to yell "duck" (and luckily he had very fast reactions) just as he pulled the shackle open. The pole swung back viciously, narrowly missing his head.

A good case for carrying a knife was made on another race I was in. The spinnaker had been doused and was being pulled aboard on the leeward side by two crew members when a wave grabbed it. It quickly pulled out underneath the lifelines and filled with water. The sheet wrapped around one crew member's leg and a stanchion, pinning him to it. Imagine the forces involved with a 50,000-pound sailboat reaching at 9 knots being held back by a spinnaker full of water. Another crew member grabbed his not-too-sharp knife and hit the ¾"-thick Dacron sheet hard. It parted in one swipe and the leg was saved. Now I happen to know that it would take about two minutes to cut through a line that thick with a knife that dull under normal circumstances with no strain on the line. For that reason I had discounted the effectiveness of using a knife in an emergency. No longer. I'm a believer.

Faulty winch handling is a cause of many more minor accidents. For instance, a crewmember may be hoisting the spinnaker and fail to get one or two wraps around the winch before the spinnaker fills with air. When it does, there are three unenviable choices: hold on tight and be pulled up in the air by the spinnaker; let go completely, allowing the spinnaker to fall into the water and most likely go under the boat, ripping on the keel; or let the halyard run through your hands until the spinnaker collapses and the halyard can be held again. The third is usually the choice selected and results in bad rope burns on the crewmember's hands. Other winch-related accidents usually come from not having enough wraps on a winch, from getting more on improperly, or from winch handles flying out of halyard winches.

Mast-Climbing Accidents

Every year there are accidents involving people climbing or being hoisted up masts. The agile sailor who climbs up the mast hand over hand and holds onto the top of the mast while accomplishing the task at hand often forgets that hands can and do cramp up and involuntarily lose their grip. The only safe way to go up is in a "bosun's chair," and in rolling conditions even using a chair can be dangerous if not done properly. A typical bosun's chair in use is shown in Photo 109. The most common halyard to use is either the jib or spinnaker halyard. The main halyard is used if nothing else is available, but usually it's being used for the mainsail.

Attach the jib halyard to the eye in the bosun's chair. A safety line should be spliced to the eye of the chair and tied to the eye in the halyard that holds the snapshackle, as in Photo 110. Thus, if the shackle fails or opens, you'll still be attached. If the conditions are very bad, it's a good idea to tape the

109. A bosun's chair for going aloft.

110. A safety line bypasses the shackle and a snatchblock keeps the chair near the mast.

snapshackle closed because the "pull" cord could easily catch on something as you go up and pull the pin, thereby opening the shackle.

Your next problem is to be sure that if you lose your grip on the mast on the way up you won't be swinging around like a paddle ball on the end of a rubber band. The mast describes a big arc in a rough sea, and it's not only hard to hold on, but if you let go you can be swinging wildly out of control. It happened to a friend of mine who went up in a blow to cut free a wrapped spinnaker. He ended up spinning around an upper shroud, all wrapped up in the halyard and unconscious. I use two methods to avoid this mishap. First, always have a downhaul line attached to the bottom of the chair with some-one feeding out slack in the line as you go up. Second, snap a snatch block to the same eye of the chair where the halyard is attached. This is shown in Photo 110 with the safety line. Snap the block over any other halyard that runs all the way up the mast so it doesn't have to be disconnected midway up. If no other halyard is available, then snap the block over the one that's tak-ing you up. This isn't as desirable as there's no way of snubbing the halyard in tight since it's pulling you up.

Photo 111 shows the proper way to crank the halyard that is pulling the chair up. The tailer is very important. If he or she slips or the coils come off the winch, the person being pulled up could easily come down in a hurry. So it should be mandatory that the tailer sit down, brace solidly, and hold the line with *both* hands. That way an unexpected wake or wave can not throw him or her off balance.

If the winch being used has a self tailing cleat on its top, *never* trust the cleat. Always use a human tailer and when the person is at the desired height,

111. This is a safe way to crank a person in a bosun's chair.

cleat the halyard on a standard type cleat and finish it off with a half-hitch for safety.

Even with all these precautions, the person going up the mast should never rely totally on the chair. There's an old axiom, "One hand for the boat and one for yourself," which means "Hold on!" Wherever possible, accomplish the task with one hand so you can save yourself with the other in case that halyard breaks or something else gives.

Steering Failures

It's fairly common to have the steering fail on a boat, particularly one with a wheel. You should inspect it often to see if the wire on the steering quadrant is frayed, burred, or damaged. Be careful not to store anything in the quadrant area that could fall and jam into the steering when the boat heels. Sometimes it falls next to the quadrant while sailing and you don't realize it until you're in a docking maneuver and need to use full rudder swing which you hadn't needed before. You suddenly find you can only turn the rudder two-thirds of the way, obviously not only embarrassing, but dangerous.

If the steering fails and you're in relatively shallow water, lower your sails and anchor immediately. Then, at your leisure, you can make repairs. In deep water, you'll have to steer by the sails for awhile until you either fix the steering or insert the emergency tiller. The latter is usually inserted onto the top of the rudder post through a plate-covered opening near the steering pedestal, as in Photo 112. Be sure you have practiced using the emergency tiller so no time is lost. Seconds could be precious.

112. An emergency steering tiller in use.

The repair might be impossible to make, as in the case of a lost rudder. Then it's a necessity to steer by the sails as described earlier. On a cruising boat the theory is the same. Trim the main and luff the jib to bring the center of effort aft in order to head up. Ease the main and trim the jib to bring the center of effort forward in order to fall off. An additional trick, and quite important for good directional control downwind, is to set a forestaysail (a small jib on the forestay) and trim it amidships. This will keep the bow heading downwind. If the boat starts to come up, the staysail will fill and push the boat down. If the boat starts to jibe, the staysail will push the bow back downwind before the main comes across. The trim of the staysail has to be varied slightly depending upon the course desired. A jib can be used instead of a staysail, but we're assuming you already have one set and winged out on a spinnaker pole.

A steering emergency occurred one year during a flotilla charter of our Offshore Sailing School graduates in Greece. The cruise was being led by our then Operations Director, Rob Eberle. He noticed that one of the boats appeared to be in trouble and was sailing toward shallow water off a point of land. He immediately raised it on the radio and asked the problem. The woman who responded was a fairly recent grad and she said they had lost their steering. Rob asked if she remembered from the "Learn to Sail" course how to tack a boat without using the rudder. She said, "Yes, luff the jib and trim the main," to which Rob replied, "Do it! Now!" He was delighted to see the boat tack and sail away from the shallow water. The point is, since it is possible to steer with the sails it is not a disaster to lose your steering. Every skipper should practice sailing without touching the steering wheel or tiller so that should a failure occur, he or she will know just how the boat handles when steered by the sails alone and would be able to sail back into safe water or to port. Unless you practice, it's easy to panic and end up in trouble. Most important about steering failure is not to panic. Boats have sailed thousands of miles without rudders so figure you can too.

Grounding

If you sail long enough there's one thing you'll eventually do—go aground. There's no real stigma in this if the grounding is one of the 90% of those that cause no damage. If you're beating up a channel and you try to hold onto one tack a little too long outside the channel and end up on a mud bank, the only thing that is hurt is your pride. Just wait for the tide to come in as the boat in Photo 113 will have to do. It's the other 10% of the groundings that get you.

For instance, take the crew that gets complacent, doesn't watch the chart carefully, doesn't even use eyeball navigation (to figure the position roughly by observation), and hits a coral reef on its windward side. They've had it. The

113. Waiting for high tide.

minute they bounce even once, the forward motion slows and the boat makes more leeway. In turning upwind and trimming the sails, the boat will heel more which may keep it from bouncing again. They might claw off to windward, but it's more likely they'll hit again, then start being pushed sideways by the wind and end up higher and higher on the reef. This is one of those cases when the first bounce is too late. The only thing that can save the boat is to get a tow immediately from a powerboat.

If the wind is light and the current is pushing you on the reef, you can try to kedge off—setting out an anchor and pulling the boat off by winching in the anchorline. Get a heavy anchor in a dinghy and attach as much line as you can find aboard the boat and drop the anchor as far out to windward in as deep water as possible. You probably will have only one chance. If the anchor drags the first time, there's not much chance of getting it up and resetting it for a second try. It will take too long and by that time the boat may be pushed too far aground for kedging to help.

So whenever you find yourself in a kedging situation, make sure you take the little extra time to row the anchor as far away from the boat as your line will allow. Though an engine won't do any good alone, it can assist if you are kedging or a powerboat is pulling you off. Also, if you put the helm hard over so the boat will turn toward deep water and rev up the engine in forward gear, it may help spin the boat off. If you don't have an anchor windlass to pull on the anchor line, use your powerful jib sheet winches.

I have dealt with the most disastrous type of grounding first. It's the kind you cannot afford to have happen—period. The first time may be the last, and the only way it can be avoided is by careful navigation. All too often, inexperienced sailors look at a chart only when close to shore. They never think that the water in the middle of a bay could be only two feet deep! As long as they're not near shore, they are lulled into a false sense of security and don't bother with the chart.

Then there's the slightly more careful navigator who is aware of a dangerous shallow spot, sets a course to miss it, and then basks in his competence. He never follows up with cross bearings to check that some unexpected current, excessive leeway, or casual steering hasn't been setting him right on the reef he was steering to miss. He may have gotten away with this type of navigation for years, but it takes only one mistake to wake him up.

Other grounding situations can be avoided by common sense. Sailing in the Grenadines, I was leading a group of four 41-foot sailboats. We lowered our sails to power through a channel to an overnight anchorage. I noticed that there was a breaking reef to leeward, so we changed our plans and went the long way around to leeward of the reef. I thought about an engine failure and didn't want any of the boats to be to windward of that reef if it happened. Sure enough, just as the last boat got dead downwind of the reef, she had a fire in her starter motor and lost her engine. Luckily, she was not to windward of the reef.

Think ahead about what can happen, expect the worst, and you may avoid some unnecessary groundings.

Now let's look at the more nuisance type of grounding, in mud with a falling tide. It's still important to waste no time getting off after you first go aground. Even if you may be unconcerned because the tide's coming in, weather conditions could change. What was a "no problem" situation could change radically if a sudden, unexpected squall comes through. If you do go aground, get all your crew weight quickly over to the lee side of the boat, then trim your sails in flat. Both maneuvers will have the effect of heeling the boat over and giving it less draft if the boat is small and light enough. You may be lucky enough to drift sideways away from the shallow spot.

If you have a spinnaker pole aboard, you can use it to help shove off. The one problem is that if the bottom is soft mud, the pole end will sink fairly deep before it becomes effective.

If worse comes to worst, don't forget that the reason you're aground is because the water is shallow. If you draw no more than five feet or so, the wind is not blowing, and there is no current, no rough sea, and wind conditions are very light, you might consider going over the side to physically shove the boat off. This can be tricky, though, and you must be very careful not to get hit by the boat or allow the boat to get away from you. First try pushing the bow up and out. If this doesn't work, alternate between the bow and stern, which will tend to spin the boat off. Surprisingly enough, using the dinghy tugboat-style is often very effective. That is, push the sailboat sideways with the bow of the dinghy against the side of the sailboat near its bow. It's best if the rest of the crew either gets way out to leeward or off the sailboat to lighten it. Sometimes it can be helpful if one or two crew members swing on a halyard or the main boom out over the water to heel the boat farther while the rest of the crew pushes against the hull.

Once the boat is free and you're sailing again, don't just assume everything is going to be fine. If you had a hard grounding with a lot of wave action, you may well have punctured the skin of a fiberglass boat or opened up some seams in a wooden boat. It is best to make a visual inspection by going over the side with a mask and flippers. At the very least, check the bilge to see if the boat is taking any water. If the boat has been built with encapsulated lead ballast in its keel, and if there are voids between the lead and the hull, this may become a source of leaks. It may take awhile for the water to fill the keel and show up in the bilge, so check every 15 minutes for a couple of hours after a bad grounding.

Night Sailing

Sailing at night is good for the soul. It can be challenging and yet peaceful. A sailboat gives a sensation of greater speed at night as bits of phosphorescence flash by and disappear. For those who live in cities and suburbs where there is always some sort of artificial light, it's easy to feel that they'd be groping in total darkness without such light. On the contrary, even with total cloud cover, visibility is rather good at sea, and on some moonlit nights one can see perfectly for miles, much like being in daylight wearing dark sunglasses. You can not imagine seeing so many stars as at sea.

Navigating at night under good conditions is even easier than in daylight. Some marks and lighthouses that can be seen only a couple of miles away in daylight can be spotted 10 miles or more away at night. And in some parts of the country, Long Island Sound, for instance, there are so many of these navigation lights that it's virtually impossible to get lost at night if the visibility is good and you're keeping track.

There are certain little tricks to using these lights. The navigation chart (and a Coast Guard publication called the *Light List)* gives the characteristics of each light. For instance, a light may be marked as "Fl 6 sec" on the chart. This means that it flashes every six seconds and is white. We know it's white because the only other possibilities are red or green, in which case the abbreviation "R" or "G" would appear after the "Fl." Now, let's say we spot a light which we think is the one above. We could use a stopwatch to determine if there are six-second intervals between flashes, but then a flashlight would be necessary to read it or we would have to go below and use a cabin light. Either way our night vision would be impaired for a short while and might make further sightings difficult. The best way is to count the seconds. After a flash, count "one thousand and one, one thousand and two, one thousand and three, etc.," until it flashes again. With just a little practice you should be able to count the seconds with very little error since the five syllables take about one second to say.

The navigator should never give the crew on deck the characteristics of the light he wishes to find. If he says he's looking for a four-second, white flashing light just off the starboard bow, the spotter is apt to accept the light seen as the one the navigator wants. However, if the navigator insists that the spotter determine the characteristics of a light seen off the starboard bow, there is much less chance for error.

One major danger in night sailing is collisions. It's imperative that anyone who sails at night knows what navigation lights other boats are carrying. The basic lights that almost all vessels have are red and green sidelights. These can be seen from dead ahead to two points abaft the beam. The red is on the port side (often remembered by the fact that port wine is red) and the green on starboard. A sailboat will carry only sidelights and a white stern light, although under power she has to carry a bowlight. Larger powerboats carry red and green sidelights, a stern light, a bowlight, and also a higher range light aft. The relationship between these last two lights tells the observer which way the boat is turning.

You may recall from an earlier chapter that a motorboat's "danger zone" is from dead ahead to two points abaft the starboard beam. At night, a motorboat in that area could be showing one of the following possible combinations of lights: (1) red and green sidelights with the bow light and range light in line, which indicates she's heading right for you or that you are crossing in front of her; (2) a green sidelight, indicating that there's little risk of collision because she's going to pass your stern, is running parallel with you, or has crossed your bow and is running away from you (depending on the relationship of the bow and range lights); (3) a low white light (her stern light), indicating that she's steaming ahead of you or you're overtaking; and (4) a red light, which means "watch out"—she may be on a collision course (depending on the angle of her range lights and her bearing) and have right of way over you since she's in your danger zone.

Here we've only described what the lights of another powerboat *might* look like in your danger zone area at night. Of course, you can see her red sidelight at many other times. If, for instance, you were sailing toward each other on parallel courses to pass port to port, you'd see her red sidelight. There's an infinite variety, but the whole idea is that by seeing those few key navigation lights and knowing their relationship you can visualize the whole boat and its direction without really seeing it.

Some special lights are very important to know. For instance, if you see three vertical lights in a row (plus a yellow towing light above the stern light) you can be sure it's a boat, usually a tugboat, with a tow far behind showing lights that are often very hard to see. Be sure you know where the tow is. If you pass behind the tug you may hit the tow line, or, worse yet, you may be smashed by the barge.

When you see two vertical lights, the barge is alongside the tug (or 200 meters or less behind it, in which case a yellow towing light will be above the stern light). This is likely the case in narrow channels. This situation poses much less of a threat since you can quite easily spot the last barge in the line.

A green light above a white light indicates a trawler dragging his nets. When dragging, this boat has right of way over all others, including sailboats, so be careful to avoid him.

Most ships have radar which they use to avoid collisions. However, sailboats don't show up very well on radar, which responds better to metal than to wood or fiberglass. A radar reflector hung high in the rigging of a sailboat will greatly improve the chances of being picked up by a ship's radar. Radar reflectors are many-sided objects usually made of wire mesh or metal sheets which can be folded away and kept in a small storage space when not in use. During periods of low visibility, the reflector should be taken out, put together, and hoisted.

If a ship is on a collision course with a sailboat at night, the crew of the sailboat must make their presence known to the helmsman of the ship. This if often done by shining spotlights on the sails of the boat, but such lights are difficult to see and not very effective. Since lives can be at stake, the best way to be seen is to shine a spotlight directly at the bridge of the ship. The spotlights aboard a sailboat are so weak that this will hardly bother the night vision of the ship's helmsman, but will at least make him aware of the sailboat.

Reading lights (determining the course, speed, and type of boat from its lights) takes experience. If you don't have it, you shouldn't venture out at night without someone on board who has. Someone has to determine if you're on a collision course and if you have right of way in order to make the proper decision as to course change. A wrong decision could be disastrous, so don't take sailing at night lightly.

If you are planning to sail night and day, you will need to split the crew into two watches. One watch sails the boat while the other watch sleeps, eats, makes repairs, and does whatever else has to be done. They are commonly called the "port" watch and the "starboard" watch. I have tried many systems, but the one I like the best is a modified Swedish watch system which divides the 24 hours of the day into watches of 4, 4, 5, 6, and 5 hours each. This means the times are as follows: midnight to 0400, starboard watch on, port watch off; 0400–0800, port watch on, starboard off; 0800–1300, starboard on, port off; l300–1900, port on, starboard off; 1900 to midnight, starboard on, port off. Now we are starting the next 24 hours with a different watch starting off. In other words, the uneven number of watches staggers them and provides both variety and an even number of hours both on or off over a two-day period. Of course, this system can start at any time, not just at midnight. As for meals, the off-watch usually eats just before coming up: 7:30 breakfast, 12:30 lunch, and 6:30 dinner. The on-watch has its meals just after being relieved: 8:00 breakfast, 1:00 lunch, and 7:00 dinner. These are close to the mealtimes most of us are accustomed to. Further, the long watches are during the day when most people are wide awake and the watches in the wee hours of the morning are short, since they tend to be the coldest, darkest, most uncomfortable time to be sailing.

Sometimes the cruise is a short one of a night or two and it's not worth setting up the long-range Swedish system. In that case, crews often use the straightforward "four hours on and four hours off" system. Or, if you have plenty of crew members, split them into three watches so that each watch is on for four hours and off for eight. A boat sailed across an ocean by six people, but normally handled by two except to change sails, will usually elect to use this leisurely type of watch system.

Steering in Darkness

Steering at night takes a combination of a sixth sense and mechanical aptitude. On reaches and runs there's not too much problem steering. The helmsman is usually trying to maintain a compass course established by the navigator. Waves on runs and wind gusts on reaches will tend to throw the boat off course and the helmsman must compensate. The extent to which he can anticipate such changes in the dark qualifies his ability as a helmsman. The helmsman whose eyes remain glued on the compass will not steer well. He only corrects his course after it has changed, rather than anticipating the change. His eyes will tire even though the red compass light is designed to be easy on the eyes. Steer for a star or a distant cloud, only looking down at the compass with short glances to check that you're still on course. Be careful that the "star" you're steering for isn't the masthead light of another sailboat (as has happened before).

Sailing upwind in the dark is more difficult. Though much of it is by "feel," for efficient sailing two other instruments are necessary: a sensitive speedometer to tell you fractions of a knot of speed gained or lost, and a wind guide to show the apparent wind direction. Some wind indicators have a scale that enlarges the movement of the wind direction arrow the first 45° or so relative from the bow. These are called "closehauled indicators" and are easy to read at night when beating. The helmsman has to juggle the instruments to maintain the best speed to windward. Let's say the boat is on starboard tack. If the helmsman heads up, three things will happen: (1) the compass will show

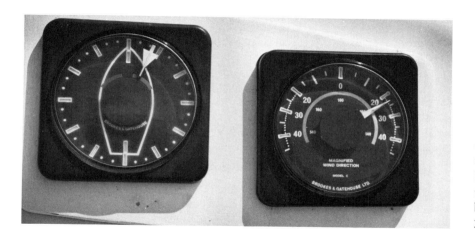

114. *Left:* a typical apparent wind direction indicator. *Right:* the dial magnifies the first 45° from the bow and stern. The dials show that the boat is closehauled on the starboard tack, with the wind at about 22° apparent.

higher numbers than previously in front of the lubberline (the line on the compass that represents the centerline or bow of the boat); (2) the apparent wind arrow (Photo 114) will show lower numbers as it moves more toward the bow of the boat on the instrument dial; and (3) the speedometer will probably show lower numbers since the helmsman is starting to pinch. These numbers all have to blend into the helmsman's mental computer so he makes the correct change of course to get the most speed from the boat.

It takes experience and concentration to do well, and is very satisfying. However, even an experienced helmsman cannot steer efficiently for long periods of time at night. It takes about ten minutes to work into the "groove" and then the next half hour the helmsman is probably steering his best. After that it's downhill; possibly imperceptibly with a better helmsman, but still downhill. Of course, if you're cruising, speed doesn't mean so much and, unless conditions are bad, a two-hour trick (period) at the wheel is fairly easy.

One of the night problems that can be avoided has to do with the dinghy. If the cruise encompasses a long stretch of open water, particularly at night, the dinghy should be brought aboard and lashed upside-down on the cabin top. A dinghy that is towed could easily swamp and capsize in heavy seas, causing it to snap the painter (the tow line) and be lost. At night you'd never find it. To bring it aboard, fashion a bridle or sling from some spare lines and use a halyard. If you are towing the dinghy in moderate weather, make sure the oars and outboard are well secured or taken off and tow it on the back of a wave so the bow is up rather than letting it scoot down the face of the stern wave.

Until you enjoy the wonderful experience of sailing all night for many nights, you have not really cruised. Some of the most beautiful, quiet, peaceful sailing can be at night.

The Galley

Probably the most important area of the boat is the galley and the most important crew member is the cook. The cook who can put out hot, tasty meals when it's cold, wet, and miserable outside and when the cabin is like the inside of a hot, tumbling clothes-dryer, deserves a medal.

Stoves

There are many types of stoves used on sailboats. Electric ones are rare because a large generator has to be run at the same time to use them. Gas is now the cooking fuel of choice. The danger in LPG (liquid petroleum gas) is that it's heavier than air and any gas leak will collect in the lowest part of the boat where a spark can cause an explosion. Therefore, the storage tanks are kept on deck in an area that has no access to the inside of the hull except through the gas lines to the stove. A solenoid cut-off valve is often installed right at the tank so that the user, after cooking is finished, flips a switch that activates the solenoid cut-off valve while the stove is still lit. The gas remaining in the line below the tank is burned off and the flame goes out. Then the stove burner is turned off. Luckily, gas used today emits quite an odor so you usually know if there's a leak. Plus a gas detector alarm can be installed on your boat in case you're asleep and don't smell the leak. A friend of mine came back to his 47-foot yacht one time and found that a burner had been left on unlit. A lot of gas had collected in the bilge. He very gingerly took a plastic bailing bucket, scooped the gas, carried it on deck, and dumped it over the side. Later, he had to use a tea cup to get the gas out of the small, deep portions of the bilge. The sight of this strapping guy carrying an empty-looking tea cup up on deck and dumping nothing over the side time after time must have both baffled and amused the other sailors in the marina.

Despite such drawbacks, gas is great. It's safe and easy to light, and cooks with a hot, even flame. It's cheaper than alcohol and is less bother.

Charter sailboats are often fueled by CNG (compressed natural gas) rather than by LPG (currently known as propane) or by alcohol. This is the safest and most efficient fuel. It is safer than propane because it is lighter than air. If there's a leak in the system, CNG will dissipate rather than drop to the lowest part of the bilge, like propane. Alcohol stoves are fairly safe, because an alcohol fire can be extinguished by water, but they are inefficient, with a cool flame compared to gas.

A tank of gas can often last a season of sailing. Usually there are two fuel tanks on deck. When one runs out, you unscrew the gas line from one tank and screw it on the full tank. The treads are *backwards* from your normal threads (left is tight and right is loose). *Never* do this operation when the barbecue is being used. I know of at least one sailboat that was lost that way. Never use any of the camping-type gas stoves, because they are not approved by the Coast Guard. Such stoves are not good for closed areas because the stove has a self-contained gas tank and any leak would go to the bilge.

Most cruising sailboats have a galley designed to allow the cook to brace against some bulkhead and use both hands for cooking regardless of the heel angle and the motion. Those that don't, usually have added belts with snaps to hold the cook near the stove even when the galley is on the high (windward) side of the boat. All good stoves are well-gimbaled so the cooking surface stays level no matter how far the boat is heeled. I've never seen any cook burned or scalded while cooking, but it does happen. Wearing foul weather gear will protect the cook. The other dangerous part seems to be passing hot items to the watch that's down below to eat. One should *never* hold a bowl or a cup and have another person pour soup or coffee into it. One person should hold both the pot and the cup. That way the pouring hand and the holding hand adjust for lurches of the boat in concert—a coordination that's impossible for two separate persons.

Food Planning

Much of this is up to personal preference. Just be sure there's plenty of it because most sailors are hungrier on the water than ashore. For a weekend cruise, casseroles that are prepared at home and heated in the oven on the boat are a great idea. There is no doubt that the charcoal barbecue grill (shown in Photo 115) which hangs off the transom is a fine invention. It can only be

115. A charcoal grill attached to the stern pulpit can easily be removed for cleaning.

used at anchor (not at a dock) though, because the boat must always be heading into the wind so any hazardous embers blow away over the water. Your grill will usually be at one corner of the stern. Hang your dinghy from the opposite corner or along the other side, so ashes and sparks don't fall into it. The grill saves some of the mess in the galley and is a nice, social way of having a fine dinner of steak, chicken, shrimp, hamburgers, or whatever. A tip, though: preboil chicken on the stove or it will take forever to cook on the grill. Use the self-starting type of charcoal that looks like egg cartons. It's clean, fast, safe, and easy to use. Line the bottom of the grill with aluminum foil to keep the grease drippings off the metal. Discard the foil after use and the grill is left relatively clean.

Water

When you are cruising over long distances between ports or in an area where good drinking water is difficult to find, water conservation aboard a sailboat is a necessity. Some sailboats have quite small water tanks, though the modern trend is toward larger and larger capacity tanks. Nevertheless, space taken for water tanks means less space for other storage, and since there's a finite amount of space on a sailboat a compromise must be reached. Once you get used to habits that conserve water, they become as second nature as the habits that waste water ashore.

Whenever you wash anything in a sink, use the drain plug and fill the bowl with water rather than let it run. Many sailboat galleys have double sinks, one for washing and one for rinsing, to help conserve water. Often they are equipped with a pressure tap and a backup hand pump or foot-operated pump in case the pressure system breaks down. On a long cruise, turn off the pressure system and rely on the manual pump. Less water is used if you have to pump it by hand or foot. On boats expecting to sail at sea, often a saltwater pump is installed in the galley. The salt water is used for the initial washing of dishes (rinsed with fresh) and for some cooking, such as boiling eggs. Even without a saltwater tap, it's common practice to wash dishes in salt water if not anchored in a polluted harbor. Just drop a plastic bucket over the side on a line, bring up the salt water, and set it in the cockpit near the companionway. Make sure no one's using the head at the same time the salt water is taken. Use liquid detergent in the bucket and pass the clean dishes down below for a freshwater rinse and for drying.

When you take a shower, a few squirts of fresh water will get you wet; then lather up and a few more squirts should be enough to rinse off. At sea, a bucket of salt water and a bottle of Joy liquid detergent are all you need to get yourself clean. Sea water is also used for brushing teeth, plus it's good for the gums. On one three-week trip across the Atlantic we averaged one quart of fresh water a day per person using such conservation measures. Remember—there's a lot of liquid in most canned foods and most boats carry adequate soft drinks to augment the water supply.

Storage

Even the finest yachts get water below in the cabin during heavy weather sailing conditions. Fiberglass has solved many of the leaking problems, but water still gets in around through-deck fittings, rudder posts, and propeller shafts. Plus, when you open the forward hatch to pull a jib out, gallons of water can charge down if you happen to hit a sea at the same time. The small amount of water collecting from these sources is nothing to worry about, but many of the smaller modern cruising boats have very shallow bilges. When the boat heels, the bilge water runs up the sides of the cabin like soup in a tilted bowl. This makes cabin drawers under the bunks very vulnerable to sloshing water as the boat pounds and rolls in the waves. Yacht designers have tried to seal off these areas, but water is fairly insidious and ferrets out dry clothing as if it had a personal vendetta. If your storage lockers have a history of leaks, it's best to keep your clothes in plastic garbage bags or in higher lockers.

Foul-weather gear should be stored near or behind the companionway if there's a spot for it. Once you track wet foul-weather gear through the cabin to store it forward, everything starts to get wet, and salt water never seems to evaporate completely because the salt absorbs any moisture in the air. After the trip, wash everything possible with fresh water so it will dry properly. Be sure to have a supply of clothes pins on hand. The lifelines around the boat make an ideal clothesline.

Glass has to be stowed very carefully. Most bottles of condiments, etc., are placed in cupboards and soft-drink bottles are stored under the cabin sole in the bilge. Eggs can stay unrefrigerated for long periods of time and often are kept in cupboards or drawers if the trip is to be a long one.

Bread, if homemade without preservatives, should be put in the icebox to avoid spoiling. This is the type of bread used in most places outside the U.S. such as the Virgin Islands, Bahamas, Grenadines, and Europe. In hot climates, fruit (other than bananas) will need to be kept in the icebox. Lettuce should be kept in the icebox but will turn brown if in direct contact with the ice, so insulate it. Wrap heads of lettuce in aluminum foil and they will keep much longer.

Ice for drinks in the evening should be removed from the icebox and put in an ice bucket so the icebox lid won't be opened every time a person needs ice for a drink. This will go a long way toward preserving the ice supply. When cold beer and soft drinks are kept on ice, a policy of "he who takes one from the icebox adds one to it" will ensure a supply of cold drinks without the need of keeping a great stock of them on ice.

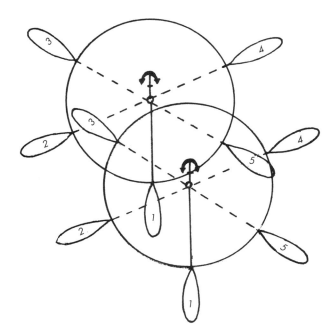

Fig. 87. By dropping an anchor alongside another anchored boat, you won't hit it as long as you both swing fairly equally.

Anchoring

Anchoring is deceptively simple. A friend of mine saw a "sailor" drop an anchor over the bow and when the anchor touched bottom the line was cleated with a report back to the skipper that "we're anchored." The report was true, but the likelihood of dragging the anchor was 100%. When we anchor, we want to reduce the possibility of dragging to the smallest percentage possible. Anyone can anchor, but not everyone will be in the same spot the next morning where they anchored the night before.

Probably the most popular type of cruising is sailing from harbor to harbor along a coast or among islands, and anchoring each night. When choosing a spot to anchor, make sure it's in sheltered water, not in a channel, and check the chart to determine if there's enough water for your boat in that location at low tide. Also, notice on the chart if the spot you've chosen for the night is a "special anchorage area." If not, you are required to have a 360° anchor light. Tie it to your headstay about seven feet high. There's a battery-powered anchor light on the market with an electric-eye switch. It turns off automatically at daybreak so you aren't wasting batteries if you sleep late. In a special anchorage area, no anchored boat needs an anchor light; those navigating in the area are aware of that fact from the chart and watch out for them.

Pick a spot that allows some room to swing on your anchor without hitting other anchored boats. Given the option, I like to drop my anchor right

116. A Danforth anchor with its wide flukes and excellent holding power is perhaps the most popular type in the U.S. today.

alongside another anchored boat and drop back from there as shown in Figure 87. As you can see from positions 2, 3, 4, and 5 for each boat, there is no chance of hitting that boat as we both swing later in the night. However, if we go forward of the anchored boat and drop our anchor, when we have let out enough line we may be too close to her. Also remember to make allowances for different types of boats. For instance, a deep-keeled sailboat will line up more with the current while a shallow draft powerboat with a high cabinhouse will line up more with the wind. So anchor near boats that are similar in design to yours.

As for holding power, the major variables are the type of anchor and its weight, the angle the anchorline makes with the bottom, and the type of bottom. For instance, a Danforth anchor (Photo 116) holds well in a muddy and rocky bottom, but poorly when the bottom is grassy (covered with seaweed). A plow-type anchor (Photo 117) is better at grabbing on a grassy bottom. A yachtsman's anchor (Photo 118) probably has the best all-around holding power, but has to be heavy to be effective and is awkward to handle. The heavier the anchor of any type, the better the holding power.

The smaller the angle the line makes with the bottom, the better the holding. If the line is almost vertical, the anchor will lift rather than dig in. However, if the line is almost horizontal, the anchor will dig in hard. The most common method to reduce this angle is to let out more line or "scope." Four to one scope is enough for temporary anchoring such as a lunch stop, but five or six to one scope is recommended if you want to sleep well at night. This means to let out anchorline equal to six times the depth of the water where you are anchoring plus your freeboard. Remember the tide factor, though. If

117. A plow anchor stored on a bow fitting for easy anchoring.

118. The yachtsman's anchor holds well on irregular bottoms. The crossbar (the stock) folds down for storage.

you anchor in 8 feet of water plus 4 feet freeboard at low tide and let out 60 feet of anchorline (five to one scope), you are only going to have about three to one scope when a 6-foot tide brings the depth up to 18 feet. Also, you may have anchored at slack tide with little current. When the current starts to flow fast, you may start to drag.

A good system is to use the fathometer to determine the depth of the water where you're anchoring, 15 feet, for example. Add the expected rise of the tide plus freeboard. Let's say we expect it to be 5 feet deeper at high tide, with 5 feet of freeboard, or 25 feet total. Multiply the result by 6 and let out 150 feet of scope. Until you are well aware of how much line this represents, place red plastic markers along the anchorline at 20-foot intervals. These markers can be bought at most nautical supply stores. You will be quite surprised in the beginning at how much line 150 feet is.

Some cruising skippers set out two anchors at 45° to 60° off the bow. This helps reduce swinging when there is limited room in an anchorage, but does not add much to the holding power. The square root of the sum of the squares of each anchor's weight gives the equivalent holding power of a single anchor. Therefore, a 30-pound and a 40-pound anchor have the holding power of a single 50-pounder, so why fuss with two? Just buy a good heavy storm anchor.

There are times when two anchors are important for peace of mind. In a tidal river where the current reverses itself 180°, the single anchor that is holding well in one direction may pull out and not hold when the current changes. The answer is to drop one anchor, drift downcurrent to the end of the anchorline, drop a second anchor, and pull or power back upcurrent to a spot midway between the two anchors. If you know they are both well set, pulling against each other, there will be no problem when the current changes.

Other than setting two anchors or letting out more scope, another common method of increasing holding power is to add a length of chain to the anchor and to attach the anchorline to the end of the chain. Then the chain has to be lifted before the anchor is affected. Also, the chain reduces the chance of the rope anchor rode chafing through on the bottom or a coral head.

Now, let's imagine we are on a cruise and have selected a harbor and anchoring spot for the evening. Lower your sails and power into the harbor. Cruising boats that don't have jib-furling gear often lower the genoa and stuff it into its sailbag for the night without even unhanking it (Photo 119). This also saves storage space below if that's where the genoa is normally stored when at home port.

Have your anchor on deck and ready. If the anchorline is stored in the forepeak, make sure plenty of it has been pulled out and is on deck so that the anchor will reach the bottom without pulling more out of the hawsehole (the hole through the deck leading into the forepeak anchorline storage area). If a tangle develops in the forepeak under the deck, it will be a nasty mess in an area that's hard to reach. Don't throw the anchor over the side or let it run free immediately, because it will run out at a tremendous speed. Lower the anchor in the water gently until some of the weight is reduced by the water pressure, and then let go. Make sure the bitter end is secure. Many anchors

119. Genoa jib bagged right on the headstay for the night. In the morning, just pull off the bag and hoist.

have been lost because the end wasn't tied and the crew member feeding out the line reached the end of it before he or she expected. It can also happen later at night when, because of an increase in the wind velocity, a crew member lets out more line to improve the holding power of the anchor and doesn't realize the end wasn't tied until it's too late. If the line comes up from the forepeak, it's a good idea to secure the end down there. Then, no matter who's on the anchoring detail, the skipper knows it can't get lost.

Make sure your dinghy is snubbed up close to the sailboat's stern. The best time to do this is as you approach the anchorage. Failure to take this precaution may result in the dinghy's painter (tow line) wrapping around the sailboat's propeller as she backs down. You might think this would cause the engine to stall out and you'd be right, but only after the whole dinghy has been pulled down under the water to the propeller, so that only the transom is left showing on the surface. I was on a privately owned boat when this happened and I can assure you it's unfortunate.

After the anchor is down, let the wind blow the boat downwind. Ease out plenty of anchorline as it goes. It's rare that you can ever let out *too much* scope, but it's common to let out too little. Err on the long side. Don't test whether the anchor is holding until you let out all the line you intend to, because if you do and it drags, you won't be anchored where you wanted to be. When enough is out, snub the anchorline around a cleat so that the momentum of the boat will set the anchor, just as one jerks a fishing line to set the hook in the fish's mouth. Next, cleat the line, reverse the engine with low RPMs, and test the set of the anchor. By grasping the anchorline you can feel if the anchor is dragging. The vibration will be transmitted through the line to your hand. Try to avoid dragging the anchor into deeper water because it surely won't catch if the water depth is increasing and the scope becomes less and less. If it is obvious that you are too close to another boat which was there first, raise your anchor and try again. The courtesy is, "He who anchors last, moves first" (if it's necessary).

Since a sailboat's bow blows off the wind so easily when attempting to back downwind, the skipper has very little control. In tight quarters, anchoring can be very difficult. One solution is to have the anchor and line at the stern of the boat. When you are dead upwind of the spot you wish to end up when anchored, drop the anchor off the stern and power slowly straight downwind. You have complete control and can power between other closely anchored boats. Snub and cleat the same way as before and, when thoroughly anchored, take the end of the anchorline up to the bow, cleat it, and release the stern attachment. Though rarely used, this system has some merit.

Next, many sailors take compass bearings on nearby landmarks or lights to determine later if they've dragged the anchor. This is better than nothing, but I've found bearings to be of limited value. If you take bearings on nearby objects, just the swinging of the boat will change the bearing and you will think you are dragging. If you take bearings on distant objects, you have to drag a long distance before the bearings change noticeably. You'll know you've dragged long before the bearings tell you. On particularly nasty nights you may want to post an "anchor watch." If you have four crew members, each one might stay on deck two hours while the others sleep, alternatively relieving one another. That way, one person is always awake in case of dragging. Sometimes the dragging is caused by a strong current that has built up over a period of hours. Be supremely careful in letting out more scope under those circumstances. In one case, a man was letting out more scope for his 40-foot sailboat in a strong current, caught his leg in a loop of the anchorline, and was pulled overboard. His son got a knife to him, but instead of cutting the line below his foot, he cut the line leading to the boat, presumably to relieve the tremendous pressure. Thus, with the boat gone and his leg "anchored," the current sucked him right under the water and he drowned. So not only cleat the end of the line with the estimated amount of slack for the extra scope, but ease the line out with a wrap or two around the base of the cleat until all the slack is absorbed.

At this point we should mention a few of the factors which go into spending a comfortable night aboard. Be sure to have screens for the boat if you're cruising in a hot, buggy area. At the very least, have bug spray and repellent aboard.

Some boats have small kerosene lanterns on the bulkheads which give a cozy illumination to the cabin. Use them and save the batteries. The less you use electric lights, the fewer hours you'll have to charge the batteries the next day.

If the sheets aren't cut and fitted to the berths, use a full-sized sheet doubled over so one half becomes the lower sheet and the other half becomes the upper. Cover naugahyde (plastic)-covered berth cushions with a blanket first and then a sheet. This makes them far more comfortable. If you use sleeping bags, be aware that Nylon, down-filled ones may be too hot for sleeping except in very cold climates.

Turn off the pressure water system, because any leak in the line will cause the pump to go on and off intermittently and wake you up.

To raise the anchor the next morning, start the engine and motor up toward it. A crew member in the bow should be pointing in the direction toward the anchor while gathering in the line as in Photo 120. Hand signals are better than verbal ones which often can't be heard over the noise of the engine. When the anchorline is vertical, snub it around a cleat and use the forward momentum of the boat to break the anchor out. The engine should be in neutral and the boat at a complete stop as the anchor is raised or the forward motion will knock the anchor against the bow of the boat as the anchor surfaces. If the anchor doesn't break out as the boat rides over it, cleat the anchor, put the engine in forward gear, and hit the throttle in an attempt to break it free. Try different angles (not just into the wind). If you can rotate the anchor, perhaps it will break free. An alternative method can be used in heavy seas. As the bow goes down, take in any slack in the anchorline and snub it. As the bow rises on the next wave, the boat's buoyancy may break it free.

120. Point toward the anchor and let the boat's engine do the work of getting the bow right over it.

For this method to be ultimately successful, the slack will have to be taken in on a series of waves before the anchorline is truly taut and vertical. If this doesn't work, take the anchorline back to a jib sheet winch and try to winch it up. Failing this, a visual inspection of the problem can often bring forth a solution, so don your mask and flippers and go for a swim, providing it's not too cold.

One other solution takes some preplanning but is useful in colder climates. This is the use of a "tripline," a light line attached to the anchor, usually near the flukes, that pulls it out backward if snagged. Some sailors attach a small buoy to an anchor tripline that floats directly above the submerged anchor. This saves letting out so much tripline that it can tangle with the regular anchorline, and also gives the skipper a mark to head for in order to get the boat right over the anchor for raising.

When the anchor breaks the surface of the water, clean the mud off, if there is any, before bringing it aboard. Stow the anchor carefully and make sure it's well lashed down on deck before setting sail.

Typical mistakes one sees in anchoring and raising the anchor are: (1) failing to snub the dinghy in close; (2) dropping the anchor as the boat is moving forward; (3) dropping it too close upwind of other boats; (4) backing down so fast that the anchorline is zinging out and there's a real threat of someone's catching a hand or leg in it; (5) too little scope; and (6) powering out of the harbor with the raised anchor still not all the way up.

Piloting

Coastwise navigation, or "piloting" as it's called, consists of transferring your actual position to an easily readable overview of your sailing area in the form of a chart. Basically, it requires that you determine your position (called a "fix"), locate the position on the chart, and then use the rest of the chart to avoid hazards such as shoals, rocks, and reefs. From your chart you can determine a course to steer for a safe passage to your destination.

The Chart

The chart is a neat "road map" of the sea printed by the U.S. Department of Commerce and available at many nautical supply stores. The area a chart covers and the identifying number is listed in a nautical chart catalog. Figure 88 shows a section of this catalog. When cruising, I find it very handy to tape the pertinent section of the catalog on a vertical surface near the navigator's station and circle the numbers of all the charts I have aboard the boat. Before leaving home, the charts are folded so that the back of the chart is on the outside. This helps keep the charts cleaner longer. Also, if the charts get wet the imprinting won't be rubbed off. Write the number of the chart on an

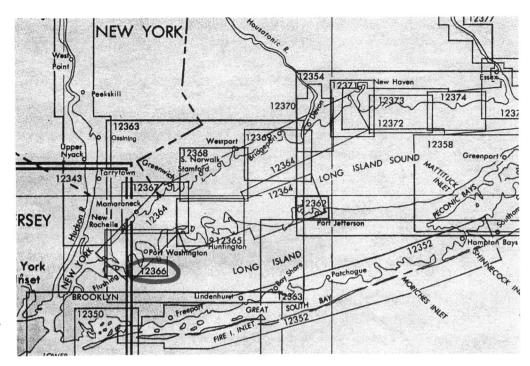

Fig. 88. A portion of a catalog of charts.

outside corner with an indelible marking pen, put all the charts in numerical order, and stow them. Under the berth cushions is a good spot if there's no chart table or if space in it is limited. Then, if I'm sailing out of Port Washington, N.Y., for instance, I look at the catalog sheet, note that chart #12366 is needed (the circle in Figure 88), and go through my stack of charts numerically until I reach #12366. This is far easier than looking at each chart until I find the right one.

For very small boats, the Small Craft Series of charts is handy because they are prefolded compactly and don't need a large, flat surface to spread on. Also, one chart, like 12364 in Figure 88, covers the same area that a number of the other charts cover, so it's more economical to purchase. My personal feeling, though, is that the Small Craft Series is harder to read and to navigate by than the larger charts.

As can be seen in the catalog, charts come in different scales. They are all roughly the same actual size, but cover different sized areas. Chart #12366, for instance, covers only a small portion of chart #12363, yet blows it up to the same size as #12363. Since #12366 enlarges a small area, it is called a "large-scale" chart. Such charts are used for entering harbors where precision and accuracy is more necessary than when in open water. If you're planning a trip, a smaller scale chart such as #12363 covers more distance and is easier to use.

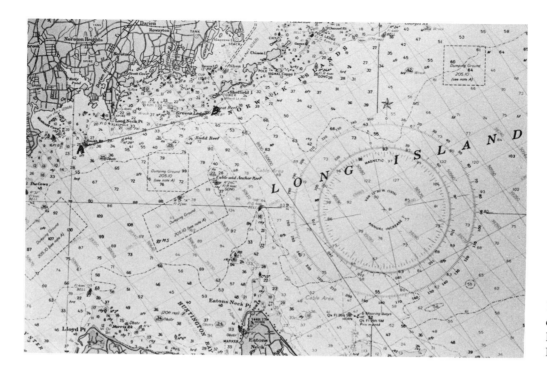

121. A course line is drawn from Smith Rock (A) to Greens Ledge (B).

Plotting

The basic tools of chartwork are sharp pencils (be sure to keep a pencil sharpener on board), parallel rulers, and dividers. If we want to travel from point A (Smith Rock) to point B (Greens Ledge), as shown on the chart in Photo 121, we draw a line which represents our proposed course. We now want to know what our sailboat's compass will read when the boat is heading in that direction. The compass rose on the chart is a circle graduated in 360 degrees. The outer circle gives you the direction to true north and the inner circle is called the magnetic rose and points to magnetic north. More on this later.

The inner compass rose, the magnetic rose, shown in the photo represents the boat's compass, which always points to north no matter which way the boat is heading. Ideally, we would like to move that compass rose over to the course line and read our course off it as if we were reading the boat's compass itself. Unfortunately, we can't move the compass rose because it's printed on the chart, so we do the next best thing: we move the course line over to the compass rose. This is done with parallel rulers that have two straight edges which remain parallel to one another at all times. Place one edge on the course line, using the edge farthest from the rose so the parallel rulers will not have to be moved so often. The fewer moves made, the less chance of a slip

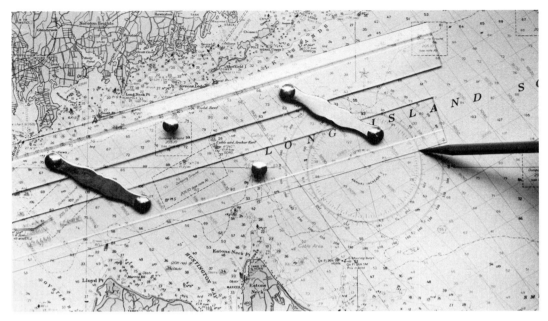

122. Lay one edge of the parallel rulers along the course line and walk the other arm so that the edge passes through the cross in the center of the compass rose. Then read the degrees off the rose.

causing an error. Press down on that leg and move the other out toward the nearest compass rose. Then press down on that leg and bring the former one back in close. Continue to spread, press, and close the legs until one edge of the parallel rulers is centered over the cross in the center of the compass rose. Read the course in degrees from the edge of the inner compass rose pointed to by the pencil in Photo 122, in this case 085°. (Always use three numbers when writing or talking about degrees of a compass lest "15 degrees" be mistaken for "115 degrees" because of a smudge, for example, or a slurring of speech.)

The most common mistakes made by sailors inexperienced in navigation are: (1) allowing the parallel rulers to slip accidentally, so they are no longer parallel to the course line; (2) reading off the outside rose (073° in this case) rather than the inside one (we'll explain this later); (3) not recognizing the increment differences between roses (in some, each line represents 2° while in the photo each line is only 1°); and (4) reading off the wrong side of the rose. For instance, one might read 265° in the photo, which is the direction you came from, not the direction you're going in our example.

Distances

For the purposes of navigation the earth is considered spherical. The north pole is named for the top of the globe and the south pole is the bottom. Lines running north and south around the earth passing through these

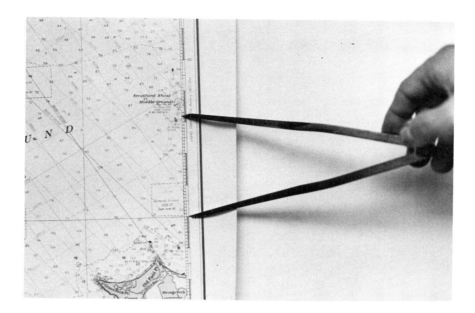

123. Place dividers along the edge of the chart to measure distance.

two imaginary poles are called meridians of longitude. The horizontal lines are parallels of latitude. Since a circle is 360 degrees, the parallel lines of latitude divide the earth into 360 equal parts of 60 nautical miles each. There are 60 minutes to a degree, so one minute of latitude is equivalent to one nautical mile, which is somewhat longer than the statute mile we use ashore.

To measure the distance between points A and B in Photo 121 we use a pair of dividers. We place one tip on point A and the other on point B. Now, place the dividers along the edge of the chart, as in Photo 123, and count the number of minutes of latitude (shown as alternate dark and light increments, each divided into tenths) that fall between the two tips. In this case it's 3.15 minutes, which converts to 3.15 nautical miles. If we sail that distance in one half hour, we are sailing at 6.3 knots. A knot is one nautical mile sailed in one hour.

If the distance you want to measure is greater than the spread attainable by the dividers, spread them along the edge of the chart a workable number of miles (minutes of latitude), say five miles from tip to tip. Then lay one tip on your starting point. The other will rest on a spot five miles down down the course. Walk the dividers so that the first tip lays five miles further down the course, and so on, until your destination is reached. It would be unusual for the last measurement to be exactly five miles, so the dividers will probably have to be pressed together so the tip rests on the destination, and this reduced distance can be measured on the edge of the chart.

To measure long distances on a 1:80,000 scale chart where only a rough estimation of distance is needed, I use my hand. The spread between my

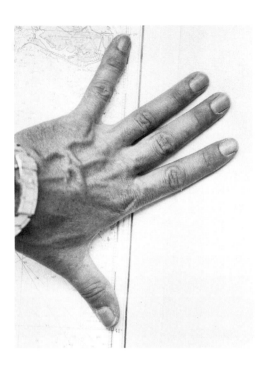

124. A handspread on many charts is almost exactly 10 miles.

thumb and little finger is almost exactly 10 miles (Photo 124) and I can measure 70- or 80-mile distances quickly and within a few miles of accuracy. Check your hand spread. Perhaps you can use this method also.

Reading a Chart

Look at the section of a chart shown in Photo 125. Buoys are shown as small diamonds with a dot or circle underneath to indicate their exact location. A purple color around the dot means it's a lighted buoy. The color of the diamond, usually red or green, corresponds to the color of the buoy. To the right of center in Photo 125 we see a green diamond in a circle. Next to it is the number "23" in quotes. Anything in quotes is written on the buoy. Even numbers are on red buoys and odd numbers are on green. The chart also indicates that the buoy is a gong.

The information on Execution Rocks lighthouse is given next to it. We interpret the information to mean that it flashes a white light every 10 seconds. The light is 62 feet above sea level and has a 16-mile visibility. It sounds a horn during foggy periods and also is a radio beacon.

The red-and-green diamond marked "RG" to the SW of Execution Rocks in Photo 125 indicates a junction buoy, meaning you can pass on either side. Since the letter "N" (nun) is under the "RB," the actual buoy (which has red and green horizontal bands) will show a red band uppermost. This means that the preferred channel would be as if the buoy were all red. We leave red buoys

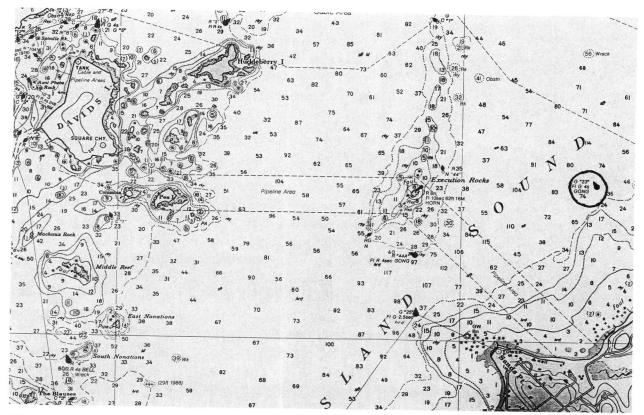

125. A section of a chart showing a wide variety of navigational aids.

to starboard as we enter a harbor or sail from a larger body of water to a smaller one. The simple phrase to remember this fact is "Red-Right-Returning."

There are many other items of information on the chart. Note chart colors. White areas are deep, navigable water, light-blue areas are usually under 20 feet deep, and green areas are out of the water at low tide. The depths of the water are usually marked in feet at mean low water. Extreme low water could mean depths four or five feet less than shown on the chart, so take that into account. Along the East Coast of the U.S. the tides are semi-diurnal: two high tides and two low tides in a 24-hour period. The tide height changes about 25% the first and last two hours of a tide, and about 50% during the middle two hours. This is a factor to take into consideration if it's necessary to cross a bar or a shoal that you know is too shallow for your boat at dead low tide, yet has deep enough water at certain times during the tidal fall. The U.S. government prints the book *Tide Tables,* giving the predicted times of high and low water and the heights of the tide. On some charts the depths (soundings) may be in meters or in fathoms (six feet equals one fathom), so check the explanation on the chart itself.

Also shown on charts are depth contours. These contour lines connect all the areas of equal depth and are very useful in navigating with the depth finder.

On the yellow part of the chart indicating dry land, any object which could be helpful in obtaining a navigational fix is located and marked. Tanks, towers, conspicuous buildings, spires, and others are all pinpointed.

Variation

Though your basic instrument is the chart, without a good compass you are lost. Compasses have a magnetized card or needle which follows the earth's magnetic field. The earth is like a huge magnet, and at any given point on the earth the boat's compass will line up with the larger earth magnet lines of force. Fortunately, the earth's lines of force generally follow fairly closely the true north-south direction on the earth, the meridians of longitude, but they tend to wander more and are not straight lines. They also tend to change with time. The magnetic north and south poles are not at the same location as the corresponding geographic poles. It is to these "magnetic meridians" that your boat compass responds, and they look something like Figure 89.

Let's say you are at the location shown in Figure 89. Your compass points in the direction indicated, following the magnetic meridians. This is obviously not toward the true north pole. The angular difference is called "variation." On most charts it is shown to you by use of the compass rose, as in Photo 122. The variation of the locality is easy to see by the angular difference of these two circles. If the magnetic north arrow points 3° to the west of the true north arrow, variation is 3° west (3° W). If it points 5° to the east of the true north arrow, variation is 5° to the east (5° E). The variation is also written at the

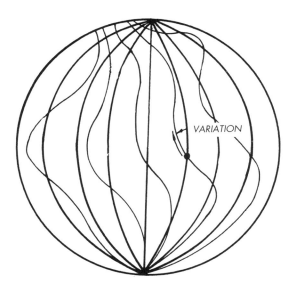

Fig. 89. Your compass points to magnetic north, not true north, and the difference is called "variation."

center of the compass rose, along with its annual rate of change. For example, in the center of the compass rose is written: "Var 14° 30' W (1989) Annual Increase 1'." This means the "variation is 14 degrees 30 minutes west as of the year 1989, with an annual increase of 1 minute per year observed." You would have to apply the annual rate according to the date and age of the chart. This usually doesn't amount to much, but the careful navigator will check this and at least be aware of this fact.

Since the inner rose already has taken variation into account, as long as we use the inner rose for plotting our courses, we can forget about having to adjust our course for variation. The course using the compass on our boat will be the same as that plotted on the chart using the magnetic compass rose, providing there is little or no deviation.

Deviation

Deviation is the angle the boat compass assumes because of ferrous metal in the vicinity of the compass. The compass will be attracted to this metal and cause errors in observed bearings. On most small sailboats this error is small, usually one or two degrees, which is difficult to read anyway, as most compasses are graduated in the five-degree increments shown in Photo 126. On sailboats, the steering compass is placed in a central location in the open cockpit, and this arrangement in itself usually insures minimum magnetic disturbances. On power boats, the compass is usually placed near many electrical instruments which, when used, cause deviation. On such boats, compass deviation is a greater problem.

126. A steering compass with 5° increments.

If you believe that your compass is being affected by some metal on your boat, check it by plotting the magnetic course on a chart between two fixed objects such as lighthouses (buoys aren't as good since they can be slightly out of place). Then, starting near one of the fixed objects, head toward the other. Your compass should agree with the computed course. If it doesn't, the difference is deviation. Run in both directions, because the deviation may be different when you're running to the south from when you're running to the north. Then use two objects lying in a east-west direction and check for deviation. An error of one or two degrees is not worth worrying about. If you sail from one buoy to another a mile away, you will be less than 90 feet from the second buoy with a one-degree compass error. Of course, over 20 miles it becomes more like 600 yards, but there's no way anybody can ever steer a sailboat as close as one degree to the course desired. Nevertheless, errors, even small ones, all can add up and carelessness cannot be condoned in navigation. You never know when you might be socked in a dense fog and need great accuracy in your course calculations. For peace of mind, have a professional compass adjuster work on reducing the deviation of your compass to zero on all headings. He will give you a deviation table for your compass that lists the number of degrees of deviation for a given heading if he is unable to zero it out.

Variation and deviation combine to make what is called "compass error" (CE). For instance, if variation is 11° E and deviation is 3° E, the compass error is 14° E. If the variation is 8° W and deviation 4° E. the CE is 4° W. If deviation is small enough to be of little concern, your compass error will be equal to variation alone. Then you can take all your bearings and courses in magnetic readings and, being careful to use only the inner circle of the compass rose (magnetic), plot directly.

On most charts this works well without difficulty. However, on many small-scale charts (portraying large areas) used for offshore work, or when planning a route between two places of considerable distance, you are not given the magnetic compass rose and must convert magnetic readings to "true" readings and vice versa. There are many methods of learning how to convert these readings. The easiest method is the simple acronym CADET. Broken down it reads: "Compass: *ADd* East to get True." Translated, this means to add easterly compass errors (combined variation and deviation as shown above) to the compass reading to get true readings. All other possibilities logically follow by common sense: (1) subtract westerly compass errors, and (2) if converting the opposite way (from true to compass), subtract easterly compass errors and add westerly ones.

Another popular method you can use if you want to check your compass for deviation is the mnemonic "TRUE VIRGINS MAKE DULL COMPANIONS." From True, apply Variation to get Magnetic. From Magnetic, apply **Deviation** to get **Compass**. You add westerly variation and deviation in this case and subtract easterly ("West is best").

To go from **Compass** to **True**, reverse the process, including subtracting westerly variation and deviation and adding easterly.

Bearings

Now you are ready to determine your position with a series of bearings transferred to your chart. In taking bearings in order to obtain a fix, the primary concern is to correctly identify a shore-based object or aid to navigation and locate this on the chart. A bearing taken on a building is fine, but unless this building is indicated on the chart it is useless to you. Study the chart looking for prominent objects in your vicinity. Good objects are lighthouses, buoys, buildings, or tangents of a prominent landmark or a hill. Try to find these by looking carefully at the shoreline or known objects (recently passed navigational aids are a good place to start, such as channel buoys). Pick at least two objects that have a good angular separation. Two objects 90° apart would be perfect, but rarely the case. Figure 90 is a diagram of bearings taken with a 5° error. Notice that the aggregate error is far more when using landmarks A and B than when using A and C, which are angled further apart. In selecting landmarks you have actually fixed the boat's position by "eyeball" navigation, and you really just need to verify your position by a more positive means, which is done by the bearings.

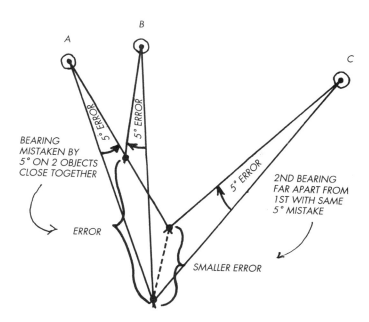

Fig. 90. Taking bearings to obtain a position. The closer to 90° apart the objects are, the less difference a sighting error will make in the final plotting.

127. A hand bearing compass in use.

Quickly sight across your steering compass, or use a hand bearing compass as shown in Photo 127, to take your bearings. Observe the bearing closest to your bow or stern first, as this will change the slowest. Then take the bearing closest to your beam last and note the time to the nearest minute. Write these down on scratch paper; then go below and plot these lines on the chart. (Never take a chart on deck unless it's absolutely necessary. It could blow overboard and leave you in a terrible predicament. When a chart is on deck, weight it down with a winch handle unless someone is holding onto the chart.) For each bearing taken, locate the number of degrees on the magnetic compass rose (the inner circle) on your chart. Put the outside edge of your parallel rulers on both that number and the cross in the center of the circle. Next, walk the parallel rulers over to the landmark on which the bearing was taken. Draw a line from it extending out into the water. This is a "line of position" and your boat is somewhere along it.

When you do the same with a second bearing, the lines will cross, as in Figure 90. Where they cross should be your position at the time of the fix, not at the present moment. You were there minutes ago when you took the bearings. Make sure you write the time of the fix on the chart. If you take bearings on three objects, you will probably get a small triangle when they are plotted. This is still usually a more accurate position than with just two bearings, unless the triangle is large. If so, one bearing is inaccurate and they should be taken again. With only two bearings there's no real way of knowing if one bearing is inaccurate. Ideally, three bearings should cross exactly at one point, your position, but in practice that rarely happens.

Assuming the boat has been underway and traveling a set course while you have been plotting your position, you have to draw this progress on the chart. Begin by plotting the course steered since the time of the fix, let's say 150° Mag. Transfer 150° from the magnetic rose to your fix on the chart and draw this line, labeling it "C 150 M," which translates as "Course 150 degrees magnetic."

It takes a bit of mathematics to figure your present position and, since this is going to take time, by the time you figure it out you won't "be" there. So predict where you will be and put this on the chart. This is called dead reckoning, which is an estimate.

Let's say your fix was taken at 1000, so pick 1015 for a DR position (dead reckoned). This gives you 15 minutes to plot your fix and work the simple time-speed-distance formula. You need to know your speed. Take an average speed from your speedometer for this value. You may have to guess at a speed if an instrument is not available. As you go along, you will begin to judge your speed fairly accurately.

Distance = Speed × Time
D = Distance in nautical miles
S = Speed in knots (nautical miles per hour)
T = Time measured in hours (15 min. = 0.25 hour)

For example, assuming a speed of 4 knots and a running time of 15 minutes,

D = (4 knots) × (0.25 hours)
D = 1.0 nautical mile

Measure one nautical mile along your course line of 150 and mark this 1015DR. This is where you expect to be at 1015. A time-speed-distance computer like the one shown in Photo 128 can hasten the computations and

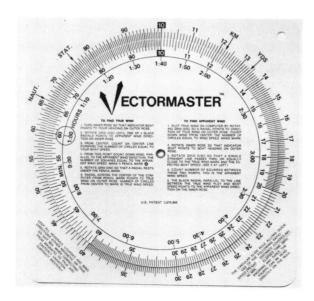

128. A time-speed-distance computer.

reduce the chance of mathematical errors. (The one shown also helps compute apparent and true wind vectors on its other side, hence the printed instructions.)

Speed-Time-Distance formulas are difficult for many people to remember, so there's a method that may be of help. Imagine a road sign in a town that says "D Street." But the sign is contracted to look like this: $\frac{D}{ST}$. Now put your thumb over the variable you want to find and what remains is the formula to find it. For instance, if you want speed, put your thumb over the "s" and what remains ($\frac{D}{T}$) tells you the formula is distance divided by time. To find "d" (distance) the formula is ST or speed times time. To find "T" (time) the formula is $\frac{D}{S}$ or distance divided by speed. Just remember "D Street."

Next question. How long can you continue this course before you are forced to change for an obstruction? In other words, is it a safe course, free of dangers? Study the chart carefully, looking at the charted depths. Look for rocks and shoals. Know the symbols on the chart.

How do you know if you are on your projected or DR course of 150°? Again, repeat the process and plot another fix with another "round of bearings." Note the time. Label this position with the time. A line drawn from one fix or position to another will be your course made good. This is really what you are interested in, as this may show setting one way or another because of wind or tidal current or both. You want to know if you are going to be set in a dangerous area. A series of fixes will show you this.

If you are sailing closehauled, leeway may be a factor. This can be measured by towing a fishing leader wire and a weight off the stern over a protractor, but most sailors just estimate leeway by past experience and adjust the compass course by a few degrees to windward.

Current

With tidal depth changes comes current. Current becomes quite a large factor in navigation as its speed becomes a large percentage of the boat's speed. Therefore, it's particularly a factor in sailing. A sailboat averaging 5 knots may be sailing in a current 20% to 40% (1 to 2 knots) of its speed.

The *Tidal Current Tables* printed by the U.S. government give the maximum flood and ebb current and the time when the current changes direction. *Tidal Current Charts* are printed for twelve bodies of water on the East and West Coasts, and are very handy in navigating and planning a cruise. These two are combined in a publication called the *Eldridge Tide and Pilot Book,* which covers the northeast coast. Photo 129 shows a page from the current tables and several of the charts (approximately one for each hour of the tide).

Assume it is now 1200 hours on August 20, 1977. The tide tables indicate that water started flooding (coming into) Long Island Sound at the Race (a narrow passage between the mainland and the tip of Long Island) at 0914

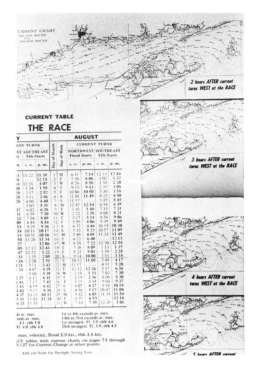

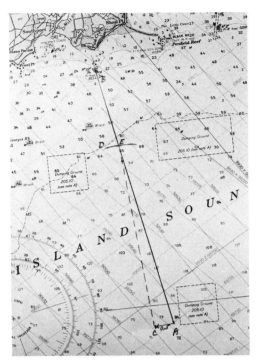

129. Locate your position on the current chart that represents the state of the current at your local time.

130. Determine the course to steer in a given current.

hours (see the underlined numbers in Photo 129). We must add an hour for Daylight Saving Time, so we get 1014 hours. It is now about two hours after the current started flooding at the Race, so the top chart is the appropriate one in the photograph. Let's say we locate our present position on the chart and find that the current is 0.5 knots in a direction of about 265° True.

We transfer this information to a chart, as in Photo 130. We are sailing from *A* to *B* on a course of 001° M. First we draw line *AC* ½ mile long, indicating the effect of the current on the boat in one hour. Next we take the boat speed (5 knots in this case) and describe arc *D* to intersect course line *AB* at point *E*. Line *CE* will be the course to steer (007° M), and *A* to *E* will be our progress toward our destination in one hour. If the current velocity or direction changes over the period of time it takes us to reach our destination, we can use an average current for our calculations.

Plotting Symbols

A fix is marked on a chart as a dot with a circle:

A DR position is shown as a dot in a half-circle:

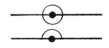

A DR position that has been upgraded by one LOP or an estimate of wind or current effect is an Estimated Position (EP) and shown as a dot in a square:

An electronic fix is a dot in a triangle:

Thus, a plot may look like this (though not labeled this way, but with courses and times):

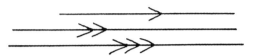

Arrowheads are used for:
Course to steer or course steered:

Track over the bottom:

Current or Tide Vector:

Courses are marked:
True heading: 090**T**
Magnetic heading: 090**M**
Compass heading: 090**C**

Keeping a Log

It must be obvious to you now that sailboat navigation is just a matter of constantly updating your position. At certain times, as while beating to windward, we cannot sail the course directly to our destination, so we just sail where we can, keep track of where we are, and gradually work our way toward our ultimate destination. When we are cruising overnight or for long distances, it is common practice to keep a log. Every half hour or every hour, depending on the navigator's desires, a crew member goes below and writes down in the logbook: (1) the time; (2) the estimated average speed for the last half-hour or hour period; and/or (3) a "log" reading (many speedometers have a "log" dial that records distance traveled in nautical miles to the hundredth of a mile, and some sailboats drag taffrail logs off the stern, a rotor on the end of a long line which rotates a pin on the back of a dial, also giving distance sailed); and (4) average course sailed in degrees. The helmsman is asked to estimate the course for the period from his observation of the compass. Any large change of course such as a jibe or tack is recorded immediately in the logbook rather than waiting until the end of the designated period. Then the navigator advances the estimated position for the boat based on three or four hours of recorded readings in the logbook thus making it unnecessary constantly to keep track of the boat's course and speed.

Navigation Shortcuts

Piloting can be made easier and faster by using your bow. If you are steering for a distant buoy or landmark, take this as your first bearing and simply read the compass heading for this number. This works well even if you have to alter your course slightly to place the object dead ahead. This will give you a very accurate bearing.

Along the same idea, let's assume you are in a boat where the only compass is mounted on the cabin bulkhead. You are unable to take accurate bearings abaft the beam as this requires looking down on the compass instead of across it. You need an accurate position to determine your location, so use the whole boat as a pointer to give you a good, accurate fix. Turn the boat in a circle, either under sail or power (power works better as the circle can be smaller), and read the heading of the boat as it passes the objects you have chosen for bearings. Settle down briefly on each heading to allow the compass to stop swinging.

When taking bearings, include a reading of the fathometer at the same time. This piece of information will help you to verify your plotted position. Another fairly good position indicator is a single bearing and a fathometer reading. In an area with a straight coast and a good, sloping bottom contour, such as along the New Jersey coast, this works excellently.

Another important aspect of navigation is the use of topographical contours and hill heights ashore. Until I started to look closely at these on a chart, every piece of shoreline looked like every other. When the contour lines are close together, indicating a steep slope, it's quite often easy to spot the hill it represents. The heights of the peaks are usually marked on the chart. Of two nearby summits, one may be 400 feet high and the other 600 feet high. When you look at the shore, the perspective of the two summits to another can give you a good idea of your geographical relationship to them.

The most accurate bearings you can take do not involve a compass or numbers. They are also the easiest to do. The only requirement is that you are sailing in an area of widely scattered landmarks, such as islands or navigational aids. Look for objects to fall in line, such as a buoy or lighthouse. Watch for two islands or points of land to come into line. Note the time. Then, on your chart, locate these objects and align them with a straight edge, draw a line, and there is your bearing; no compass required. Add a fathometer reading of the water depth and you may get a good EP (Estimated Position). It's a simple procedure, but very accurate and fast.

The other secret to safe navigation is to be very skeptical of your work. Once a fix is plotted, check it by looking around to see if it makes sense. According to your position, do nearby objects appear in the proper perspective? Is that island really on your starboard bow as your fix shows? This is the type of reasoning you follow to check yourself.

Nothing beats reading the number right off a buoy if it's close enough in order to verify that it's the right one. Once you've navigated awhile you'll find—because of fog, low visibility, current, excessive leeway, or some other factor—that buoys that seem to confirm your position often turn out to be the wrong ones on closer inspection. If you don't check the number or otherwise confirm your position, you might make a course alteration on the assumption that your navigation is correct and really end up in trouble. If you aren't sure, quickly plot a second fix to check the first, and so on. With practice you will gain confidence in your work and will more easily be able to catch mistakes before they can cause danger.

If you don't have a computer and have to work out fixes mathematically, use minutes evenly divided by six when noting time. For example, use 06, 12, 18, 24, 30, etc., for your time, because 06 min. = 0.1 hour, 12 min. = 0.2 hour, 18 min. = 0.3 hour and so on. This puts your time in even tenths of an hour and your time-speed-distance formula becomes easier to work.

GPS and Loran

GPS (Global Positioning System) and loran (long-range navigation) are a mixed blessing. On the plus side, they can pinpoint your position with a direct reading of latitude and longitude. All you need to do is plot it on a chart. However, it tends to make navigators very lazy because of the misguided confidence with which they regard the machine. There are times, just around sunrise and sunset, when sky wave effects make loran reading unreliable. There are geographical areas, such as the Virgin Islands, where loran readings are unreliable. Of course, if the boat's battery power is lost or the loran or GPS malfunctions, you are without its services. If you are dependent on electronic navigation, when it goes out you are not only lost, but have reduced ability to navigate the normal way, because of lack of practice and because you haven't been checking your position by other methods.

Another of their mixed blessings is their ability to give you a range and bearing to a destination. All you need to do is input the latitude and longitude of your destination as a "way point." The GPS or loran does the rest. Beside range and bearing, the cross-track error (the amount you are to one side or the other of your intended track), the speed over the bottom (not through the water) you are making good towards your destination and the ETA (estimated time of arrival) all are constantly updated. The problem arises when the navigator gets a bearing (course) for the destination and doesn't plot it carefully on the chart to make sure the course doesn't pass across shoal areas, through buoys, or even over land. Most navigators are careful enough to check the course initially, but fail to re-plot it a few hours later when, due to leeway, current, wind direction, or whatever, GPS or the loran show a different course to the destination. The tendency is to forget the original course and constantly change the course to that which the machine tells you is the direction to your destination. Because of such sloppiness you may end up on the rocks.

The way electronic navigation should be used is as a check to your piloting. Rely on it as a backup, not as your only or primary source of navigational information.

Courtesy

Yachting is steeped in a long tradition of courtesy. Sailing off the coast of England, when you pass another boat a crew member will often run aft and dip the yacht ensign (or sometimes the national flag) to half-staff. In response, you must dip yours.

Though the above is a little more than we're apt to find sailing along our coasts, we too adhere to our courtesies. For instance, you always ask permission of the owner or skipper before setting foot on a boat.

If you've been invited aboard for cocktails, let's say, and your friend is below, don't climb aboard and poke your head down the companionway. Your friend may not be ready for guests yet and, after all, this is his or her home. Just as you ring a doorbell at a house, make your presence known with a hail. If there's no answer, gently rap on the hull. This generally can be heard throughout the boat, which acts like a large sounding board. When your friend appears, check if your shoes are alright (unless they're rubber-sole boating shoes). Street shoes tend to scratch, mar, and dirty decks.

You might also check the owner's feeling about smoking. Some owners are very finicky about the chance of cigarette ashes falling on their decks or on the cabin sole below. The couple who may be very casual and careless about the condition of their home may be completely the opposite when it comes to their boat. Don't assume that they are the same persons you know ashore. A boat can bring out the best and the worst in people.

If you are chartering a sailboat or going on a cruise as guests, pack clothes very sparingly and never bring hard luggage. An empty suitcase uses a great deal of valuable space and will definitely not be appreciated. My wife and I usually pack clothes for a two-week, warm-weather cruise into two small duffels that fit in the overhead compartment in the airplane, and we always have enough to wear.

One of the most common discourtesies has become an everyday part of the English language for upsetting a peaceful setting—"making waves." Luckily, most sailboats cut through the water neatly without making a great deal of wake. Even small waves in a narrow waterway can bounce off walls and upset the peace aboard boats in slips. On a calm day waves can seriously slow down the progress of racing sailboats. Great consideration should be shown to yachts in a race that are trying to catch every zephyr to keep the boat moving, however slowly, through the water. Any bouncing breaks the airflow over the sails and hurts their efficiency.

The same consideration should be shown to the racing skipper in situations concerning right-of-way. Most skippers will show their appreciation with a wave and a "thanks" if you waive your right-of-way and let them sail through without an alteration of course. When you find yourself unavoidably sailing in the middle of a fleet of racing yachts, try to stay "off their wind." In other words, stay downwind of the boats rather than between them and the wind. Also, try to avoid running over the lines of fishermen trolling from a powerboat. Stay alert and there's less chance of getting others upset.

Unless you're out at sea and have no other option, no garbage should go overboard. In December, 1988, the first international agreement to clean up the oceans went into effect when the U.S. ratified it by passing Public Law 100–200. Under the agreement called the MARPOL (Marine Pollution) Protocol, Annex V, it is illegal for any vessel to dump plastic anywhere in the ocean. Violators can be fined up to $50,000. It is illegal to dump garbage (victual waste), paper, rags, glass, metal, bottles, crockery, and similar refuse inside of 12 miles from the nearest land. Place all cans, bottles, and other debris in containers and take it ashore for disposal. The water is for everyone, but a few can mess it up.

There has been great emphasis on flag etiquette in the past: which flag to fly, where, and when. Such traditions are of lesser importance in modern sailing, but a few items should be pointed out. It is proper to "make colors" (raise and lower the flags) at 0800 and sunset, respectively. The yacht ensign or national flag is raised first, followed by the yacht club burgee and the owner's private signal. Flags are lowered in reverse order. If you see a solid blue rectangular flag flying from the starboard spreader of a yacht, it signifies that the owner is absent. A blue flag with a diagonal white stripe signifies that the owner is absent and the yacht is under command of a guest. By the time you learn enough about sailing to cruise to a foreign country, you'll know enough to buy courtesy flags of each country you visit. These, too, are flown from the spreader. You'll have to remember to keep a "Q" flag aboard (solid yellow rectangle) to summon customs officials to clear you into the country you are entering. This is called the "quarantine" flag, and remains up until you are cleared.

Everyone likes a good party, but the host of any held on board a boat should keep the uninvited neighbors in mind. Sound carries very well across water since obstructions are few, and a noisy party is just as loud for a nearby boat. Keep it down, particularly late at night when others are trying to sleep.

If you borrow or charter a sailboat, make it your policy to leave it in as good (or better) condition than you received it. Have pride in keeping a sailboat shipshape. Have pride in your seamanship. Have pride that you're part of the sailing community. There's a general helpfulness, sharing, and camaraderie among sailors that needs to be nurtured lest it be lost to the onslaught of today's rampant selfishness. When another yacht is tying up at a slip, offer to take his lines if you're standing there. If you see a boat aground, offer to help tow him off if your boat is capable of it and can get close enough. More and more, such aid is results in a bill for services sent to the boat that innocently accepted the aid. It's a shame that some sailors don't still come to the aid of other sailors without charging for it (unless, of course, the service was a costly one).

Let's keep the pleasure in the sport of sailing by extending courtesy to others involved in it with us. Everyone will enjoy it more.

TEST QUESTIONS ON PART II

1. What are spring lines?
2. What is a seacock?
3. If the engine quits while you've powering in a congested area, what is the first thing to do?
4. What are scallops?
5. What is "to tail" a winch?
6. What is an easy way of lowering a jib if you're shorthanded?
7. What is a boom preventer?
8. What is a "jiffy" reef?
9. What is scooping?
10. If you are going up the mast in a bosun's chair, what should be attached to the chair?
11. At night you see a boat with three vertical white lights. What is it?
12. Which is lighter than air: LPG? CNG?
13. What is scope?
14. What is an "anchor watch"?
15. What is a "tripline"?
16. What is variation?
17. What is deviation?
18. Can a bearing be taken without a compass?
19. How many nautical miles are there in a degree of latitude?
20. Why tie halyards away from the mast at night?

PART III

Fundamentals
of Racing

Introduction

There's an innate competitive nature in humans which invariably surfaces when two sailboats out for a casual sail find themselves near one another heading in the same direction. An informal race inevitably results. They may not try to give the impression they are racing one another, but attention to sail trim and other details sharpens when in the company of another sailboat. What starts as an informal brush with another boat whets the appetite for more serious racing.

Racing is both cerebral and physical. We'll try to take care of the cerebral part in this book. The physical part is practical experience on the race course. The differences between individuals will be determined by not only how well they master each separately, but how well they can combine the two. I've known sailors who can really make their boats go. If you sail alongside them, they leave you behind. But during a race they usually make some strategic or tactical blunder that causes them to finish way back. I've known others who are rules experts, tactical experts, and really know their theory. However, they are so uncoordinated and inept on the boat that other sailors pass them right and left on the race course. Combine the good qualities of the two and we have a sailor who is practically unbeatable.

Preparation

The Hull

Many races are lost before the skipper even gets to the race course due to lack of preparation. The more meticulous the sailor is in his preparation, the better results he will have when racing.

The hull of a boat needs special attention. First and foremost, the bottom must be clean and smooth. It's incredible how little marine growth is needed on the bottom to make a considerable difference in speed. If a boat is left in sea water for two days without anti-fouling paint, she will be slower. Most competitive small racing sailboats are "drysailed" (taken out of the water after racing) in order to keep the bottom clean of marine growth.

Often a racing sailor will buy a shiny new fiberglass boat. A boat right out of the mould will have an incredibly smooth, shiny bottom, and the natural reaction is to believe that the bottom can't be improved upon, particularly if the owner is drysailing and doesn't intend to paint the bottom with anti-fouling. To leave it alone is a mistake. Spray the bottom with water from a hose and most likely the water will coagulate into beads. This indicates that there is a wax-like substance on the surface which is a very slow finish for racing. After wet-sanding the hull to get rid of the wax, you will notice that a spray with the hose reacts completely differently. The surface stays wet over a large area until the water evaporates. The surface is now called a "wetting" type, which is much faster than a waxed type.

Weight

The weight of the boat is also of paramount importance. Of two boats, equal in all other ways—size, shape, crew, sails, etc.—the lighter boat will be faster because less water is displaced by the hull. The Soling, for instance, is an Olympic class and is allowed to weigh no less than 2,282 pounds. Most competitive Solings at a recent U.S. Olympic Trial weighed from one to eight pounds over the minimum. This shows a tremendous amount of attention to weight on the part of the skipper and the manufacturer.

To attain this lightness, much of a racing yacht's equipment is down to the minimum size and weight capable of withstanding loads generated by most wind and sea conditions. If a fitting is too light and breaks, it is replaced by a heavier one. However, a fitting that never breaks may be overly strong and too heavy for its purpose, but the sailor will never know. You must constantly be on the lookout for equipment showing signs of stress. A breakdown during a race may force you to drop out. A "DNF" (did not finish) is usually equivalent in points to finishing last. Check all standing and running rigging, cam cleats, spinnaker pole ends, hiking aids, cotter pins, and sails. Make sure all required equipment is on board, such as life vests, anchor, paddle, bailer or pump, and any other items listed in the class rules.

The Race Circular

Next, study the "race circular" or "racing instructions." These lay down the conditions of the race. Since they are often copied from previous circulars, they all read somewhat alike, lulling competitors into a quick prerace scan of the circular, which can be disastrous. A new or unusual requirement might be missed. For instance, the racing instructions for the 1976 Olympic Trials required all yachts to pass close astern of the Race Committee boat before the start of the race in order to be recognized as a starter. Of 24 Solings, only 12 either read or remembered the race circular well enough to fulfill this requirement before the first race. Some of the best sailors in the country slipped up.

In one 5.5-meter World Championship, the Russians totally missed a race because they failed to look at the Official Bulletin Board (as required by the racing instructions). So be sure you read and know the contents of the racing instructions before you start a race.

Nonrequired Items

Other preparation involves obtaining as good a weather report as possible and making sure you have nonrequired items for racing, such as a stop-watch, protest flag, code flag identification (unless you know them all), rule book, current tables, times of high and low tides, tools, knife, grease pencils, tape, etc. By "nonrequired" items, I mean you can't be disqualified if they are not aboard but most are very necessary for successful racing. You cannot protest another yacht, for example, unless you fly a protest flag, and you obviously can't fly it if you didn't bring it aboard.

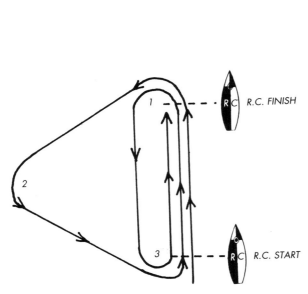

Fig. 91. A common race course consists of a triangle followed by windward, leeward, and windward legs.

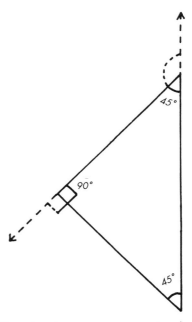

Fig. 92. For the given race course triangle, compass courses can be figured out by subtracting 135°, 90°, and 135°.

The Course

Be aware of the type of course you'll be sailing. Many races are being held nowadays on Olympic courses. Three buoys are anchored as in Figure 91. You start at the leeward mark, beat to windward to mark #1, reach to mark #2, jibe, reach to mark #3, and then sail to windward (to mark #1), to leeward (to mark #3), and to windward again to the finish. The triangle is 45°, 90°, 45°, as in Figure 92. The Race Committee boat will usually post the course to the weather mark in degrees and you figure out the rest. For instance, a posted course of 90° means that mark #1 is dead upwind at 90°. By subtracting 135° (the dotted angle in Figure 92) we get a course for the first reach of 315° (90° from 135° = 45°, 360° less 45° = 315°). Subtract 90° from 315° to get the course for the second reach, or 225°. The beat is still 90°, the run is the reciprocal of 90° or 270°, and the beat to the finish is 90°. Now, rather than do this in your head and be open to a mathematical error, course computers are available, such as the one shown in Figure 93, to quickly give you the reaching and running courses. If such a course is expected, don't forget to bring your course computer. New Olympic courses such as the trapezoidal are being used, but are not popular yet.

You may be given a totally different course, one that uses government navigation marks, for instance. Your race circular will give you the information

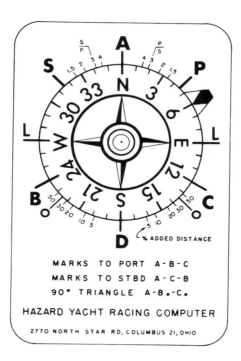

Fig. 93. A typical computer for determining compass headings on an equilateral or an Olympic-style racing course (45°, 90°, 45° triangle).

and may even give you the compass direction to each mark. If not, figure out the compass courses before you set sail. Many a race has been lost because the lead boat headed in the wrong direction for a mark, and others followed.

Now that you have adequately prepared for the race and have sailed to the race course, you will be confronted with certainly the most critical and most stressful situation of the whole race: the start. The degree to which you get a good start will have a great bearing on your finishing position. It is beneficial, therefore, for us to pay particular attention to the tactics and information needed to make a good start.

◆ 2 ◆

The Start

The Starting Signals

Most races use a standard starting sequence of signals. A gun is fired and a white shape is raised. Five minutes later a second gun is fired and a blue shape is raised. Five minutes later a third gun is fired and a red shape is raised. This last is the "start." The white shape is called the "warning" signal and the blue shape is called the "preparatory" signal. These are important insofar as you are technically "racing" from the "preparatory" signal. in other words, if you foul a boat or touch a mark or have your engine running after the "prep," you're in trouble. When I was young I used to use a little memory aid for these signals that may be helpful in the beginning. I noticed that the two Ws go together. The warning signal is white. Then I remembered the sequence of signals from the name of a class of boat called a *Wood Pussy*: the "*w*arning" is followed by the "*p*reparatory." Or perhaps you can use some other "*W.P.*" (like *Water Polo*) which may be easier for you to remember.

Exactly one minute before each shape goes up, the preceding one is lowered. In other words, four minutes after the white shape goes up, it comes down. At nine minutes, the blue shape is lowered. So if you missed getting the time at the first shape, you have one minute's warning when it is lowered to get the time at the next shape.

The gun or horn or whatever your Race Committee uses is a device to draw attention to the signal. There is nothing official about the sound device. If it misfires or is early or late, that's tough. It's the shape that counts, and the exact timing for a signal depends on the instant that the shape hits the top of the hoist. For that reason, in more important regattas the Race Committee will tie the shape up in breakable "stops" (light line), secure it at the top of the hoist, and pull down on the bottom of it to open the shape. The shape is cylindrical, made of cloth, with wire hoops at the top and bottom, so it collapses like an old-fashioned top hat and can be pulled open with a jerk of the downhaul line. Since the gun is fired when the shape reaches the top or is broken out, if you don't hear the sound, start your watch when you see the shape.

Crew and Skipper Responsibilities

Be sure to assign specific duties to the various crew members. The smaller the number of crew, the more duties each has to assume. The singlehanded skipper, of course, has to do them all. Typical of such duties are: (1) spotting potential collisions and right-of-way boats; (2) calling the time remaining; (3) judging how close to the line you are; (4) sail control; (5) noting any last-minute wind shifts; (6) spotting potential tactical problems like a competitor overlapping your lee quarter; and (7) observing whether you are being called back by the committee for being over the line early.

Added to this list of duties are what I call "input considerations." These are facts that the skipper should know that will have a bearing on his start, such as: (1) wind direction; (2) wind type; (3) which end of the line is favored; (4) how long it takes to run the line; (5) current; and (6) the course to the windward mark.

Let's go into more detail about both the duties and the input considerations.

Crew Duties

Collisions and Right-of-Way

The crew member who is spotting potential collisions needs to have a good 360° view of all the surrounding boats. On most boats it is not important to hike out over the side until just before the starting gun on the final approach. The crew may be able to crouch in the cockpit if the boat is large enough, and be able to see to leeward. On cruising boats, a lookout is often posted in the bow before a start. Weight in the bow is very detrimental to the speed of the boat though, so the crew member must run aft quickly after the start and should not distract the skipper with a constant barrage of boat locations. Only call attention to boats which could become a potential hazard. Even though you have right-of-way, don't relax your vigil, because you can be disqualified along with the other boat if you fail "to make a reasonable attempt to avoid a collision resulting in serious damage." The basic rules that most often come into play before the start are: "a port tack yacht shall keep clear of a starboard tack yacht," "a windward yacht shall keep clear of a leeward yacht," and "a yacht clear astern shall keep clear of a yacht clear ahead."

Timing

Watch for the shape to go up and start your watch when it hits the top of the hoist. Sometimes it's hard to see the shape from a distance. If so, take the time from the smoke that comes from the gun. It will take a few seconds for the noise to reach you, so don't rely on the sound of the gun for your timing. The skipper should make every attempt to place the boat in a position for the timer to get an unobstructed view of the shape going up. Never be far away from the committee boat or be in the process of tacking or jibing about the time a signal is expected to be raised or lowered. Such a maneuver takes the timer's attention away from timing. Since the sails of competitors can obstruct the view of the signal and since most boats sail back and forth to leeward of the committee boat (when the first leg is a beat), a good position from which to get the time is upwind of the committee boat to one side or the other (not in front of its bow).

It is best, in a boat with two or more crew members, to have two stopwatches timing the start in case one is stopped accidentally. Often skippers can improve their judgment of the approach by glancing at their own watch rather than just hearing the seconds remaining being called out by a crew member. Don't buy the type of watch that hangs around your neck. One that straps to your wrist is far better because it can't bounce around hitting things. Also, you don't have to fumble to find it. When the time remaining is being called out by a crew member, it should be done clearly and succinctly in half-minute intervals until the last half minute before the start. Then "20 seconds," "15 seconds," "10 seconds," and "5, 4, 3, 2, 1, start" should be called out.

The relationship of time and distance to the start has a great deal to do with the type of boat you're sailing. If it's a light boat that accelerates rapidly, you can just about sit on the line luffing your sails and trim them in just before the gun. Catamaran sailors do this all the time. If you're racing a heavy-displacement type of boat, it will take a long time to get it sailing at top speed, so you can't afford to slow up much as you approach the starting line.

One method for timing the start for a displacement boat is known as the "Vanderbilt" start. Cross the starting line going away from it on a reach and note the time remaining. Add to it the amount of time it should take to complete the tack or jibe to return toward the line. Divide by two and the result is the time remaining on your watch when you start your tack or jibe. For example, your watch shows a minute and 20 seconds remaining as you cross the line going away. It takes you 12 seconds to tack. At 46 seconds left on your watch ($92 \div 2$), start your tack to start back to the line. You should arrive on the line at the gun. Bear in mind that this method was devised by Cornelius Vanderbilt for the enormous J-boats competing for the America's Cup in the 1930s. These boats sailed closehauled almost as fast as on a reach. Plus, they were match racing (only two boats), so the wind was not being broken up by other boats. In practice, nowadays, one has to allow a little extra time for the approach to the line since modern boats will reach faster away from the line than they will sail close-hauled toward it, and, in fleet starts, boats to windward will interfere with your wind and slow the boat down on the return to the line.

Judging the Line

If the starting line is a long one and you intend to start near the middle, it's very difficult to judge accurately the point at which you are right on the line. Skippers in this situation tend to play it cautiously with the result that there's apt to be a big sag in the middle of a long starting line of boats.

You can minimize your loss by sailing beyond the buoy end of the line and lining up the buoy and the white flag on the committee boat (which indicates the other end of the line) with any convenient landmark ashore, such as a rooftop or a tree, providing, of course, there is land in that direction.

It may be possible to get a range from the committee boat end, but often the committee boat itself blocks you from getting a good view of the buoy and the land. This range should not be taken too early, because the committee boat may shift position, or a change of current may cause it to swing, which would change the range.

As you are approaching the starting line to start, watch the white flag on the committee boat against the shore very carefully. It will move along the shore toward your landmark (see Figure 94). If the two line up just as the gun goes, your bow will be over early because of your physical position in the boat when you noted the range. So hang back slightly from lining them up at the gun.

In an International 14 regatta, using this method I found that the sag in the middle of the line was two boat lengths of open water between my boat and the other starters. You will have a decided advantage over the other boats starting in the middle of the line if you can get two boat lengths ahead of a bunch who think they are getting a perfect start or even feel they might be early.

One Finn dinghy sailor I know decided to play for starting line sag even though there were no landmarks to confirm it. He started dead ahead of the boats with the best starts in the middle of the line each race of a big regatta,

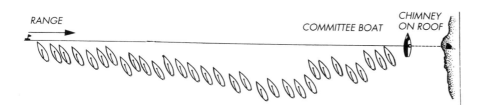

RANGE · · · COMMITTEE BOAT · CHIMNEY ON ROOF

Fig. 94. A range can aid in judging a long starting line.

and never was called back for being over early! That's playing it risky, though, because sometimes the sag just isn't there.

There are other starting lines, with no landmarks available for ranges, where the Regatta Committee conveniently, and certainly unintentionally, helps the competitors judge the line. When they are starting a large fleet they must have a long line. Since it is difficult for the people on the Race Committee boat to read the sail numbers of the boats over the line before the gun if they're far away, they station another boat beyond the buoy end of the line. A person on this anchored boat radios back to the committee boat the numbers of the near-by competitors who are over early. To do so accurately, he or she must line up a post on the stake boat with the buoy and the white flag on the committee boat. As a competitor sails along the line on starboard tack toward the buoy, the skipper can sight the buoy in line with the post or spotter on the anchored boat and know for certain whether or not he is over the line.

There's another way to judge the location of the starting line in boats like a Soling. If there's no chance for a range, lean way out over the side of the boat to windward. Look forward and aft at the two ends of the line as you are reaching along it. Sitting on the rail, it might appear you are right on the line. But when you lean way out, the perspective changes and you can see how far from it you really are.

Sail Control

Before the start, large adjustments in speed are necessary. We're not thinking about the fine nuances of sail trim. It is crucial that the skipper state clearly exactly what he wants. If he wants to slow down he may say "kill it," whereupon the crew will let the main and jib luff. If he wants to stop dead he'll probably say "back it," meaning to back the main against the wind. If he wants to accelerate rapidly, he'll probably say "trim for speed."

Many skippers concentrate their practice on accelerating the boat, but very few practice what is equally important—stopping the boat. Practice the drills described earlier. Head up and back the main. Work toward ultimate control of your boat. If you don't learn to stop the boat in a hurry, you may find yourself needlessly across the starting line too early, with little hope of doing well in the race after restarting.

Last-Minute Wind Shifts

On light, fluky days, a wind shift just before the start of a race can mean the difference between winning and losing. An observant crew can be very valuable in such instances. In one national championship I sailed, the buoy end was favored in very light breezes. We noticed some dark patches on the water approaching the committee boat end and immediately sailed over there.

We reached the new breeze just as the starting gun sounded and won the race easily. One other lesson learned: a crew member of another boat also saw the dark patches of wind, but instead of just verbally describing the location of the breeze to his skipper, he pointed to it. I expected that the mistake would draw many boats from the rest of the fleet over to the new wind. Fortunately, however, only one other boat noticed the crew member point. The third boat to notice the new wind placed second in the race, while the one with the pointing crewman lost a sure second place and wound up third, So never point at anything unless you are doing so deliberately to mislead your competitors.

Though the above is an extreme example, there are many times when a lesser wind shift can have a great effect on the start of a race. Later we will discuss the favored end of the line, which is the upwind end. A small wind shift can change one end of the line from being favored and make the other end favored. It's important to be aware of such shifts, since they can account for many boat lengths when the race starts.

Potential Tactical Problems

The skipper and his crew have to be constantly aware of the position of competitors before the start. They particularly have to keep another boat from getting an overlap to leeward and forcing them over the line early or closing any opening they might have at the committee boat. Often, boats approach on port tack and tack onto starboard, to leeward of other starboard tack boats. The skipper and crew need to anticipate this, possibly by heading off and discouraging the port tack boat from tacking, though not obstructing her from keeping clear. If she tacks anyway, then head back up again to increase the lateral distance between your boat and the other. A crew member should be calling to the skipper the likelihood of port tack boats attempting this maneuver. He should also advise the skipper whether it looks as if they are "running out of line." In other words, are they going to reach the end of the line before the gun goes off. If that happens, they have only two choices, neither good: (1) go over the line early, in which case they must return to restart; or (2) go under (to leeward of) the starting mark which, though more desirable, can't be done if a boat is to leeward of them holding them up (since windward boats must keep clear of leeward boats). They could avoid running out of line by controlling their progress along the line by judicious luffing and speed control.

Over Early

One crew member must determine if the Race Committee is calling the boat back for being over the line early. Sometimes it's hard to judge if your bow or other part of the boat is over before the gun. Race Committees have different ways of informing you. Sometimes a board is held up with your sail number on it. Usually a gun or horn is sounded for each boat over early and the number called out on a megaphone. On cruising boat starts in major races, the premature starters are often announced on a certain frequency on the radiotelephone. Whatever method is used will be written in the racing instructions passed out to the competitors before the race. However, it's the obligation of each boat to sail the course properly, and not being aware of the Race Committee's recall signal is no excuse. So it's very important, if it's a close start, for the skipper to know whether they are over early, and someone should be assigned the task of watching the Race Committee for the recall. Many times a skipper has raced the entire race, crossed the finishing line first, and not received the traditional gun for first place, only to find out that the boat was a premature starter and technically hadn't raced the course properly.

A boat that is over the starting line early has to return and start properly. While she is returning to start, and until she has crossed to the prestart side of the starting line or its extensions, she has no rights over boats who have started properly. If she were running back to the line on starboard tack, for instance, a port tack boat which had started correctly would have right-of-way over her.

Those are the various duties of the crew. Following are input considerations which are primarily the concern of the skipper.

Skipper's Input Decisions

Wind Direction

Finding wind direction is fairly easy. Just shoot the boat dead into the wind and let the sails luff. When the main and jib are right over the center-line of the boat, you are headed directly into the wind. Wait until the boat has lost all headway before doing this (particularly in light airs) because, if it is moving forward, the wind will appear to be dead ahead long before it really is. If there is a sea that is slightly angled to the wind direction, the jib (if it isn't a genoa) is a better indicator than the main because the weight of the main boom tends to make it swing more. When you are dead into the wind, read the compass to get the wind direction.

Wind Type

You want to know, though it often ends up as an educated guess, whether the wind is shifting back and forth (oscillating) or gradually veering or backing in one direction (a continual shift). Oscillating shifts are usually associated with unstable conditions. Upper air, for example, may be coming down to the water surface in gusts as the air above the land rises.

Look at smoke coming from chimneys ashore. If it's a clear day with cumulus clouds, and if the wind is cool and from the northwest, you can be fairly sure that the mean direction of the wind will remain fairly consistent, but the wind itself may shift back and forth in oscillating shifts. If it's a hazy day, the smoke from the stacks may go up a short way and then stratify along with the clouds. If the wind has a southerly trend, the weather will be stable and the mean direction of the wind will probably shift one way or the other in a continual shift.

Another way to check out shifts before the start is to sail closehauled on the port and starboard tacks for awhile and record the high and low compass headings on both tacks. If you do this, you'll know right after the start whether you are sailing in a header or a lift.

Favored End

Once you have determined the wind direction and decided what type it is, find out which end of the line is favored.

First, let's straighten out a few terms. Boats normally cross the starting line on starboard tack. The port end of the line, therefore, is called the leeward end because it is to leeward of the starboard tack boats. We usually leave marks to port in the United States, so the buoy is normally placed at the port end of the starting line. The Race Committee boat is at the starboard end. (By leaving a mark to port, we mean the mark will be on the port side of your boat as you pass it. We do *not* mean to sail to the port side of the mark.)

You might think the upwind end should be called the "windward" end of the line, and some people do call it that. But this gets confusing when the buoy end, or the leeward end, is upwind. It is preferable to call the upwind end the "favored" end of the starting line.

If the first leg is a beat, we want to know which end is more upwind. The position of the first mark has nothing to do with the end of the starting line you choose. For instance, the first mark could be so far over to the right side of the course that you could practically reach it on port tack. The natural assumption would be that the starboard end is closer, and so it is (by straight-line distance). But if no boat on the line can lay the weather mark (reach it without tacking) and at least one tack must be made, and if the port end is more upwind, the port end is favored.

Look at Figure 95. If the wind is square, or perpendicular to the starting line, boat A on port tack starting at the buoy end will meet boat B starting at the other end on starboard tack at position A-1/B-1. It doesn't matter if they start on opposite tacks as diagrammed, or start on the same tack and meet later going up the weather leg. Assuming equal speed and no wind shifts, the effect will be the same.

Now, shift the wind 10° to the left. Boat A is sailing 10° higher and boat B 10° lower. After they have sailed the same distance as before, their positions will be A-2/B-2 in Figure 95. The boat that started at the port end of the line now is able to cross the boat that started at the committee boat end.

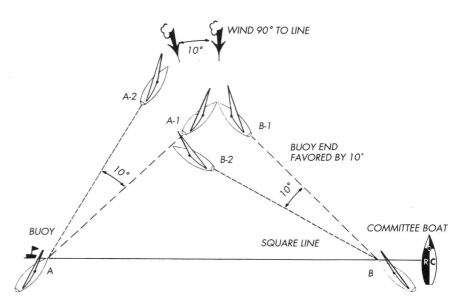

Fig. 95. A wind shift toward one end of the starting line favors that end.

As long as there is at least one tack on the weather leg that will make their paths cross, boat A will have an advantage over boat B.

The often-recommended length of a starting line in heavy air is 125% of the aggregate length of all the boats crossing it. For example, if you had twenty 30-foot sailboats on a line, it should be 750 feet long. If the wind is 5° off a perfect 90° angle, a boat starting at the upwind end will be 65.6 feet ahead of a boat at the other end, right at the start! This is over two boat lengths! Imagine the penalty you would pay if you started at the wrong end if the wind were 15° off square, which is common.

Many good sailors get the feel of which end of the line is upwind by sailing along the line in one direction with their sails trimmed perfectly. Then they return and run the line in the opposite direction without changing the sail trim. If the line isn't square to the wind, the sails will either luff or be overtrimmed (stalled) when they return. A luff indicates that the starting mark ahead of them is upwind and a stall tells them that the mark astern of them is upwind. This system tends to average out the wind shifts, but is more intuitive than scientific.

There are a number of ways to determine the favored end. Possibly the most popular is shooting head-to-wind in the middle of the starting line. The upwind end will be forward of abeam. The bow of the boat will be pointing more toward the favored end. A more accurate way of doing the same thing is to shoot the wind just outside the buoy end and sight in one direction, toward the committee boat. This halves any potential error. If the committee boat is forward of abeam, that end is favored.

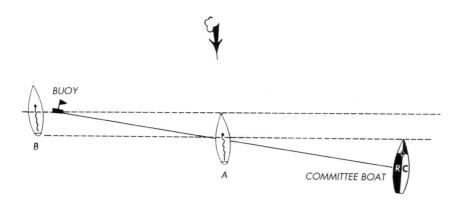

Fig. 96. To judge the favored end, shoot into the wind near one end. The same can be done in the center of the line, but there's more chance of error.

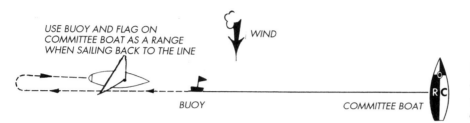

Fig. 97. Determine the compass course of the starting line by lining up the starting mark with the committee boat.

Most boats have a thwart or a traveler that runs directly across the boat, and this can facilitate sighting. If these aren't available, lines painted on the deck perpendicular to the centerline will do the same thing. Note that in Figure 96 boat A shoots the wind in the middle of the line, sights abeam, and concludes that the buoy end seems to be favored. But when boat B shoots into the wind near the buoy it is obvious which end is favored.

If you have a boat with a steady compass, an accurate method is to compare the compass course of the starting line with the compass reading of wind direction. Sail directly away from the buoy end of the starting line on the extension of the line. Then sail back toward it, lining up the buoy with the white flag on the committee boat. When you are sailing that range, check the compass heading (see Figure 97).

Let's say you find the line to be 100° as you sail toward the committee boat. That means the wind direction should be 010° (100° minus 90°) if the wind were absolutely square to the line and neither end were favored. Then remember this "magic number" of 010° every time you shoot the wind thereafter. Check the wind direction quite often to make sure that there hasn't been a shift in the interim. If you find that the wind is 015°, the committee boat end is favored by 5°. One major advantage in this system is that you don't have to be near or on the starting line every time you check the wind. Quite often there are other classes which may start ahead of you and you won't be allowed near the line until five or ten minutes before you start, which is usually too late to get all the other input considerations. There's normally just enough time to get where you want to be, and then make one last wind check to be sure nothing has changed. Another reason to check wind direction away from the line is that the wind can be "chewed up" (disturbed) by the many boats sailing around at the start. Getting an accurate wind direction there may be very difficult.

Running the Line

There are very few fixed points in the water one can use as a reference with which to judge distance. There are at the start, however, two fixed points you can use, and those are the buoy end of the line and the committee boat. By sailing the length of a short line and timing it, you can get a good feel for time and distance as you approach the line to start. If the line is long, there's another good reason to time it. You may make a last-minute decision to start at the other end of the line. You had better know how long it will take you to get there.

Current

Nothing is more frustrating or disastrous than misjudging the current and being swept across the starting line early, before the starting gun. It's particularly bad when it happens in a light breeze and you have to fight your way back upcurrent on a run in order to start correctly. Equally bad is being caught far away from the line with the current against you when the wind dies. You may end up taking an hour to cross the starting line. So the trick is to determine the current's speed and direction.

Observation is the key. Observe the angle the committee boat or other boats lie at anchor. Look at the mark end and see if it leaves a wake (as if it were moving through the water). Look at small objects, preferably below the surface, that may float past the mark. Or better yet, toss a current stick (a two- to three-foot stick weighted to remain upright with a few inches of it breaking the surface) overboard near the mark and observe its speed and direction of drift. One hundred feet of drift in a minute equals a knot of current.

Course to the Windward Mark

Most skippers shoot the boat into the wind to determine wind direction, but few point the boat in the direction of the first mark before the start. Useful information may be obtained. If the course is a windward-leeward one, pointing your boat at the windward mark will tell you which side to set your spinnaker on—which tack you'll be on as you return on the run. When you point the boat at the mark with sheets eased, the sails will be luffing. If the

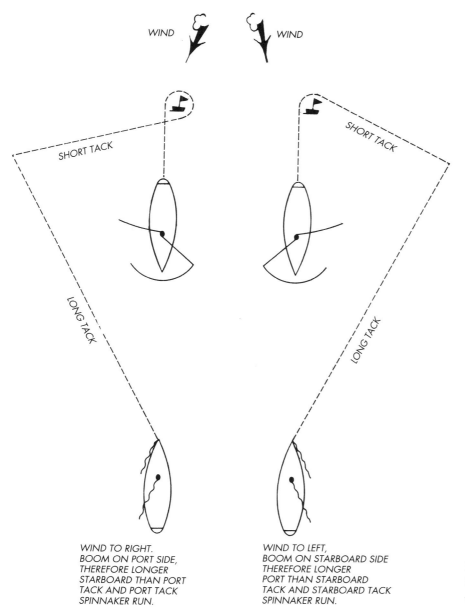

WIND

WIND

SHORT TACK

SHORT TACK

LONG TACK

LONG TACK

WIND TO RIGHT.
BOOM ON PORT SIDE,
THEREFORE LONGER
STARBOARD THAN PORT
TACK AND PORT TACK
SPINNAKER RUN.

WIND TO LEFT,
BOOM ON STARBOARD SIDE
THEREFORE LONGER
PORT THAN STARBOARD
TACK AND STARBOARD TACK
SPINNAKER RUN.

Fig. 98. Shoot the weather mark before the start to determine which tack is longer.

mainsail is off-center more to the port side of the boat (as it would be on starboard tack), the wind is to the right of the weather mark and the starboard tack will be the long tack up. If the starboard tack is the long tack when beating, you will be on the port tack on the run (see Figure 98). Of course, as you beat up to the weather mark you must watch for further wind shifts which may change this information.

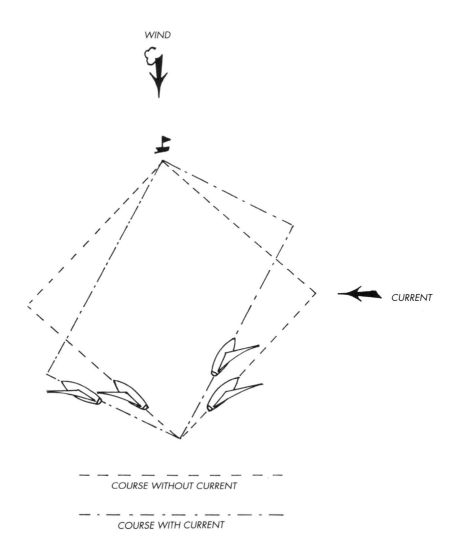

WIND

CURRENT

COURSE WITHOUT CURRENT

COURSE WITH CURRENT

Fig. 99. Current will cause a normally square windward leg to become lopsided, with more time spent on one tack than on the other.

It's a racing axiom that, if all else is equal, it is best to take the long tack first since it takes you closer to the windward mark. Figure 98 also shows that by pointing your boat at the windward mark you can easily determine which is the long track.

Another racing axiom is shown in Figure 99. Take the upcurrent tack first. In the diagram the wind is square, but the current is from the right. On the starboard tack the boat is being set away from the windward mark, effectively making the port tack the "long" tack which should be taken first (all else being equal).

Now that we have covered the duties and input considerations necessary to enable the skipper to make reasonable starting decisions, let's look at the actual start.

Where to Start

At some point a decision must be made as to exactly where along the line you want to start. The choice is based on which end of the line is favored and how the wind is expected to shift right after the start. For instance, the buoy end may be favored because the wind has shifted to the left momentarily. That means right after the start you'd be sailing in a starboard tack header and would want to tack away.

In this situation you might try starting a short distance from the buoy end in hopes you won't be pinned by other starboard tack boats when you want to tack over to port. If, however, you don't expect the wind to swing back to the right, but rather to swing further to the left due to either meteorological or geographical reasons, the best start would be right at the buoy.

If the committee boat end is favored or if you expect the wind to swing to the right, that's the end to start at. In this case, you should avoid being squeezed out by leeward boats. If the wind is steady and you want to remain on starboard tack, be one of the first boats to cross the starting line, but not necessarily right next to the committee boat.

You want to have good speed and open space to leeward in order to reach off and increase your speed. Otherwise you may end up in the bad air (airflow that has been disturbed) of some other boat and have to tack away to get clear air. On the other hand, when you expect the wind to shift to the right, you must be next to the committee boat so you can tack right after the start. You want to be sure no boat can get on your weather quarter and keep you from tacking from starboard.

The Starting Approach

When you trim in the sails just before the start, you won't be able to gain much speed unless you can bear off slightly. Just trimming in the sails when you are heading on a closehauled course will cause the boat to make a great deal of leeway until it picks up sufficient speed to create adequate lift on the keel and rudder. It's impossible to bear off to pick up speed if there's a leeward boat right there, so avoid getting yourself into this predicament.

If you see a boat attempting to get his bow to leeward of your stem, discourage him by bearing off unless the gun is just about to go. When overlapped by a windward boat, try to open up a hole to leeward by luffing up. At the last moment you can reach off into this hole and pick up speed.

Another reason to avoid letting a boat get close to leeward of you is more serious. They can luff you right over the line before the gun and you will have to restart.

Special Starts

The Dip Start

The dip start is used quite often when there is a strong current running with the wind or a large sag in the middle of the starting line. It consists of dipping across the line from the course side and starting. It's dangerous on two counts. First, you are on the wrong side of the line and have to get completely over to the other side of the line before the starting gun goes off. If any part of your boat or crew is on the line when the gun goes off, you are considered over the line early and have to restart. Along with this problem is the fact that you are not hidden from the view of the committee boat. Many of the boats approaching on starboard tack are hidden by the sails of others. You stick out like a sore thumb, and even if you get completely over to the proper side of the line before the gun goes off, you may be called over early by an overzealous Race Committee member. The second problem is that, being weather boat you have no "rights" (right-of-way) over leeward boats approaching the line on the same tack. They can hold you up and keep you on the wrong side of the line if they want to. This type of start is advantageous (see Figure 100) when a light wind combines with a strong current in the same direction.

Note that boat A is on the upcurrent side of the line. This is good practice in light air since, if the breeze dies, when you are downcurrent of the starting line the current can carry you far downwind of the line and it may take a very long time to get back. Often the other boats haven't allowed for current and are late for the start. This opens a hole for boat A, and just before the gun she dips over the line to the proper side and starts.

There is one situation when one should not consider a dip start. After a general recall (a start when the whole fleet is recalled because so many boats

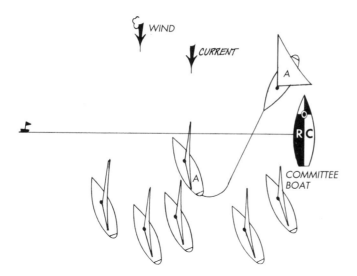

Fig. 100. A dip start can often be successful when the wind and current are together.

are over early the committee can't identify specific boats), a boat on the wrong side of the line during the last minute before the starting signal has to go around either end of the line to start. This is called the "One Minute Rule."

The Delayed Start

If the committee boat end of the starting line is well favored, many boats will decide to start at that end. However, it is very important to be able to tack away and clear your air, but this may be difficult if there's a jam-up at the committee boat. You can't tack onto port if there are starboard tack boats to windward and behind you. You have to wait until they tack away first. One

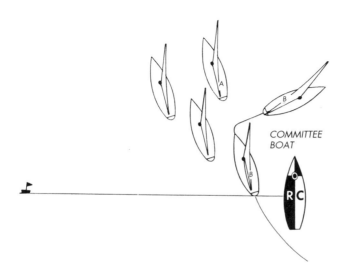

Fig. 101. A delayed start allows boat B to tack away, rather than be pinned on starboard tack.

solution, if you see a jam-up developing before the start, is to be in the second wave, but right next to the committee boat. As you cross the line, therefore, there is no way for a boat to be to windward of you and prevent you from tacking to port to clear your air. This is accepting second-best since the best start is made by the one boat that is closest to the committee boat at the gun, but the delayed start is far better than being buried in a pile of boats and pinned down. In Figure 101, boat B has made a delayed start right behind boat A and is free to tack over to port.

The Port Tack Approach

This is a start that takes guts. The whole fleet may be approaching the line on starboard tack with right-of-way and you are converging with them on port tack "across the grain." After the gun the starboard tack boats can assume their proper course. This means that if they were reaching along the line, they can come up to closehauled when the gun goes off, and if you're in the way on port tack, that's just too bad. The advantage of a port tack approach is that you can look for an open area with clear air in a fleet of starboard tack boats and tack into it, if you find one. Once on starboard, you are pretty well committed to the same general area in the fleet. If you get on starboard early, you will find boats tacking in front of you, to leeward of you, and swooping down from the windward side. You can find yourself virtually boxed in by other boats and unable to get away from their "dirty" (disturbed, turbulent) air.

In Figure 102, boat A started approaching the starting line closehauled on starboard tack from quite a long way out. Boats B, C, D, E, F, and G, in delaying their final approach, have completely surrounded her. Boat D has made

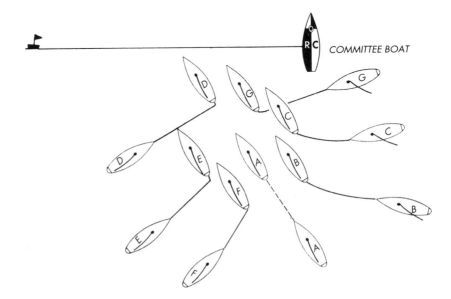

Fig. 102. A port tack approach allows boat D to choose a favorable position to start.

a port tack approach, found a good hole, and is in a fine position to bear off for speed to make a good start.

Light Air Starts

The most crucial thing in a light air start is to stay near the starting line. I've seen boats that in normal wind conditions would be no more than 30 seconds from the line take an hour to cross the line, while the rest of the fleet sails merrily up the windward leg in a local breeze. Second, always have the anchor ready to put over the side if the breeze dies completely, particularly if a current is carrying you away from the line.

For light air starts, keep your speed up, because it's very difficult to get moving again if you luff your sails and kill your speed. Also, don't rely on a timed start, because the breeze may be fresher when you go away from the line than when you return.

When you make any maneuver, a tack or a jibe, in current and light air, keep in mind what effect the current will have on your relationship to the starting line after the maneuver is completed. It is usually best to choose between tacking or jibing based upon which heads you into the current. For instance, if the current is carrying you downwind away from the line and you jibe to come back toward the line, by the time you complete your jibe you will be much further away from the line than before. However, if you tack, you will most likely be almost the same distance away from the line at the end of the tack as you were when you started the tack.

The Barging Start

There is a racing rule that gives boats certain rights to room when rounding marks. These rights do not exist "at a starting mark surrounded by navigable water . . . when approaching the starting line to start until clearing the starting marks." This means that boat A in Figure 103 doesn't have to let boat B have room to pass between her and the committee boat, and boat B doesn't have to leave room for boat C. Technically, both boats B and C are "barging" in relation to boat A.

In the absence of boats A and B, however, it's perfectly legal for boat C to make this "barging" approach since there are no boats to leeward to "close the door" on her. The approach isn't illegal, as long as you don't get caught.

There are times when boat C's approach is a good one. Like the dip start, she can sail around upcurrent of the starting line when the current is setting her downwind. In the last few seconds she can dip under the stern of the committee boat and start. Since the current is setting the leeward closehauled boats like A and B away from the line, it's unlikely that they will give her any

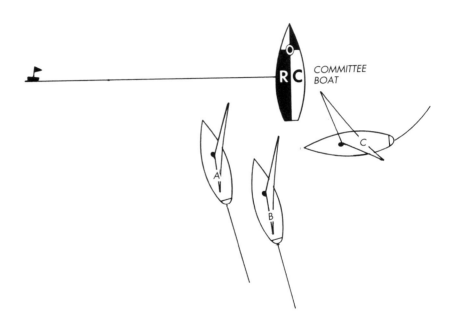

Fig. 103. Boats B and C can be squeezed out at the committee boat.

trouble. In addition, boat C was not seen on the wrong side of the line by any committee member and the latter can't be biased into calling her over early. One disadvantage, however, is that a barging start cannot be made in a large fleet, because most certainly some boat will be on time at the committee boat and catch the boat barging.

Sail Shape and Control

There is probably no other speed determinant so important as a sailboat's sails and the manner in which they are set or trimmed. Keep in mind that some sail material, such as Dacron, is constantly stretching as the forces on it change. The forces change not only when the wind strength changes, but also when the boat slows down as when plowing into waves or speeds up as when surfing or sailing in smooth water. To control this stretch, and thereby the shape of the sail, numerous adjustment devices are found on many classes of boats. Before we look at the specific devices, let's discuss the desirable end result.

Sails power a sailboat much like an engine powers a car. When a car is moving slowly, uphill or over a bumpy terrain, you keep it in low (first) gear. As it picks up speed and the ground levels off, you shift to second gear. When the car is moving fast on a smooth road, you shift to high. So with a sailboat. Full sails are the low gear and flat sails are high. When the seas are heavy and the boat is sailing slowly ("stop and go" as it hits each wave), the sails need power. Full sails are the answer. In smooth water and high winds when the sailboat is moving its fastest, flat sails are desirable.

Draft

The mainsail is a very versatile sail and can be made flat or full at will. But, you may ask, what is a "full sail" or a "flat sail"? The terms are relative. A sail is flatter or fuller than another based on the relationship of the maximum depth of the curvature (the draft) to the distance from luff to leech (the chord). Photo 131 shows the cross-section of a mainsail. An imaginary line drawn from luff to leech is the chord. A line drawn perpendicular to the chord

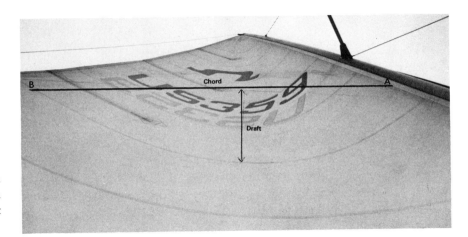

131. "Draft" is the maximum depth of the sail measured from the chord—an imaginary straight line from luff to leech.

at the point where the sail is the greatest distance from the chord is the "draft" or "camber." The "camber-to-chord ratio" is the relation of this distance to the chord, usually expressed as a percentage. If the chord is 120" and the draft or camber is 12" deep, the camber-to-chord ratio is 10 to 1 or 10%. Sails can be used effectively as flat as 5% or as full as 20%, depending on the class of boat and the sailing conditions.

Of even more importance to the racing sailor is the position of maximum draft in the sail. Figure 104 shows three sails all with the same camber-to-chord ratio, but with quite different locations of the maximum draft. A has the draft in the desirable location for a mainsail—40% to 50% aft from the leading edge (the luff). B shows the draft forward, near the mast. This can happen when a sail is designed to accept a certain amount of mast bend, but the sailor doesn't bend the mast enough.

The sailmaker puts draft into the sail in two ways: by a "luff and foot round" and by "broadseaming." If you laid a mainsail on the floor and "luff and foot round" was the only draft producer, it would look like Figure 105. However, when it is put on a straight mast and boom (the dotted lines) the

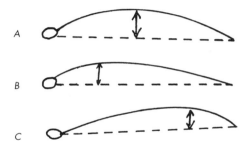

Fig. 104. The maximum draft of a sail may be found in numerous locations.

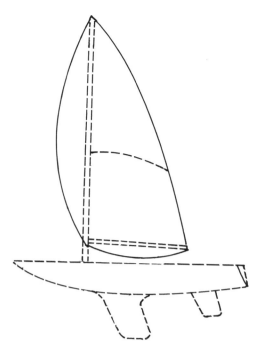

Fig. 105. The curves along the foot and luff of a mainsail become draft when on a straight mast and boom.

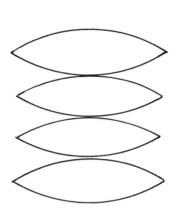

Fig. 106. Before it's sewn together, a football may look something like this.

Fig. 107. A sailmaker also gets draft by curving the panels and then sewing them together.

excess material becomes draft. As the material stretches in the wind, this draft moves aft toward the desired location in the middle of the sail. In light winds on a straight mast, the draft created by luff round will be forward, near the mast. If you bend the mast and boom to conform with the designed edge round, then the sail will be flat as a board.

The other method of obtaining draft, broadseaming, is simply narrowing the panels of cloth before they are stitched together. To understand how this creates draft, imagine a football that has been taken apart. It looks somewhat like Figure 106. Sewn together, it becomes a football. The same method is practiced in sailmaking, as in Figure 107. Draft created in this manner is placed exactly where the sailmaker wants it and does not depend on mast bend or stretch to place its location. A combination of both methods is used in the manufacture of all sails.

C in Figure 104 shows the maximum draft aft, near the leech of the mainsail. As the breeze freshens, sail material stretches and the draft tends to move aft toward the leech. This movement will cause the battens to cock to windward in the mainsail and produce a less efficient air foil. Increased tension on the luff can keep this movement to a minimum.

Sail Construction

But first, just a bit about how a sail is constructed. The threads that run across a panel of sailcloth are called the filling threads, otherwise known as the "weft" or the "fill." The threads that run lengthwise are called the "warp." Warp stretches more than weft, but the greatest stretch comes in a diagonal direction, called the "bias." Most Dacron sails are designed with this stretch in mind.

For example, the mainsheet will exert the greatest force on a mainsail, and most of it will fall on the leech. Consequently, the panels of cloth are sewn together so that the crosswise threads, or filling threads, lie along the leech of the sail (see Figure 108).

This means that all the panels along the luff of the sail must be cut on the bias, where stretch is greatest. If we were to blow up a small section of the sail along the mast, we would see that the threads look like a whole bunch of little diamonds at the bias (Figure 109). As we pull down on the luff and increase the tension, each diamond elongates (the dotted lines) and pulls material in from the center of the sail (see Figure 110). If we pull down hard on the luff when there is not enough wind to warrant it, vertical troughs or creases will appear, running parallel to the mast (see Photo 132).

You can simulate this effect by taking a handkerchief and pulling it at two diagonally opposite corners, as in Photo 133. The same troughs will appear, just as they will when there is too much luff tension. Photo 134 shows that as the corners are stretched apart on the bias, the material moves upward. The lower corner was even with the instructor's waist and is now a few inches higher.

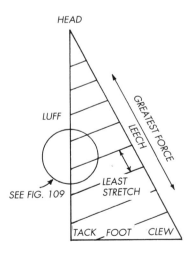

Fig. 108. Panels meet the mast on a bias.

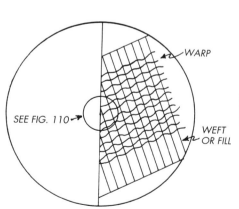

Fig. 109. The threads form little diamonds near the luff.

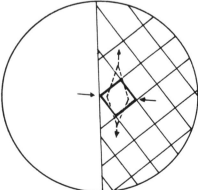

Fig. 110. As the top and bottom of the diamonds are stretched, material is pulled in from the middle of the sail.

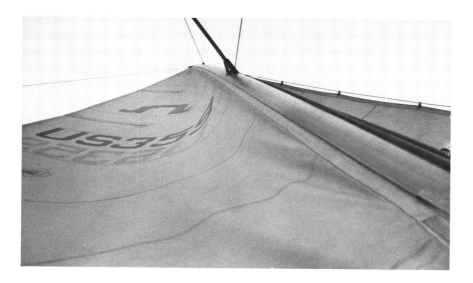

132. Excessive luff tension causes wrinkles near the mast.

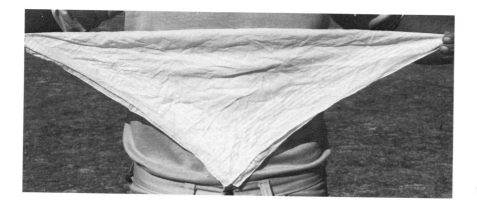

133. Hold the handkerchief at two corners on the bias.

134. Pull outward and creases appear as the bottom corners pull up.

Proper Mainsail Adjustment

Tensioning the Luff

There are two ways to tension a mainsail's luff: with a downhaul and with a cunningham. In the days of cotton sails, you would buy a sail that was actually too small in light air. This would allow you to stretch it to the legal size limits to flatten it when the wind velocity increased. Of course, this meant that you would automatically penalize yourself in light air by having reduced sail area.

To solve this little dilemma, Briggs Cunningham, skipper of *Columbia*, winner of the 1958 America's Cup, chose the simple expedient of placing a grommet above the mainsail tack fitting in a full-sized sail. When the tack reached the lower black band on the mast (and had been stretched as far as it could be legally), a block and tackle arrangement was attached to a line running through the grommet. Tightening it added more tension to the luff, and legally so. Though some wrinkles do appear along the foot below the grommet when the cunningham is in use, they don't seem to make an appreciable difference in the efficiency of the sail.

This grommeted hole in the mainsail has become known as a "cunningham hole" and it is now commonplace in most Dacron sails. With a cunningham, a sail can be made full-sized for light air performance and still be tensioned along the luff to keep the draft from moving aft when the breeze increases.

A variation of the cunningham is also used on Dacron jibs. Many small boats have a cloth tension device attached to the jib near the tack, and a wire that leads to the cockpit can be adjusted to increase or decrease the tension of the luff. Larger boats use something that looks more like the mainsail cunningham. A line is dead-ended at the deck near the tack, and is run up through a grommet hole in the luff of the jib about a foot or so off the deck. Then it is run back down through a block and taken to a winch. The theory is the same for both a jib and a main. But the jib is much more sensitive to luff tension than is the main.

When sailing to windward, the point of maximum draft on a jib should be about 35% of the chord behind the luff, compared to about 50% of the chord in a mainsail. If the wind increases, it's far easier for the draft of a Dacron jib to work aft of its normal location, and this means that you must constantly change the jib luff tension for highest efficiency whenever the wind changes.

Luff tension must also be changed depending upon what point of sail the boat is on. When reaching or running, you want a very full sail with the draft well aft. You should ease off the downhaul and cunningham in this situation.

The Traveler

The traveler is an important mainsail adjuster often found on racing sailboats. It is a track with a sliding mainsheet block which runs across the boat beneath the main boom. The better travelers have ball-bearing cars because, when closehauled, the nonball-bearing types have a tendency to stick under the pressure of the mainsheet.

The traveler's function is to allow the angle of the boom relative to the centerline of the boat to change without allowing the boom to rise. If, instead of using a traveler, we eased the mainsheet, the force of the wind on the sail would lift the boom in the air and the top part of the leech would fall off to leeward.

Figure 111 shows the constant angle the apparent wind makes with the luff of the sail for its full length when the mainsheet is trimmed in tight. Figure 112 shows how this angle changes in the upper part of the sail when the mainsheet

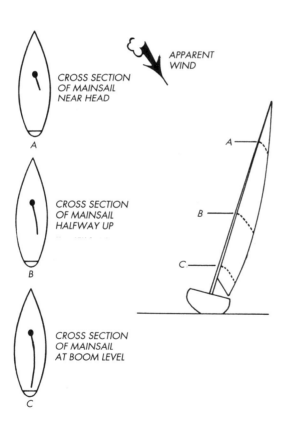

Fig. 111. With the mainsheet trimmed tightly, the sail near the top of the mast has almost the same angle to the wind as the bottom.

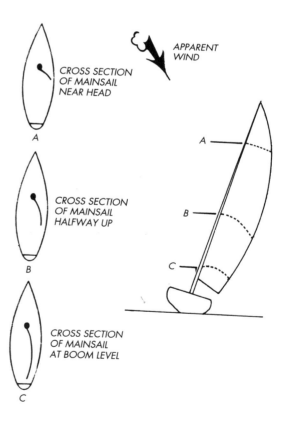

Fig. 112. When the mainsheet is eased, the top part of the sail falls off to leeward.

is eased. The upper part can actually be luffing even though the bottom part is full of air. This effect is called "twist," and is usually undesirable.

There are a couple of exceptions. The wind on the surface of the water is slowed down by friction, so the wind at the top of the mast has a greater velocity than at deck level. Thus, the top of the sail is sailing in a continual puff relative to the bottom of the sail. Apparent wind comes aft in a puff. And in order for the apparent wind to have the same angle to the luff all the way up and down, a slight twist at the head of the sail is necessary.

The other exception to the harmful effects of twist is when there is very heavy air. The upper part of the sail greatly affects a boat's heeling, just as weight at the top of the mast does. If you want to reduce heeling, simply reduce the effectiveness of the upper part of the sail by inducing twist. Instead of easing the traveler out, ease the mainsheet.

The traveler is also used to help control heeling. We all know that as a sailboat turns from closehauled to a reach, one should ease the sails (see Figure 113a). If you didn't, the boat would heel way over as the wind hits the windward side of the sail at right angles to it. Forward drive would be reduced because of the lack of drive-producing airflow over the lee side of the sail (Figure 113b). We know that if sails are trimmed properly for a reach, the boat heels less than it does when closehauled because the drive from the sails is more in the direction of the boat's heading, and heeling force is reduced (Figure 113c).

If we are heeling excessively when closehauled, we can reduce the heeling by easing the traveler. Many good small-boat sailors use the traveler rather than the mainsheet to adjust to changes in wind velocity. Every novice has learned that when you are hit by a puff, you ease the mainsheet and head up into the wind to reduce heeling and avoid a capsize. The advanced sailor does much the same thing, but eases the traveler instead, though this depends to an extent on the type of sailboat being raced. Since the apparent wind comes aft in a puff, easing the traveler maintains the angle the apparent wind makes with the luff of the sail.

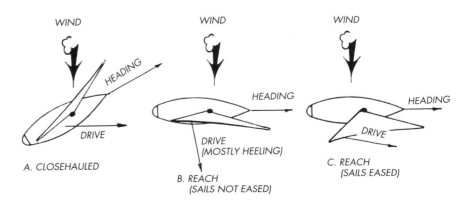

Fig. 113. Heeling is reduced when drive and heading line up together.

As you fall off on a true reach, easing the traveler acts like a boom vang, keeps the boom from rising, and reduces twist. However, its effectiveness ends when the traveler car reaches the outboard end of the track, and the mainsail must go out still further. Now the mainsheet, instead of pulling down, is angled out over the water and a boom vang has to do the work of keeping twist out of the sail. In Photo 135 the vang is not in use and the sail is badly twisted. Photo 136 shows the difference in the leech when the boom vang is pulled tight. The farther forward in the boat the traveler is located (and some boats have them in the middle of the cockpit), the farther out the boom can go before the traveler car reaches the end of the track and the vang must take over. And the closer the traveler is to the boom, the more positive is its control. If the traveler is mounted way down on the cockpit floor a number of feet

135. With no vang tension, the mainsail is twisted so that the top part is useless.

136. With the vang tight, the mainsail presents its full area to the wind.

137. Pull the traveler car to windward to get boom near center without pulling hard on the mainsheet.

beneath the boom, a puff may cause the mainsheet to stretch. The boom will lift and move outboard, negating some of the traveler's usefulness.

There is one other use for the traveler. You can trim the main boom up to the centerline of the boat without pulling down hard on the mainsheet. The closer the boom comes to the center of the boat, the higher you can theoretically point. On a light day, however, trimming the main tight can result in a very tight leech. The solution is to leave the mainsheet lightly trimmed and pull the traveler car up to windward, bringing the boom toward the middle of the boat without pulling it down at the same time, as in Photo 137. Now let's look at the backstay.

The Backstay

The adjustable backstay is a mast-bending device. On small boats, a block-and-tackle arrangement is attached to the lower end of the backstay and produces the leverage for bending the mast with a minimum of effort. Other factors are involved in mastbend such as leech tension, angle and length of the spreaders, placement of the partners where the mast goes through the deck (if any), tension on the jumpers (if any), location of the mainsheet blocks along the boom, etc. But for now let's just analyze the backstay. Tightening the backstay bends the mast and flattens the mainsail. But what is meant by a "flatter mainsail"? The fullness of any sail is the relationship between its chord length at a given height and its maximum draft. The chord is the straight-line distance from luff to leech, as described before.

When the backstay is tensioned, the middle of the mast bows forward, lengthening the chord, as the dotted lines in Figure 114 indicate, and decreasing the draft. With a longer chord distance and the same amount of sailcloth

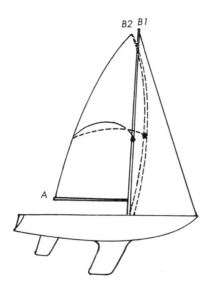

Fig. 114. Bending the mast changes the camber-to-chord ratio and flattens the sail.

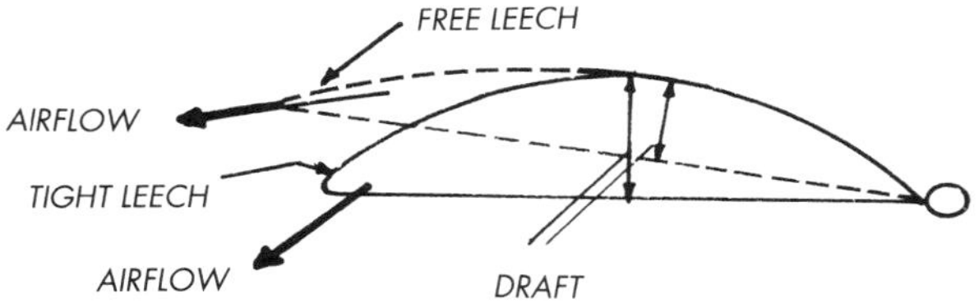

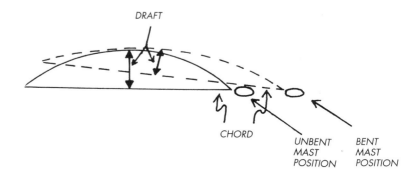

Fig. 115. Bending the mast frees the leech and flattens the sail.

Fig. 116. The combination of moving the mast forward and freeing the leech really flattens the sail.

as before, the draft has to be less as the excess material built by the sailmakers into the sail along the luff is stretched out and the sail flattened. But also note the action at the top of the mast. It is pulled back and down, which effectively shortens the distance between the top of the mast and the end of the boom. The distance A to B_2 is shorter than the distance A to B_1 in Figure 114. This frees the leech of the sail because the material sags off rather than being pulled tight. The end result is indicated by the dotted lines in Figure 115. Even if the chord length remains the same, a free leech creates a flatter sail since the draft is less. The figure also shows that the drive will be in a more forward direction, which reduces heeling.

Weather helm is reduced as the leech is freed. With a tight leech, airflow on the windward side of the sail is bent around until it exits off the leech in a windward direction. The tight leech acts like a rudder, forcing the stern to leeward and creating weather helm. But when the leech is freed, the air can flow straight aft or slightly to leeward, which minimizes turning effect of the leech. Figure 116 shows how the combination of the mast moving forward and a freer leech creates a much flatter sail.

The Mainsheet

Mainsheet tension, particularly on light days, will harden up the leech and cock the battens to windward. The sail will look much like the solid lines in Figure 115. Photo 138 shows a cocked leech on the boat to the left caused by overtrimming the mainsheet. Because this is a fuller shape, we can say that

mainsheet tension makes any cross section of the sail fuller, whereas an eased mainsheet, and the corresponding twist in the sail as the boom rises, makes a high cross section of the sail flatter.

The Outhaul

The outhaul mainly affects the draft in the lower part of the sail near the boom. Figure 117 shows the outhaul eased, and it is obvious that it creates a greater draft in the sail. Even if the actual draft remained the same, the shortening of the chord makes the camber-to-chord ratio larger, thereby making the sail fuller. Easing the outhaul excessively will cause wrinkles along the foot of the mainsail, as in Photo 139.

OUTHAUL EASED
(EXAGGERATED)
OUTHAUL OUT

Fig. 117. An eased outhaul creates a fuller sail.

139. Easing the outhaul can cause undesirable wrinkles.

How to "See" Sail Shape

It's difficult for many sailors to see fine adjustments in sail shape so it's best to use visual aids. In order to determine how much mast bend you have, with an indelible pen draw short vertical lines on the mainsail at spreader height, evenly spaced about three inches apart. Sight up from under the gooseneck to the masthead and determine where an imaginary straight line would fall. With this method we can determine that the mast in Figure 118 has about 13 inches of mast bend.

To see how much twist the mainsail has, sight up the sail from under the boom and line up the top batten with the boom. It should be parallel or falling off a little, but should not be cocked to weather. And if there is room to stand on the afterdeck behind the main boom, one can obtain a good overall perspective of the mainsail from that position.

Obviously, these sightings would be disruptive while racing when it is necessary to stay hiked out, so they should be made while closehauled before racing. Colored tape can be placed on the backstay in small boats to correspond with a certain amount of mast bend. Colored marks on the mainsheet can give you a guide as to how much twist there is in the mainsail leech for given wind conditions. Marks next to the traveler at one inch increments can help you duplicate the traveler car position. Also, a mark on the jib halyard against a series of marks spaced at equal intervals on the mast can be helpful in duplicating luff tension.

The jib is a little harder to judge. When it is a genoa, overlapping outside of the spreader, use the spreader tip as a guideline. Depending on the type of genoa, the lateral jib lead placement, the wind and sea conditions, and the

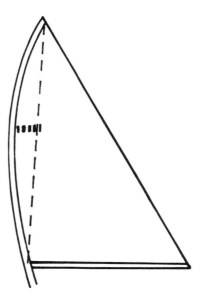

Fig. 118. The amount of mast bend can be determined by sighting up the mast past marks placed at known intervals.

luff tension, the cloth should be trimmed anywhere from a point a few inches off the spreader tips to just touching them.

If the jib does not overlap the spreaders the leech will probably point right at them. Place a piece of tape on the spreaders as a guideline and trim the sail until the leech points at the tape.

One way of knowing whether the jib is trimmed in too tight or the draft is too far aft is to observe the amount of backwind in the mainsail. If the backwind extends further back than usual, it is probably caused by over-trimming the jib.

Last, for an overall look at the jib shape, go to the bow and look at the leeward side. This can help you see if the draft has been blown aft.

All the above helps you to duplicate the same shape at another time, but only testing alongside another sailboat will tell you which shape or which sail is fastest. Sailmakers do this all the time when testing sails, so it can help you too if you can find a willing collaborator with a boat equal to yours. Sail side by side closehauled, each with clear air, keeping one boat as a "control" (don't change anything on it) and changing only one variable (such as the mainsheet tension or mast bend) on the other at any one time.

Proper Jib Adjustment

Twist in the mainsail results from the top part of the sail's falling off to leeward because of inadequate leech tension. The same problem exists with the jib, but it is the fore and aft placement of the jib lead (the block that the jib sheets run through) that determines how much twist a jib will have when beating. If the lead is too far aft, the jib sheet will pull along the foot of the sail but there won't be enough downward tension on the leech. The result is that the top part of the sail will tend to luff first.

However, other things can have the same effect as moving the jib lead block forward or aft. For instance, if the mast is raked (leaned) aft by lengthening the jibstay (see Figures 119 and 120), it effectively moves the head of the sail aft and the clew is lowered. If the jib lead remains in the same place, raking the mast frees the leech of the jib. Flying Dutchman class sailors often use this to free their leech in heavy weather since their jib leads are placed a maximum distance aft and it is illegal for them to move them further back.

A good rule of thumb is that the opening or slot between the jib leech and the body of the mainsail should remain parallel. This means that if we induce twist in the mainsail in heavy weather to reduce drive in the upper part of the main, thereby reducing heeling, we must also do the same to the jib.

In light air, any fullness should be down low in the jib. You can accomplish this by easing the jib sheet. This has the same effect as easing the outhaul on the main along the boom. Easing the jib sheet increases draft by shortening the distance between the tack and the clew, and this gives you greater

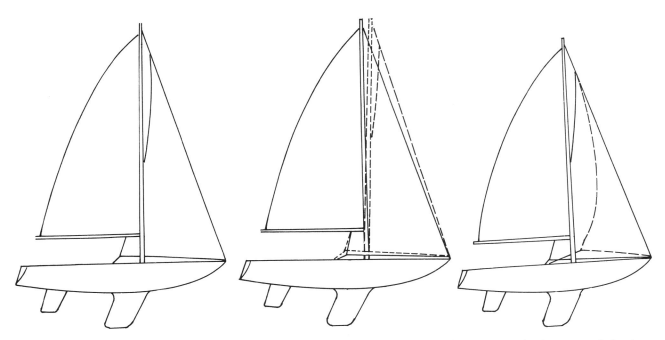

Fig. 119. Mast straight.

Fig. 120. Mast raked aft. The clew is moved lower and forward, the effective lead moved aft, and the leech is freed.

Fig. 121. As the sheet is eased, the clew rises and goes forward, the sheet angle is lowered, the effective lead goes aft, and twist develops.

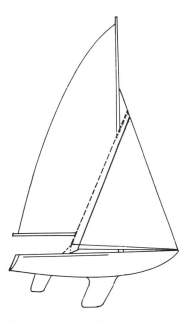

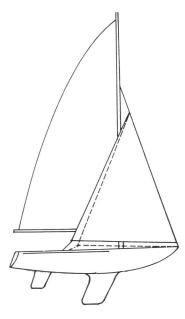

Fig. 122. As the jib halyard is tensioned, move the lead aft.

Fig. 123. As the jib downhaul is tensioned, move the lead forward.

drive in light airs and lumpy seas. However, there is one detrimental side effect to easing the sheet. As the clew goes out, the angle of the jib sheet is lowered and frees the leech (see Figure 121). Therefore, to regain the proper leech tension, you must move the jib lead forward.

The jib tack, jib halyard tension, and jib downhaul, or cunningham, also affect the location of the clew and the jib lead. One usually increases the tension on the luff of the sail to control the jib's shape as the wind increases. As a Dacron jib stretches under the force of the increased wind velocity, the draft tends to move aft in the sail, and more luff tension is required to keep the draft in the same location. But when the luff tension is increased by tightening the jib halyard, pulling the head of the sail higher, the clew is lifted higher also, and the lead will need to be placed further aft (see Figure 122). In heavy air you may even want a little twist in the sail, and the lead may need to come back even further.

However, if you get your luff tension by pulling down the luff downhaul or jib cunningham, the clew will be lowered and the lead will appear to be aft of its previous location (see Figure 123). Since the wind is blowing relatively hard when this is done, you may not want to change the jib lead position. It is now effectively aft of where it had been. This may produce the desired twist.

Observe what jib halyard tension does to the leech of the sail. As draft is pulled forward, the leech should become free and flatter. On high-aspect sails (those that are tall and narrow rather than wide and squat), the opposite can sometimes happen. The halyard pulls on the leech almost as much as on the luff, because the angle is about the same, so luff tension cups the leech instead of freeing it.

As a boat falls off onto a reach, the jib sheet is eased and a great deal of twist can develop. In order to correct this, the lead must go forward again. In the old days, sailboats did not have effective boom vangs for their mains and the top part of the mainsail twisted off to leeward when reaching. In order to make the jib leech match the curve of the main, sailors would move the jib lead aft.

Not so, today. Effective boom vangs keep twist in the main to a minimum and, therefore, little twist is needed in the jib. So in most cases the lead, when on a reach, should go forward, not aft, to pull down on the leech and reduce twist.One other sensitive adjustment for the jib lead is its correct distance outboard from the centerline of the boat. To find this point, first draw a line from the tack of the jib to the jib lead and measure the angle it makes with the centerline of the boat. This is called the "jib lead angle," and it will vary greatly from boat to boat.

A narrow keelboat will get away with having the jib lead fairly well inboard and still maintain speed while pointing high. A beamy center-

.0875	5 00'	.1405	8 00'	.1944	11 00'
904	10'	435	10'	974	10'
934	20'	465	20'	.2004	20'
.0963	30'	.1495	30'	.2035	30'
992	40'	524	40'	065	40'
.1022	50'	554	50'	095	50'
.1051	6 00'	.1584	9 00'	.2126	12 00'
080	10'	614	10'	156	10'
110	20'	644	20'	186	20'
.1139	30'	.1673	30'	.2217	30'
169	40'	703	40'	247	40'
198	50'	733	50'	278	50'
.1228	7 00'	.1763	10 00'	.2309	13 00'
257	10'	793	10'	339	10'
287	20'	823	20'	370	20'
.1317	30'	.1853	30'	.2401	30'
346	40'	883	40'	432	40'
376	50'	914	50'	462	50'
				.2493	14 00'

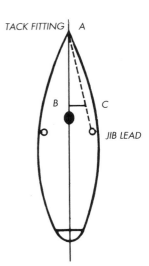

Fig. 124. Use this table to determine jib lead angle.

boarder, though, would have her jib leads further outboard in order to obtain enough drive to go through the seas.

Think of the lateral placement of the jib lead in the same terms as the mainsheet traveler. If the traveler needs to be eased, the jib lead should probably be eased outboard, too. The best way to tell whether your jib lead angle is correct is to test your boat against another. Sail closehauled alongside another boat of the same class and vary the lateral position in or out. The correct location will show up in increased speed.

You can measure the angle by using the table and diagram in Figure 124. To do so, first measure along the centerline from the tack fitting to any point just forward of the mast (distance *AB* on the diagram). From *B*, measure at right angles to the point that intersects a straight line running from the tack fitting to the jib lead (distance *BC*). Divide *BC* by *AB* and carry it to four places. Then consult the table for the jib lead angle in degrees. Example: *AB* is 59" and *BC* is 11". Eleven divided by 59 is .1864, which is a hair over $10\frac{1}{2}°$ in the table.

Start at about 9° on your boat and, in light air, come inboard with light jib sheet tension to about 8°. In heavy air you may be able to go outboard to 11° or even 12° with success. But remember—these adjustments always vary with boat type and the wind and sea conditions.

Tuning

The very word "tuning" conjures up visions of a virtuoso violinist delicately, and with an ear unattainable to the everyday man, adjusting his instrument so that it plays perfectly. It's a common word used in reference to preparing a cruising boat for sailing, but is misleading. When the stick (slang for mast) is placed in the boat in the early spring, the rigging is tightened to keep the mast straight. Usually the main halyard or a steel tape is led from the top of the mast to either side of the boat to make sure the mast is plumb. If the whole rig is leaning to one side a few inches, the boat will not sail well on one tack. Once the upper shrouds are tightened so that the mast is amidships, the lower shrouds are adjusted to get the mast straight. Many sailors think they have now finished tuning their boat. Actually, they have barely started. The *only* way to be sure the mast will be straight under load is to go out on a breezy day and sail upwind, first on one tack and then on the other. Get right behind the mast and sight up along the mainsail track or groove. You will most likely find that the uppers aren't tight enough and the top of the mast falls off to leeward. If, after tightening them up considerably, the top still looks like it's falling off to leeward, the lowers are probably too tight, bowing the mast to windward. Easing off on the lowers can cure this. Because the uppers are so much longer than the lowers, they stretch a longer distance under load, and therefore the lowers must be looser than the uppers so the stretch equals out.

If your boat has two lowers, forward and aft on each side of the boat, the forward lowers need to be tighter than the after lowers. The mast is designed to take a forward bend, but not the reverse. In a heavy breeze, this forward bow flattens the mainsail and frees the leech, which is good. Having tighter forward lowers prevents the bend from reversing itself in a seaway as the boat pounds into the waves.

Once the mast is straight athwartships (sideways), tighten the backstay in order to tension the headstay. If you lie on your back on the foredeck near the jib tack and sight up the headstay while beating to windward, you can see how much sag there is in the stay. Excessive sag will reduce the pointing ability of the boat. In other words, the boat won't point as close to the wind as she would with less sag. The sailmaker allows for a certain amount of jib-stay sag when he designs and cuts the sail, but when it sags excessively, it sags not only to leeward but aft. The sag aft shortens the distance between the luff and the leech and makes the sail fuller. This results in the airflow off the jib being curved into the main, causing backwind. Also the leading edge luffs easier and you have to fall off to fill the sail. Just remember that the net effect of inadequate headstay tension is to reduce windward performance.

Most cruising boats position the headstay turnbuckle so that when the backstay is tightened, the mast is straight fore and aft. If, however, you lengthen the headstay, the mast will be leaning aft. This rake tends to help the pointing ability of the boat, but decreases its ability to foot with other boats. If you keep the mast straight, the boat will foot well (sail fast), but will not point as well (sail close to the wind). There is no time I know of when you'd ever want to rake your mast forward when sailing closehauled. In other words, the headstay should never be tightened so much that the mast is leaning forward. If it is, the main boom will tend to be up in the air and airflow near the foot of the sail will be disrupted by the boom. The escaping air under the boom will equalize the pressure between the two sides of the sail and reduce the effectiveness of the mainsail. If the mainsail is recut so the boom remains level with the deck, though the mast is leaning forward, too much sail area is lost. Forward rake when running, however, is definitely faster. Some modern boats have lowers in line with the mast and hydraulic headstay and backstay adjusters for ease in varying the rake of the mast.

Light Air Sail Shape

It has long been thought that one should have flat sails in heavy air and full sails in light air. However, most top sailors in the country have come to recognize that a full sail is needed only when power is required, no matter whether the wind is light or heavy. In *drifting* conditions, it is conceded by most that one needs a flat sail.

When there is practically no wind, sails have to be set to maximize fully any puff that comes along. If there is a deep curvature in the sail, a puff is unable to attach itself readily to the lee side of the sail, since the airflow has to make too large a turn. A flat sail is, therefore, desirable in such conditions, for it doesn't require the air to deflect far from its normal direction to attach to the sail.

As soon as there's a breeze of 2 or 3 knots, full sails are required for low-speed power and acceleration. The racing sailor will start flattening the sails again at 10 or 12 knots of wind speed. A small sailboat that uses crew weight to stay flat may need to flatten sails earlier. A heavy keelboat sailing in heavy seas may need full sails up to a higher wind velocity. It all depends on the boat, the crew, and the wind and sea conditions.

In light air conditions, be careful not to overbend the mast or you will "turn the sail inside out." This occurs when the mast is bent more than the amount of luff roach that has been built into the sail. The visual result will be obvious by the wrinkles emanating from the clew (see Photo 140).

In purely drifting conditions, the cunningham and the main boom downhaul should not be tensioned. Both tend to pull the position of maximum draft forward, but neither one will flatten the sail. If you pull down hard on the cunningham in light air, the draft will go all the way forward and form a cup along the mast. Any puff hitting the sail will be unable to make such a sharp bend, and will fail to produce adequate airflow to produce lift. However, you want to avoid the wrinkles near the mast, shown in Photo 141, caused by no luff tension at all.

In drifting conditions, in addition to having flat sails and light trim, you also must trim the sails as if you were close reaching. The boom, for exam-

140. Wrinkles from the clew to the mast indicate that the mast is overbent.

141. The small wrinkles along the luff can be cured by tightening the cunningham. Straighten the mast a little to cure the large wrinkles from the clew.

ple, never should be over the centerline of the boat because if a zephyr does hit the sail, the force is translated into leeway rather than forward motion. The jib should be led further outboard than when there is a breeze. In light air you cannot "strap" the sails in. Doing so just slows the boat down.

The jib is played in much the same way as the main in light air. A jib should have very light halyard and sheet tension, and little to no luff tension. In some cases, the jib sheet should be hand-held so its weight doesn't tighten or collapse the jib leech. A jib is shaped so that the clew is aft of a point directly below the head. When there is no wind to fill the sail, gravity causes the heavy clew to fall forward directly beneath the head. This cups the foot of the sail and tightens the leech. The effect is similar to releasing the outhaul on the main boom (see Figure 117).

Balance

To sail properly, and certainly to race successfully, one must always consider a boat's balance. By "balance" we mean the tendency of a boat's heading either to deviate to one side or to continue in a straight line when the helmsman releases the tiller or wheel. As we mentioned earlier, if the tiller is released and the boat turns away from the wind to leeward, the boat is said to have "lee helm." Conversely, if the boat turns to windward, it has "weather helm." If it sails straight ahead, the boat is balanced.

Though these are useful guidelines, be careful not to be misled by "artificial" weather helm. A boat will normally turn into the wind when the tiller is released. Because of the forces acting on the rudder's windward side, "lift" is generated due to the angle of attack with the water flow. If the rudder post is located on the leading edge of the rudder and attached to the trailing edge of the keel, all the area aft of the post is pulling to windward, which tends to turn the boat into the wind.

Separated or "spade" rudders have become common on modern boats, large and small. The rudder is usually placed near the stern, where it can have maximum steering leverage. These rudders usually are "balanced" in that the rudder post is located on the rudder about one-fourth of the way back rather than attached along the leading edge. The designer intends the center of pull to windward to be at the post. The rudder, therefore, will remain straight. Balancing the rudder this way reduces artificial weather helm. It also decreases true weather helm because the rudder, as a lifting surface, pulls the stern of the boat to windward a small amount.

Excessive leeway can also cause artificial weather helm. Take an extreme example of a boat with no forward motion, slipping straight sideways through the water. The water on the leeward side of the rudder behind the rudder post will push the rudder blade to windward, giving the appearance of weather helm (the tiller will be pulling to leeward).

To distinguish artificial from true weather helm, determine whether the rudder must be deflected from the centerline in order to make the boat sail straight. If the tiller must be held constantly a few degrees to windward to make the boat sail a straight line, it does have true weather helm.

I've sailed on cruising boats with balanced spade rudders where the owners swore they sailed fastest with a "neutral" helm, and that once they had developed a slight weather helm, the boat slowed down. However, I observed that, although the helm "felt" neutral (there was no tug on it because the rudder post entered the rudder well aft of its leading edge) there was indeed a slight weather helm because the tiller was being held to windward a few degrees. But when the helm was increased to a point where the helmsman could actually feel it, there was a large enough rudder angle to slow the boat down by creating rudder drag.

◆ 5 ◆

Racing Rules

The racing rules have evolved over many years. The governing body of sail-boat racing is the International Sailing Federation (formerly the International Yacht Racing Union). The United States Sailing Association adopts the racing rules from the Federation. The rule book is divided into six parts plus some appendices: (I) Status of the Rules, Fundamental Rules, and Definitions; (II) Management of Races; (III) General Requirements; (IV) Right-of-Way Rules; (V) Other Sailing Rules; and (VI) Protests, Penalties, and Appeals. Parts I and IV are those of most concern to the racing sailor. While we have already mentioned a few of the racing rules as they apply to special situations, every racing sailor should thoroughly study the rules or his ignorance may cause him to be needlessly disqualified.

Rather than quote all the rules, we will paraphase the important parts the sailor starting to race should know. In particular, be sure to read, study, and know the definitions from Part I. The following is an explanation of the more common rules that cause confusion.

Definitions (from Part I of the Racing Rules)

Racing

Under the definitions we find that a yacht is racing from her preparatory signal until she has finished and cleared the finishing line or retired. This means that a boat can use her engine right up to her preparatory signal, but not afterward. If she hits a starting mark or fouls another boat after the warning signal, she is not disqualified or subject to penalties unless the foul occurs after the preparatory signal.

Starting and Finishing

When any part of the boat's hull, crew, or equipment, in normal position, crosses the line, she has started or finished. "In normal position" are words added to the finishing definition so a crew member can't legally run up to the bow and hold a paddle or other piece of equipment out ahead of the boat in order to beat another boat. The start must be in the direction of the first mark and the finish must be from the direction of the last mark.

Since you have finished when any part of the boat crosses the line, you don't have to cross it completely, but can turn around and sail home if you'd like to. However, you are still racing until you have cleared the finishing line. In other words, you are subject to the racing rules until no part of your boat or equipment remains on the line sighted from the flag on the committee boat to the buoy. Thus, if you hit the mark, foul another boat, or start your engine before you have cleared the line, you are subject to the appropriate penalties.

Luffing and Tacking

It's important to understand that luffing is simply altering course toward the wind *until* head-to-wind, and tacking is *from* head-to-wind until the boat is on a closehauled course if beating (or her sail is filled if not beating). A boat that is tacking must keep clear of a boat on a tack, and it's a common mistake for a beginning racer to feel he is being fouled by a boat who intends to tack and turns as if to tack. However, until head-to-wind, the skipper of the other boat is only luffing, and if he has luffing rights (discussed later) he is not fouling the other boat, even if he forces her to change her course.

Another common error in this regard occurs when two boats converge on the same tack. If the leeward boat does not have luffing rights, she is not allowed to luff and must sail a straight course. Since this may still be a collision course with the windward boat, the latter often feels put upon by a boat without luffing rights and calls out for the leeward boat to stop luffing. Remember that a prerequisite for luffing is "altering course toward the wind," and when the leeward boat is not sailing above her proper course and is only sailing straight ahead, she is not luffing. The rule that applies is "a windward yacht shall keep clear of a leeward yacht."

Bearing Away, Jibing, and On a Tack

Jibing is spelled "gybing" in the rulebook. This variant of the word is most used in Great Britain, but in the U.S. we spell it "jibe." A boat starts to jibe when the foot of her mainsail crosses the centerline. Up to that point, she is just bearing away downwind and maintains her rights as being on a tack. She completes her jibe when the mainsail has filled on the other tack.

A boat is on a tack except when she is actually in the process of tacking or jibing. Thus, a boat on the starboard tack (with right-of-way over a port tack boat) maintains her rights *up to* head-to-wind if tacking, and *until* the main boom crosses the centerline if jibing. However, a boat in the process of tacking or jibing must keep clear of a boat on a tack, so, when the starboard tack boat in our example above passes head-to-wind, she must then keep clear of the port tack boat. A boat is on a tack corresponding to her windward side, so if a boat's starboard side is to windward, she is on the starboard tack.

Leeward and Windward

The leeward side is the side on which the boat is carrying her mainsail or, if head-to-wind, the side on which the mainsail was before heading up. If you're heeling the boat to windward on a light-air run and gravity is causing the boom to swing over, you can hold the boom out and stay on that tack.

Clear Astern, Clear Ahead, Overlap

If you project an imaginary line abeam from the aftermost part of a leading boat, any boat behind that line is clear astern. The leading boat is clear ahead. They overlap if neither is clear astern or an intervening boat overlaps them both. These terms apply only to boats on the same tack, with the exception that boats can be overlapped on opposite tacks when in the process of rounding marks other than when beating.

Proper Course

This is the course a boat might sail in a race in which she was the only competitor racing against the clock. There is no proper course before the starting signal. The "proper course" is mentioned in a number of rules. For instance, a boat on a free leg of the course (a reach or a run) shall not sail below her proper course when she is within three boat lengths of another boat trying to pass to leeward. If she does, in an attempt to blanket the other boat and keep it from passing her, her skipper may have to explain in a protest meeting (if the leeward boat skipper protests) that the course steered was the one that he would have elected to steer, in the absence of the leeward boat, to finish as quickly as possible. The skipper may be justified in not heading directly at the next mark. For instance, there may be a current to stem, shallow water he's heading for in order to get out of the current, or a wind shift expected to be obtained by heading low. The skipper may be heading low early in the leg, expecting the wind to die and allow a faster point of sailing coming up for the mark, or more breeze may be spotted in the area to leeward. There may be any number of reasons why the proper course may not necessarily be the one that takes the boat directly to the next mark.

Mark

A mark is any object specified in the sailing instructions that a boat must round or pass on a required side. If a boat hits a mark, she is out of the race unless she exonerates herself by sailing well clear of all other yachts and, while remaining clear, immediately makes one complete 360° turn including one tack and one jibe. If another boat wrongfully forces her to hit the mark, the skipper can protest and doesn't have to make the penalty turn, but he had better win the protest. If he loses, he'll be out of the race. Some skippers protest *and* make the turn, just to be safe. Ground tackle or anything accidentally or temporarily attached to the mark does not count as part of it.

Further about marks, a boat must pass each one on the required side in the correct sequence, so that a string representing her wake, when pulled taut, will lie on the correct side of each mark. A mark has a required side for a boat only as long as the boat is on a leg which it begins, bounds, or ends. Both these rules came into effect graphically for me during a cruising boat race a few years ago. Figure 125 shows the course as it was meant to be. The mark boat was to be left to port, the buoy to starboard, and thence to the finish. However,

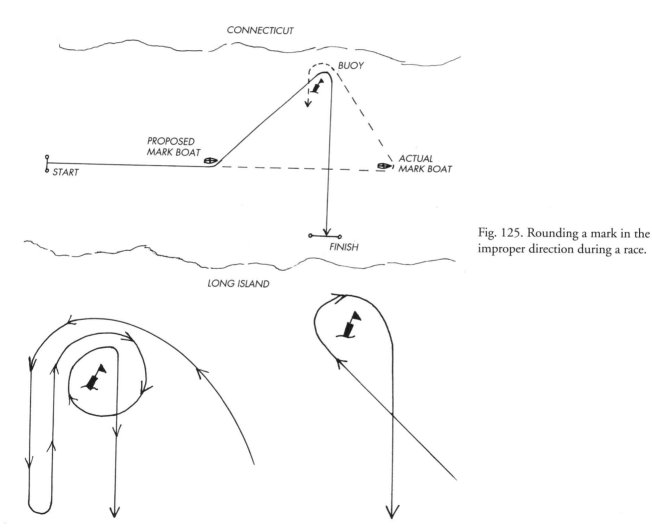

Fig. 125. Rounding a mark in the improper direction during a race.

Fig. 126. This is the method of correcting the error.

Fig. 127. This is the way it was supposed to be rounded.

the mark boat was late getting fueled and by the time it got ahead of the leaders and set an anchor, it was way past the point it should have anchored. We inadvertently sailed the course shown by the dotted lines but immediately realized that we had left the buoy to port instead of to starboard and went back to correct our mistake. First we had to return the way we had come to undo the error and then pass the buoy, leaving it to starboard as in Figure 126. Note that if this were a string, when pulled tight it would look like Figure 127, which was the correct rounding. Now, on the way to the finish we are leaving the mark boat on a different side than the way the race was originally planned, but this doesn't matter since the mark boat is not part of the leg we are sailing.

Obstruction

An obstruction is as it sounds: any object that will cause a boat to make a substantial alteration of course when more than one boat length of it. It can be another sailboat in the race or any object which can be passed one side only. The rules that apply for passing and rounding marks also apply for obstructions.

Other Definitions

We haven't mentioned all of the definitions in Part I, but the few others are not very important. Of interest are some listed in Rule 54. "Pumping," "ooching," and "rocking" are illegal. "Pumping" is the frequent, rapid trimming of sails. It has been made illegal to prevent a crew from "fanning" a boat around a course in light wind days by flapping the sail back and forth like a bird's wing in flight. Repeated jibing or roll tacking (described later) in calm conditions fall in the same category as pumping. "Ooching" is lunging forward and stopping abruptly, and "rocking" is persistently rolling the boat from side to side. These also are methods that develop forward propulsion, but are illegal.

The Right-of-Way Rules
(from Part IV of the Racing Rules)

We have mentioned many times that a starboard tack boat has right-of-way over a port tack boat, a leeward boat over a windward boat, and a boat clear ahead over one clear astern. These are the basic rules. Let's look at some of the more complicated ones.

Luffing after Starting

Probably the rule that causes more confusion than any other is the luffing rule. Luffing after starting is a defensive maneuver to keep a boat from passing you to windward. A leeward boat may luff a windward boat. However, if at any time during the overlap the helmsman of the windward boat is abeam or forward of the mast of the leeward boat, the latter must not sail above her proper course. This precludes the possibility of a leeward boat's catching up from astern, getting her mast forward of the windward helmsman, and then luffing, because when the overlap was established her mast was aft of the windward helmsman.

As the leeward boat legally luffs a windward boat attempting to pass her, the relationship of her mast to the windward helmsman changes. In Figure 128, the mast of boat A is well forward of the helmsman of boat B catching up to windward. As boat A luffs, she finds herself on the outside of a circle and soon the helmsman of boat B is abeam of A's mast. If boat A is in the position indicated by the dotted lines, further away from boat B, the mast abeam position is reached even earlier as A luffs and B responds. One learns through experience that it isn't worth luffing at all if you're too far to leeward of your competitor or if you wait until the overlap is well established. Luff early, close, and decisively to luff effectively and to discourage the windward boat from trying to pass.

When the boats reach the position where the windward boat's helmsman is even with the leeward boat's mast, he should hail "Mast abeam," because without such a hail the leeward boat may assume she still has the right to luff (if there is any doubt).

When "Mast abeam" is called out, the leeward boat must cease luffing and fall back down to her proper course. If she deems the hail to be improper, her only remedy is to protest. While the overlap continues to exist the leeward boat can no longer luff. As the leeward boat falls back off to her proper course, her mast may very well go forward of the windward helmsman since now the

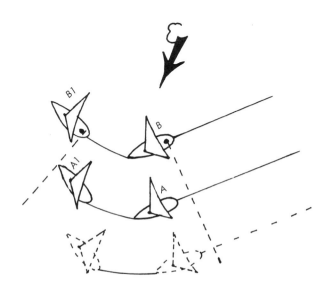

Fig. 128. As one boat luffs another, the "mast abeam" line rotates forward.

leeward boat is on the inside of the turn. Nevertheless, she must not luff again during that overlap. How, then, is the overlap broken?

1. If the windward boat drops back clear astern or goes clear ahead, the overlap is broken. If the windward boat goes clear ahead, luffing rights cannot be regained by the leeward boat when the overlap is reestablished to leeward, because her mast is aft of the windward boat's helmsman. If the overlap is broken by the windward boat's falling clear astern, then the leeward boat can again luff as the windward boat tries to pass her on the windward side.

2. The overlap is broken when the boats are more than two overall lengths of the longer boat apart from one another. Thus, a leeward boat without luffing rights on a reaching or running leg of the course could diverge from the windward boat a few boat lengths and then converge with her again after luffing rights were established (her mast forward of the other's helmsman). In practice this is rarely done deliberately, because if the leeward boat is sailing fast enough to catch up and go through the windward boat to leeward, she hardly needs to luff for protection. Nevertheless, if she decides she wants to get up in front of the windward boat to consolidate her position, she can do so legally.

3. Since overlaps only exist for boats on the same tack (except when rounding marks), the overlap is broken if one or the other tacks or jibes to the opposite tack. It is reestablished as a new overlap when a tack or jibe puts them both on the same tack again. At that point, if the leeward boat's mast is forward of the windward boat's helmsman, she has luffing rights.

4. A new overlap is established for the purposes of this rule when the leeward boat has started and cleared the starting line. If her mast is forward of the windward boat's helmsman, she can luff as she pleases to keep windward from passing her. This brings up the differences between luffing after starting, which we have been discussing so far, and luffing before starting.

After the start, the leeward boat can luff sharply and without warning if she pleases.

Luffing before Starting

A luff before the boat has started and cleared the starting line is covered by a completely different rule. Most importantly, there's no limitation on how the overlap is established. A leeward boat can come from clear astern, create an overlap, and have the right to luff. Unlike the "luffing after starting" rule, she must luff only slowly and must give the windward boat room and opportunity to keep clear. Though she can luff with just an overlap, she may only luff to a closehauled course until her mast is forward of the windward helmsman. At that point she may luff the windward boat head-to-wind. There is no restriction on luffing past closehauled a second, third, or fourth time during the same overlap, as long as each time leeward's mast is forward of windward's helmsman. Whether before or after the start, a boat that luffs must have luffing rights on all boats affected by her luff. All must respond, even boats caught in the middle who would not otherwise be allowed to luff.

Mark-Rounding Rules

The basic purpose of the mark-rounding rules is to allow boats on the inside, near the mark, to round safely without hitting the mark or other boats. "Room" includes room to tack or jibe in order to round the mark. Outside boats, therefore, must give the inside boats such room even if they normally wouldn't have to stay clear. For instance, an outside leeward boat with luffing rights is not allowed to luff the inside boat into the mark. Nor can a starboard tack boat on a run force a port tack boat into a mark. In both cases they must give the inside boat room to round the mark safely.

Obviously there has to be a time when these unusual rights are established. Otherwise the windward boat or the port tack boat might demand them halfway down the leg of the course. So it is written in the rules that the inside boat obtains her right for room at the mark when the outside boat comes within two of her overall lengths of the mark. We call this the two-boat-lengths circle. The inside boat must be overlapped with the outside boat (or overlapped with the intervening boat or boats that overlap the outside boat).

The scenario goes like this: the bow of an inside boat is about even with the stern of an outside boat which has reached the two-boat-lengths circle. The helmsman on the inside calls out for "buoy room" The outside helmsman, if he considers that the boats are not overlapped, may call out "no room" or "no overlap," in which case the inside boat had better swing outside past the stern of the outside boat lest she get squeezed between the mark and outside boat. If she doesn't swing out, but insists on room against the judgment of the outside boat, she will have the responsibility of proving to the Protest Committee that the overlap was established in proper time. This is commonly called the "burden of proof" and is very difficult to overcome. The rule makers assume that the helmsman of the outside boat is in a far better position to see the bow of the inside boat and to know if there's an overlap than vice versa. It is accepted by many, but certainly not all, that if the inside boat swings out immediately after being told "no room" and her bow hits the stern of the outside boat or her spinnaker hits the backstay, there really was overlap and the outside boat was wrong. However, the outside boat must have reached the two-boat-lengths circle before the rule takes effect and such a collision constitutes proof of an overlap.

The burden of proof isn't all one-sided, though. A few years ago, to offset a spate of burden-of-proof rulings against the inside boat, the rules makers came up with another rule. The outside boat must prove that an earlier established overlap she claims to have broken before reaching the two-boat-lengths circle actually was broken in time. Thus, we currently find inside boats trying to establish by hails, well before the circle is reached, that an overlap exists, thereby transferring the onus to the outside boat to prove she broke the overlap in time, if in fact she did.

The plethora of mark-rounding rules is justified when you consider that sailboats may be converging on the mark in a large group at a fast speed. Overlaps are established and broken at a dizzying rate as boats surf and then fall back on waves. The rule takes this into account by granting an inside boat room even though the overlap may be broken inside the two-boat-lengths circle (as long as she had the overlap at the proper time).

Sometimes we run across the situation shown in Figure 129, where the inside boat has not only the right to buoy room, but is also on starboard tack. To keep her from carrying the outside port tack boat way past the mark, another rule states she must jibe at the first reasonable opportunity to assume most directly a proper course to the next mark. The same rule applies to the boats on the same tack, as in Figure 130, if we assume the inside leeward boat does not have luffing rights. However, in Figure 131 the inside boat does have luffing rights and can carry the outside boat past the mark as she pleases.

When two boats on opposite tacks are on a beat, or when one will have to tack to round the mark, the only rules that apply are the starboard/port rule and the rule on changing tacks mentioned before: a boat which is tacking or jibing shall keep clear of a boat on a tack. In order to clarify the changing-tacks rule, let's say that a boat is tacking into a position that will subsequently give her right-of-way to leeward of another boat (windward must keep clear) or

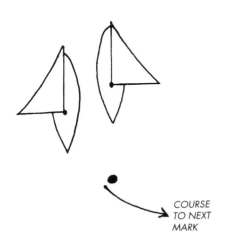

Fig. 129. The boat on starboard tack must jibe at the mark.

Fig. 130. If it has no luffing rights, the leeward boat must jibe at the mark.

Fig. 131. With luffing rights the leeward boat may jibe when she pleases.

in front of another boat (the boat clear astern must keep clear of a boat clear ahead). She must complete her tack before the other boat has to alter course to avoid a collision. The onus is on the tacking boat to prove that she completed her tack early enough. If beating, she only has to get to a closehauled course, but after a tack she has slowed down so much that an overtaking boat can catch up in a matter of seconds. It is very easy for the overtaking boat to win the protest if it's a close call. So, near the weather mark, two boats beating on opposite tacks really act as if the mark isn't there. If, however, they approach on the same tack, the same overlap and room requirements mentioned before apply.

There are many other rules, but the ones above are those that come into play most often on the race course. New, simplified rules are being tested and may be adopted in 1997. Look for them, as they change many of the rules I've described here.

◆ 6 ◆

Tactics

Clear Air and Covering

Once the starting gun has fired, getting and keeping clear air becomes of prime importance. Wind in the proximity of a starting line is always chopped up by the other boats, so those that get away from the starting area into clear air first will be able to stretch their lead. If you find yourself boxed in between boats to windward and leeward of you, get out of there! This may mean killing your speed, if necessary, so that you can let the windward boat pass. Then you can tack and cross under its stern.

Clear air is important anywhere on the course, but particularly so near the start. Figure 132 shows the various zones of disturbed air coming from a sailboat. The shadings indicate the intensity of the effect. The darker the area, the more detrimental it is for you to be there.

The distance the disturbed air extends to leeward and astern will depend on the wind conditions. As a general rule, air is disturbed at a greater distance in light air than it is in heavy. You probably will be affected adversely by a boat two to four lengths to windward in heavy air, but it can run up to seven lengths in light air.

The worst area is the blanket zone, where a boat is ahead and upwind of you. Boat B is in boat A's blanket zone in Figure 132. Most of the diagrams I've seen show this zone as a cone flowing straight to leeward of the windward boat's sails, and though this is technically correct, I prefer to show it as a curve. For some reason, possibly having to do with the fact that the apparent wind is further aft at the top of the mast than at the bottom, a curve seem better to depict what actually happens on the boat. This will become appar-

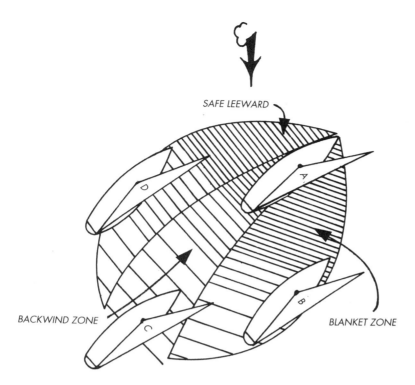

Fig. 132. The "bad air" areas in sailing.

ent if you've ever been on a large cruising boat on a beam reach and have passed a small boat to leeward of you. Your bow must be well past his bow before you cause him to straighten up. If you're racing a class boat and are trying to hurt a competitor on a reach, you'll find it insufficient to have your masthead fly pointing at his mast. You will probably have to get well past him, so that your fly points ahead of his bow, before the large lower part of your sail area has any effect on him. Once you do get a boat in your blanket zone, however, he will drop back quickly.

When closehauled, a boat behind or slightly to leeward will be in the backwind zone. Though this is bad position to be in, it's not as harmful as being blanketed and you won't drop back as fast. Still, the turbulent airflow you are receiving from the other boat's sail is usually sufficient to necessitate a tack to clear your air. Boat C is in A's backwind in Figure 132.

The safe leeward zone is just to windward of the backwind zone. A boat sailing in this area generally will not be able to pass to windward of the leading boat. The lead boat has what is called a "safe leeward position," and as the wind hits the sails of the lead boat, it is bent aft, causing the boat in the safe leeward zone to be sailing in an apparent header. The wind is more on the bow than it is for the lead boat. In this situation, the boat is affected more by a change in wind direction than it is by turbulence. Boat A has a safe leeward position on boat D in Figure 132. An aggressive sailor will try to slow other boats in a race by keeping all these zones in mind and using them properly.

Because there are many potential winners in a race and you can't slow them all, you should only cover those who might provide a serious threat to your own position. The basic rule in all covering situations is to stay between your competition and the mark.

If you are headed for the windward mark and you tack hard on the wind of a competitor, placing him in your blanket zone, he will be forced to tack away. To cover him, you will have to tack as well. This is called a "close cover," and should be used only when you want a competitor to tack. A loose cover is one where you allow your competitor to have free air so he won't be inclined to tack away.

The close cover is used when a rival is sailing away from the desired side of the course or away from a group of boats you should cover. Here, it is important to force him to tack. In effect, you shepherd him back in the desired direction. A loose cover can be used when the rival boat is on the tack on which you want to remain.

Breaking a close cover depends a great deal on the exact positions of the boats. Let's assume you are sailing bow to bow on port tack with a boat just to weather of you. You are both approaching the layline, the imaginary line which takes you to the mark on the other tack without having to tack again. He has you pinned, and every time you bear off to try and get tacking room, he bears off too.

If you have luffing rights, a sharp luff head-to-wind can do wonders. But make sure you ease your jib so that it doesn't back you over onto the other tack (particularly important with a genoa). You may very well catch him enough by surprise that he will fail to ease his jib in time. The result will be that he will fall off on the other tack short of the layline. You can now go on until you reach the layline and starboard tack him near the mark when you come together again (assuming marks are rounded to port).

However, a luff may be impossible if you are well to leeward and behind. Here, a series of tacks may just discourage the boat covering especially if the skipper feels they are losing ground to other boats by engaging in this private tacking duel. If the covering skipper is not discouraged, which would be the case if you are the only boat that poses an immediate threat, or if it's a match race series, a "false" tack can sometimes work. This tack is executed exactly like a tack up to the head-to-wind point, but at that point you fall back on the original tack.

Your crew must know that the tack will be a false one, but must make it appear to be authentic by freeing the jib, crossing the boat, and doing whatever else is normally done on the boat during a tack. Hopefully, an overanxious coverer will tack too quickly and, after completing the tack, will have to regain speed in order to tack back again.

A false tack rarely works when the covering boat's crew is looking for it and is prepared to delay their tack until your intentions are obvious. In that case, you had better complete your own tack, because any hesitation when head-to-wind will cause you to lose ground. Theatrical acting, along with a louder than usual "ready about," rarely works either, although some sailors try it.

If you are still unable to shake clear of the covering boat and you are approaching the layline to leeward and behind the covering boat, your only hope is that they will overstand (go past the layline). If they are so intent on covering you, they may not notice that they are on the layline. The proper thing to do is to keep on going. Don't tack until the covering boat tacks. Pinch your boat to get as far to windward as possible. This will slow you down, and your coverer may become gleeful at how badly he's "hurting" you and how much he's pulling ahead.

Actually, the further he goes, the greater the distance he sails away from the mark. Figure 133 shows B pinching with A footing out. At position 1, A is closer to the mark and, because A is on the layline, she will obviously beat B to the mark. At position 2, however, B is closer to the mark (the dotted radius lines) and when they tack, B will have at least an inside overlap at the mark, which basically means that she has taken over the lead. B may even be totally clear ahead of A, and though it is possible for A (on a broader reach) to pass B if they are planing boats, getting A to overstand is the only chance B has to gain the lead in this situation.

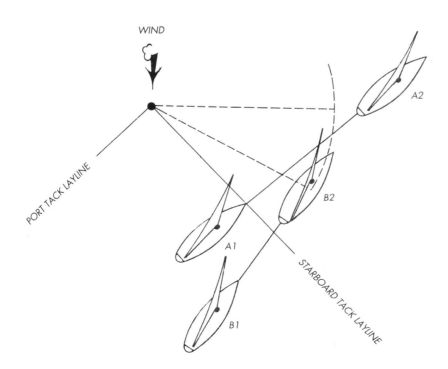

Fig. 133. Overstanding a mark can be a grave mistake for a windward boat covering a leeward one.

Opportunities for breaking cover sometimes will appear as some problem aboard the covering boat. You may round a leeward mark behind and want to tack, but you know that if you do, you will be covered by the lead boat. Wait until their crew is engrossed in some problem or action, and then tack. If crew members on the other boat are up on the foredeck getting the spinnaker pole down, that is the time to tack away. Always try to tack when their attention is focused on something else.

Another way to break a cover is to get a third boat to run interference. If you are being covered, you may see another boat, possibly in another class up ahead. Time your tack so that if the covering boat tacks when you do, she will be sailing right up the backwind of the disinterested third boat. When they realize their mistake, they will have to tack away and you'll have broken the cover. Tugboats, their tows, fishing boats, or anything else that will take a substantial alteration of course to avoid can be used to benefit in breaking cover.

Wind Shifts

More can be gained or lost in one healthy wind shift than can usually be made up by any amount of boat speed or superior sailing. But a beginning racing skipper often is so concerned about whether his boat is sailing faster than the one next to him that he neglects to consider the effect of wind shifts. He fails to recognize them when they arrive and doesn't know how to handle them properly.

However, discussing any wind shift with a skipper who can't steer within 10° of a closehauled course (because he's too worried about other boats) is useless. Half the time, the boat is either luffing or hard and a shift is not noticed even if it is 20°! So a basic premise is that one must at least be able to sail the boat well enough to know that a luff can indicate a large wind shift, and is not caused by erratic steering.

How do we determine a shift? Many people use landmarks, but this is only good for short runs, in fact only for one tack. Once a boat has tacked twice, the angle to the landmark is different and is no longer reliable.

For boats having compasses, a crew member should continuously call the compass readings. A skipper can get confused about just which way the wind has shifted. As a memory aid, make two assumptions: (1) that a boat on starboard tack is superior to a boat on port tack, and (2) that a lift is better than a header. Thus, on the starboard tack the higher the numbers (indicating a lift), the better off you are, but on the port tack the higher numbers are bad. This may be a little oblique but it can tend to eliminate confusion. Thus, if you are sailing 275° on starboard tack and a short time later the crew calls out 280°, you have been lifted. On port tack you have, of course, taken a header.

A third way to determine wind shifts is by your relative position to other boats. This is used most often on single-handed small boats, that either don't carry compasses or are bouncing around too much for them to be dependable. Of course, the skipper of a single-handed boat doesn't have a crew to read compass headings to him.

In Figure 134, the two boats, A and B, are abeam of each other. In Figure 135, the wind has headed the boats and A has "shot" ahead, even though the distance between the boats hasn't changed (note the dotted line through the mast). In Figure 136, both have been lifted and B is well ahead of A.

If you're sailing A in Figure 135, it's quite easy to attribute the sudden lead to superior helmsmanship, some extra little trim on the mainsheet, or a minor

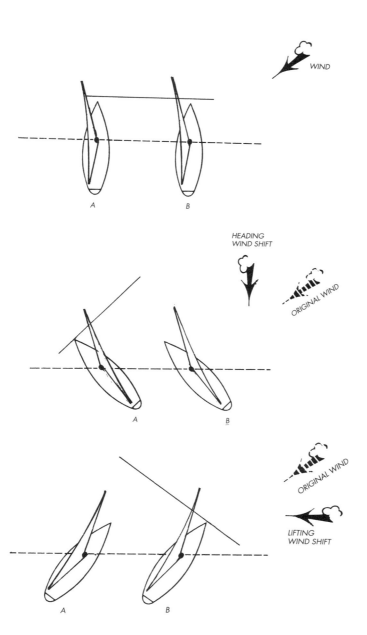

Figs. 134–136. Wind shifts change the relative positions of boats sailing close together.

adjustment to the traveler. In fact, anything that suits the ego will do except the real reason—that you've both been headed and you ought to tack.

Why should you tack in a header? The classic description of why one tacks in headers can be shown by exaggeration. Imagine a wind that's shifting back and forth from NE to NW. The boat in Figure 137 tacks on headers and is on port tack in the NW wind. When the wind heads him, he tacks to starboard and is on starboard tack in the NE wind. The boat in Figure 138 tacks on lifts. He is on starboard tack in the NW wind and port in the NE wind. One can see that the boat which tacks in headers is sailing straight up the course toward the windward mark while the other is sailing back and forth across the course. This never happens to such extremes, but the same occurs in small wind shifts with small gains and losses.

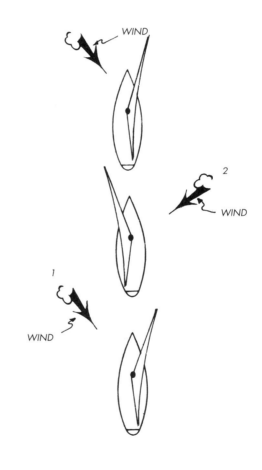

Fig. 137. A boat that tacks when headed sails more toward an upwind destination.

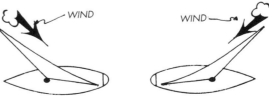

Fig. 138. A boat that tacks in every lift goes nowhere.

For this reason, given the choice between the two boats shown in Figure 134, a novice skipper would usually elect to be on boat B. Not only is he to windward of the other boat, but if a lift comes, he goes well ahead of A. This is called being on the inside of a lift. The only hitch is that if the wind continues to shift in the same direction (see Figure 139), every time the skipper wants to tack to lay the windward mark he gets lifted more and, as a result, cannot lay it. Most racing skippers call this "sailing the great circle route." Instead of gloating over how they are putting it to boat A (see Figure 136), the crew of boat B should be concerned that this may be a permanent shift to the right (see Figure 139). Perhaps they should tack when they get further lifted at point B. If they had tacked at point B, taken their beating (sailing in a header), and tacked again at point C when they were headed further, they would have come out far better in the long run.

It's this very problem that makes boat A's position (in Figure 134) slightly superior. If permanently lifted, they are more apt to tack away from B and get on the proper side of the shift. If headed, A is ahead of B, remains ahead after tacking, and increases its lead as the wind lifts A up to the mark.

Boats are even with each other upwind if they are all on a line perpendicular to the wind direction—the "line of equal position." In Figure 140, boats A, B, and C are all equally upwind. If either A or B tacked, they would meet C bow to bow. None is ahead of the others. Boat D, however, is tail-end Charlie, well behind and to leeward. Along comes a backing wind shift (see dotted lines). If lines of equal position are drawn perpendicular to the new

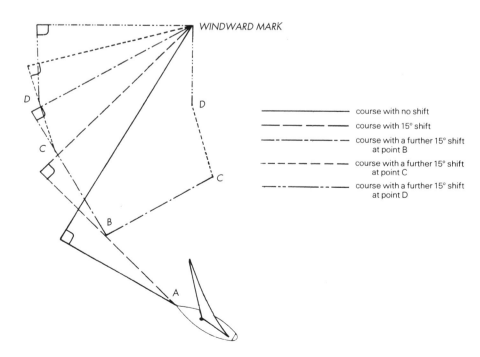

WINDWARD MARK

————————	course with no shift
— — — — — —	course with 15° shift
—·—·—·—·—	course with a further 15° shift at point B
– – – – – –	course with a further 15° shift at point C
—··—··—··	course with a further 15° shift at point D

Fig. 139. Sailing a "great circle" in a continuing lift.

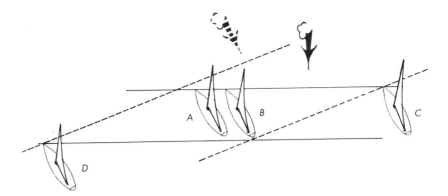

Fig. 140. The boat the greatest distance toward the next wind shift gains the most when it comes.

wind direction, we see that tail-end Charlie, boat D, now leads the fleet, with boat A in second place, B third, and C running a poor last. Therefore, if you expect a header, for some meteorological or geographical reason, always sail to the side of the course it is expected to come from.

Laylines

Though a great deal of importance is always placed on getting a good start, making the turn at the windward mark, which is often more congested than the start, is usually overlooked.

One universal comment made concerning the windward mark approach is "never get to the layline too early." The layline is the imaginary line on which a boat can reach a mark without having to tack again. Any boat that goes past this imaginary line has "overstood" the mark and will have to ease sheets and reach down for it. If you are a few hundred yards from the mark, it is practically impossible to judge accurately whether or not you can lay it. If you've gone too far, you have overstood and wasted distance. If you haven't gone far enough, you will have to tack twice again.

However, even if you've judged the layline accurately, a wind shift can hurt you. In Figure 141, boat, A is on the layline and boat B is the same linear distance away from the mark. But a header (W_2) places the boats in positions A_2 and B_2. Boat B is now well ahead of A. Or a lift (W_8) causes A to overstand the mark and have to reach down for it while boat B can practically lay it from a much shorter distance out. Another disadvantage of getting to the layline early concerns the possibility that boats which are ahead of you will reach the layline first, tack in front of you, and give you bad air all the way to the mark.

The best approach is: hit the starboard tack layline (for a port rounding) only four to ten boat lengths from the mark, depending on the size of the fleet. The larger the fleet, the further out from the mark you have to be, because

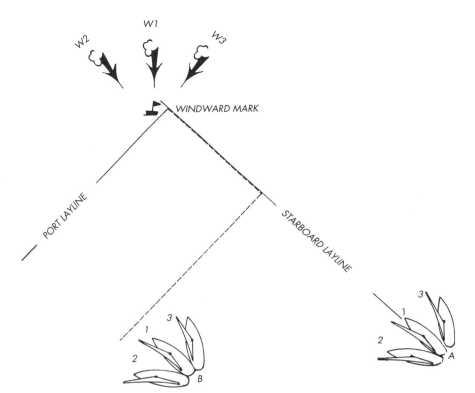

Fig. 141. Never get to a layline too early. You lose on any wind shift.

of congestion. You can usually find a hole to tack into, because as boats tack on the layline they tend to stack up to windward. Either they overstand or pinch up to avoid being directly behind another boat in his backwind.

If you are close to the mark, you can probably tack right behind one boat and on the lee bow of another (Figure 142). Even though you may have to duck under a few sterns to find a hole, generally you can gain many more boats than by getting to the layline early. One disadvantage to this approach, even though it is a slight one, is the lack of time available on the starboard tack to prepare for a spinnaker set. This may not be terribly important on a small boat, but as the boat gets larger, more time is needed.

The beginning racing sailor often makes the mistake of concentrating on the mark. I call it "mark fixation." As he approaches the mark, the novice will get on the layline quite a distance out. Then, because of current or windshift, the layline changes. When this happens, the boat is either overstanding or not making the mark. But because the beginner is steering for the mark and not by the wind, he will either bear off without adjusting sheets or pinch.

With a current setting the boat to leeward, I've often seen skippers pinch (sail close to a luff) more and more as they approach the mark until they're right next to it. By pinching they have lost speed, are now in irons, and drift

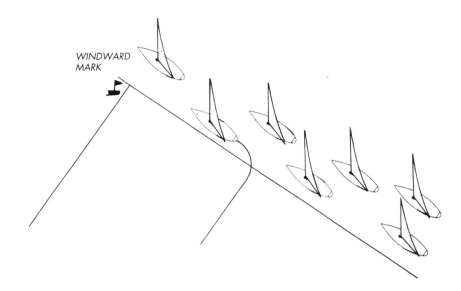

Fig. 142. There are many advantages (and a few disadvantages) to approaching the layline near the windward mark on port tack.

WINDWARD
MARK

into the mark. They don't realize what they are doing until the very end, and then do not have enough forward motion to tack.

When you have tacked for the mark from a good distance out, ignore the mark until getting close. Have your crew tell you if you need to ease off or if you're not making it. Take two extra tacks if necessary, though you may be able to shoot head-to-wind at the last moment to round it if you have good boat speed. Once you pinch, though, you're dead.

"Tacking lines" are often painted on the decks of racing sailboats by their skippers. If you are approaching the starboard tack layline on port tack from a distance out, you can judge when the mark comes in line with the painted line. If a boat tacks in 90°, the line would be painted on the deck perpendicular to the centerline of the boat. If it can tack in less than 90°, the line would point more toward the bow of the boat.

Many skippers paint additional lines on their deck to help them judge whether or not they are ahead of other boats. Look at Figure 143. The crew of boat B sights along the forward leeward line and can see that A is forward of the line and therefore is ahead. The angle these lines make with the bow of the boat is determined by how close to the wind the boat sails. The crew of boat A can quickly see, by sighting along the after windward line, that they are ahead of boat B. They can also see that they are on the layline to the mark. These lines are similar to the "lines of equal position" mentioned earlier.

Such lines are used as a rough guide, and only hold true if (1) the skipper is right on the wind when the sighting is taken, (2) there is no wind shift, (3) there is no current, and (4) the boat will point as high on one tack as it will on the other, which is a rare occurrence unless the seas and the wind are running parallel.

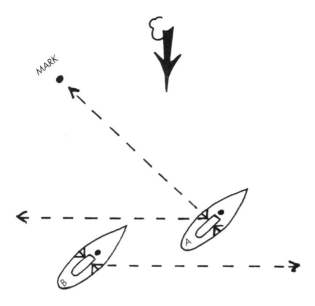

Fig. 143. Lines painted on the deck can aid in determining the layline, and whether the competition is ahead or behind.

If you are sailing closehauled on port tack toward the starboard tack layline and you pass under the stern of a starboard tack boat, often you can see how far he is from laying the mark and can estimate how much further you yourself have to go. This can be done with accuracy only if you make your sighting just as his headstay and mast line up. Be aware that a foxy competitor may head down just at that moment to make you believe he is far from laying the mark to trick you into overstanding.

One of the worst mistakes, and one frequently made by beginning racing sailors, is to be surprised by a starboard tack boat at or near the layline as the former approaches it on port tack. You should always be looking for right-of-way boats when you are sailing on port tack, but particularly so near the layline. If you are surprised by a "starboard" hail, and you have to do a panic tack to starboard, the other boat will most likely ride right over you before you pick up speed. This will slow you enough for other boats on the layline to pass you.

It's also very possible that you won't fetch the mark because of the leeway you will make by being slowed down by other boats. You must be aware of the starboard boat early enough to make the decision either to tack, if you feel he is laying the mark and you can get a safe leeward position on him, or to go under his stern if he isn't laying. If you decide on the latter, then bear off early and substantially, easing both jib and mainsheets as you do, and aim your bow at his stern. As he passes, you should be coming up and trimming in both the main and jib sheets for acceleration.

We mentioned earlier that by taking compass bearings on the other boat you can determine if you are on a collision course. If the bearing doesn't change and you are converging, eventually you will collide. By the way, the bearing doesn't change if two boats are sailing parallel courses at the same speed, so competitive racers use bearings to compare speed, with increases shown in bearing changes. If you are on port tack, you can determine without a compass whether a starboard tack boat is on a collision course with you by watching the land in the distance behind him. If the land doesn't move relative to his boat, watch out! But if the land is disappearing behind his sails, he is "making land" on you and will pass ahead of you. Or, conversely, if he is falling back on the land (giving the appearance of sailing backward vis-à-vis the land behind him), you will cross in front of him. This method is simple, really works, and I recommend it highly.

Often novice racers wonder why they can't luff up to kill their speed a little and then pass under the stern of a right-of-way boat slightly more to windward. They feel that the more to windward one gets, the better it is. The answer is that one's position is being controlled by the starboard tack boat, and whether a port tack boat passes a foot further to leeward or a foot further to windward, he is still a foot from the other fellow's stern.

If you do bear off, it is a good idea to yell: "Hold your course, I'm going under you." This has no basis in the rules, but the other skipper may not know this or may have to take time to think about it. Legally, he can ignore the hail and tack right on top of you, as long as he keeps clear of you as he does. However, since you have passed his stern before he tacked and are sailing fast, you have a good chance at achieving a safe leeward position on him. Always keep in mind, as you approach a starboard tack boat, that when you reach the mark you will want to starboard tack him. You can't afford to be pinned down short of the mark, so it's crucial to judge whether or not he is laying it.

Another mistake often made by a beginning racing sailor is to be so ecstatic by having starboard tack right-of-way over a port tack boat that he always yells "starboard." There are times, particularly when one is on the starboard tack layline, that such a hail is detrimental. The port tack boat, if it is close to crossing, will be feeding you backwind after the tack. Because you are already on the layline, you can't tack away and make a gain. A better hail is "Go across, you can make it." That way, the port tack boat might go far enough past not to bother you when he does tack, and he might even overstand the mark!

Mark Rounding

The important part of rounding a mark is your position not at the time of rounding, but about one minute later. You must anticipate where the other boats are going to end up after they round the mark, and what effect they will have on you. Your own rounding must take their movements into account and minimize their impact on you.

Though you can pretty much choose how you want to round a leeward mark, your options are more limited when rounding a windward mark. However, there are several alternatives. If you've overstood, you may want to reach down to the layline outside the two-boat-lengths circle in order to break any possible overlap you might have created while reaching.

Let's look at the mark-rounding rule again. An outside boat must give room to round the mark to any boat that is overlapped on the inside providing that overlap was established by the time the outside yacht comes within two of her own boat lengths of the mark. For clarity we draw a "two-boat-lengths circle" in diagrams describing the rule. Boats are overlapped if neither is clear astern or clear ahead. One is clear astern (and the other is clear ahead) when she's abaft an imaginary line projected abeam from the aftermost point of the other's hull with equipment in normal position.

Figure 144 shows boat A with an inside overlap on boat B. But the overlap is broken when the boats arrive at positions (A_2 and B_2, because boat B now has hardened up for the mark. If B had continued to head straight to the mark from the overstanding position, her angle would have kept A in an overlapped position.

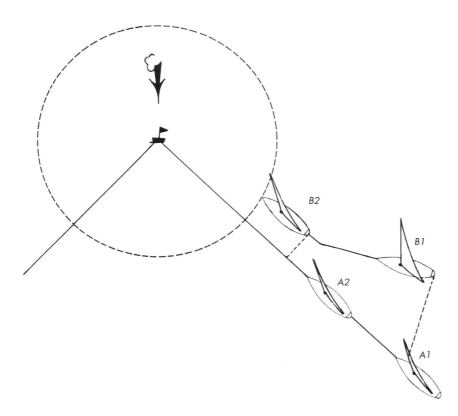

Fig. 144. An overlap can be broken by an approach like the one shown.

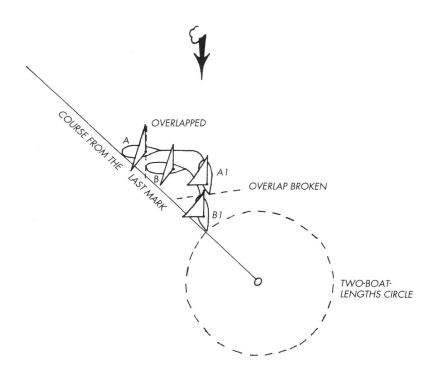

Fig. 145. An overlap can be broken by a sharp luff followed by a dip to the two-boat-lengths circle.

On the second reach of a triangular course with marks to port, the overlap can be broken in the same manner (see Figure 145). Boat B sails high of the course on port tack and holds boat A up. As they both head off for the mark at the two-boat-lengths circle, the perpendicular off boat B's stern rotates forward and the overlap is broken.

Another situation occurs on the weather leg when B is near the port tack layline and has A behind and to windward (as in Figure 146). When B reaches the two-boat-lengths circle, A is not overlapped and not entitled to room. Only the basic port/starboard, windward/leeward, and tacking-too-close rules apply. So, though A can't demand room, she can keep B from tacking around the mark until she tacks (if A merely sails straight ahead). However, B does have one recourse. Because she isn't tacking until she is past head-to-wind, B simply luffs right up next to the buoy. A can't afford to luff because she will find herself on the wrong side of the mark, so she dips under B's stern. At that point, B completes her tack around the mark, and goes into the lead.

The situation can be slightly different. When boat B approaches the two-boat-lengths circle, she is slightly overlapped by boat A. A good tactic for B is to luff A sharply, provided, of course, she has luffing rights. This can often break the overlap by the time the two-boat-lengths circle is reached.

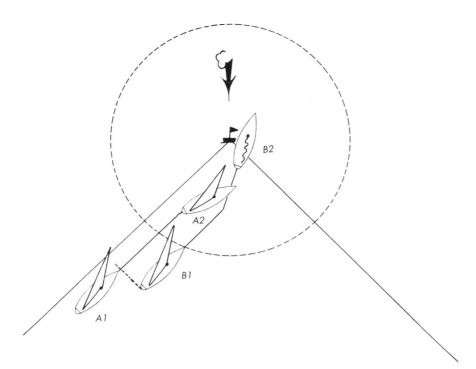

Fig. 146. A luff before tacking can discourage a windward boat from preventing the tack.

Remember that if two boats on a beat are approaching the mark on opposite tacks, the rules that apply stand as though the mark weren't there. Don't, for example, tack right between a starboard tack boat and the mark and claim room while luffing, unless you can get completely over to a closehauled course on starboard and then luff up to get around the mark. You have to complete your tack before you have the right to luff a windward boat, and you never have the right to room if the other boat is unable to give it. If you tack and luff too quickly for the other boat to respond, and you hit the mark because of it, that's your tough luck.

Windward Mark Rounding to a Run

One of the most important immediate decisions when heading off downwind is which jibe to take first. If the wind is parallel to the course of the downwind leg and the weather mark is left to port, the safest and most natural first tack is to starboard. Since you will come around the mark on starboard, the spinnaker should be ready for setting on that tack. A jibe to port and then a spinnaker set is a more complicated maneuver. There are other difficulties with a quick jibe to port after rounding: (1) if it's a large fleet, you will be sailing in the disturbed air to leeward of all the boats on the starboard tack layline to the mark; (2) you don't have right-of-way on any closehauled boat—a leeward port tack boat has right-of-way over you because you're to windward, and a starboard tack boat has right over you because you're on port; (3) you are sailing toward a more congested area of right-of-way boats which are approaching the starboard tack layline; (4) if you are prepared for a port tack spinnaker set, you have to get on port to set. A boat on starboard tack inside of you at the mark can keep you from jibing, since he's leeward boat, until he has set his spinnaker on starboard tack and sailed merrily ahead of you. At that point you can jibe and set, but you have lost distance.

However, if the wind has gone clockwise on the beat, a port tack run becomes necessary and the longer you stay on starboard the further you sail at an angle away from the next mark instead of toward it. On the beat, based on your closehauled compass headings, determine whether the wind is to the right or the left of the course and set up for the spinnaker accordingly.

When the wind is oscillating back and forth, great gains can be made over the competition on a run by playing the wind shifts. On a beat, you gain by *tacking in headers.* When running, you gain by *jibing in lifts.* Photo 142 shows a type of masthead fly that is very helpful in determining wind shifts while running. The arrow tails are at a fixed angle and the centerline of the boat bisects that angle. Line up the rotating wind fly with one fixed arrow tail, as in the photo, which indicates a starboard tack run. Glance at your compass and get your heading. While keeping the masthead fly lined up with the tail, if the compass indicates you are sailing higher than before (more toward the original wind), you are being lifted and should jibe. On the run, when the

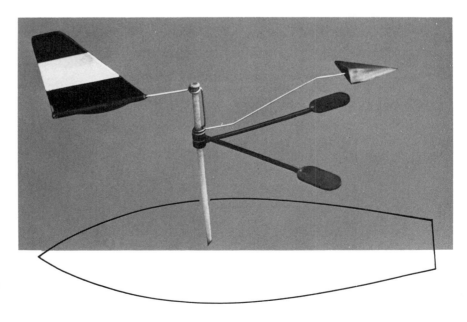

142. A helpful masthead fly for tacking downwind.

wind comes forward toward a reach, the boat sails faster. When the wind shifts aft, the boat speed lessens. In other words, the boat sails faster in headers than in lifts. For that reason, by jibing every time you get lifted, rather than following the lift toward the wind, you will be sailing more toward your destination. Figure 147 shows boat A on a port tack run heading up on every lift. Boat B jibes on every lift and sails more toward the desired destination. Boat A could have sailed straight, but would sail much slower during each lift.

Even if there are wind shifts to play, a common technique practiced in light air is "tacking downwind." It is called "tacking" because the boat is zigzagging back and forth much like beating, even though each zigzag is actually a jibe. By heading up from a dead run, a sailboat will sail faster. Air starts to flow over the lee side of the main and spinnaker, creating a suction and making their aerodynamic shapes work. However, if your destination is dead downwind, extra distance must be covered.

Look at Figure 148. Boat A sails straight downwind to the mark. Boat B sails 25° higher, on a reach, jibes halfway down the leg, and converges on the mark on starboard tack. It should be noted here that when the two-boat-lengths circle is reached at a leeward mark, it doesn't matter whether a boat is on starboard or port tack. The inside boat has right to buoy room if overlapped. Boat B has to cover slightly over 11% greater distance than A. Thus

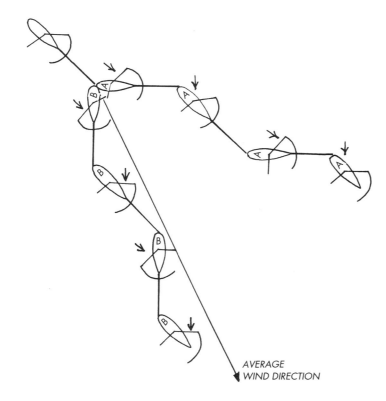

AVERAGE
WIND DIRECTION

Fig. 147. Jibe on lifts.

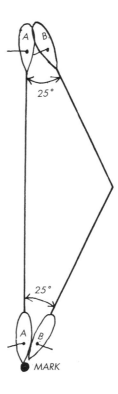

Fig. 148. Tacking downwind.

B must sail 11% faster than A to reach the mark at the same time. If A is sailing at 3 knots in a light breeze, B only has to sail at about 3.3 knots. Since B is heading up at a large angle, 25°, substantial increase of speed will probably result, possibly to 4 knots or more, and B will easily beat A. At higher initial speeds, as in heavy weather, it is more difficult for B to increase speed enough to cover the extra distance sailed. Boat A could be traveling at close to maximum speed, say 9 knots. Boat B would have to sail at close to 10 knots, which would be well nigh impossible in heavy winds on a reach. So in light winds, tack downwind; in heavy wind, just play the shifts.

Windward Mark Rounding to a Reach

As you round a windward mark and head off on a reach, a lot depends on whether you have strong competition right on your heels. If so, a sharp luff is apt to discourage a boat astern from trying to pass to windward. If you have to hold low for the next mark, the trailing boat may delay his spinnaker set, assuming, of course, you're racing sailboats with spinnakers.

No matter how efficient your own crew work is, setting a spinnaker will slow you up slightly. The trailing skipper will set his sails for a reach, hike out hard, and concentrate on boat speed in an attempt to get on your wind. Once he's there and hurting you, he can set his own spinnaker at his leisure and still control you. You can't luff beneficially because you have your spinnaker set and he has none. Your only defense is to anticipate his intentions and not set until he does.

The decision whether to go high or low on the first reach should be made at the time you round the mark. There are many factors. If you expect the wind to increase, you can go high early in the light air for better boat speed and come down later in the leg when the wind is strong enough to maintain speed on a freer point of sail. If the wind is light but the current is strong, it's mandatory to stay upcurrent in case the breeze continues to drop.

If the wind is gusty, head down in the puffs and up in the lulls. When beating, we head up in the puffs to reduce heeling, but downwind or reaching it's the opposite. Heading up can cause a broach. Moreover, by heading down you are traveling in the direction of the gust and staying in it a longer period. Heading down when it's blowing hardest may also help you get on a plane if you are sailing a planing-type hull, or a surf if the waves are high. In the lulls, head high of the mark to make up the distance you went to leeward of the straight-line course in the puffs. On most boats, you will be sailing faster or at least just as fast by heading high in the lulls.

The fastest course in gusty wind conditions on the reaching leg, therefore, will be a series of wiggles to windward and to leeward of the straight-line course (the rhumb line).

Even on light days a good racing sailor heads off when the puff comes and up in the lulls on reaches and runs. In this case, the process is called "ventilating." When you head up, airflow is able to get around to the lee side of the main and spinnaker rather than the two being in a stalled condition. The sails come to life and the boat starts moving. Once the momentum is built up, it remains for awhile as you head back downwind. When the momentum and the breeze die, head up and ventilate the sails again for speed. Most important, think ahead to the next mark so that you end up on the inside of your competitors with buoy room on them.

On the first reach of a triangular course leaving marks to port, to be inside at the mark requires sailing low of the competition. There's an added advantage that at the end of the leg you will be sailing on a higher, and therefore faster, angle toward the mark. If any boat has sailed lower on the leg than you did and is even but not ahead of you, when you head up for the mark you will break the overlap he needs at the two-boat-lengths circle to demand buoy room (note Figure 149). Boats that held high on the leg must come down for the mark on a slower point of sailing.

If you do find yourself on the outside of a bunch of boats at the jibing mark, consider slowing the boat down, jibing early, and crossing their sterns to get inside and to windward on the next leg.

To slow the boat on a reach, luff the sails, collapse the spinnaker, and head up. On a run, trim the main amidships and collapse the spinnaker. When

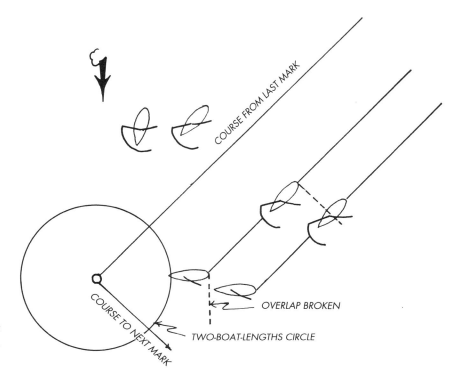

Fig. 149. Sailing low on the first reach can sometimes be beneficial.

COURSE FROM LAST MARK

COURSE TO NEXT MARK

OVERLAP BROKEN

TWO-BOAT-LENGTHS CIRCLE

closehauled, head up, luff the main and jib, and push the main boom out against the wind. And in all cases steer the boat through a series of sharp S turns.

By slowing up, the overlap is broken and an outside boat is able to jibe over and head for the mark. By the time she gets there, the group should be well past the mark. But even if they aren't, the inside boat will have been kept so close to the mark on the near side by the other boats that when she jibes, she will have rounded quite wide on the other side. This should allow the outside boat room to sneak in.

Even if you aren't entitled to room, it's perfectly legal to take it if there's an opening available. A leeward boat can luff you up into the mark though, so there's an element of risk.

Leeward Mark Rounding to a Beat

Rounding the leeward mark is even more important. If you have a poor leeward mark rounding, you may never recover on the windward leg. Slowing down to break an overlap and then cutting in from the outside is very tricky, and the maneuver has to be started quite early or you will find yourself hard on the wind while you're trying to get inside.

If there is a tremendous jam-up at the leeward mark, often aggravated by light air and an adverse current, sometimes you can stay way wide of the mark and sail right around the fleet on the outside. If you are the inside or the lead boat under these conditions, leave your spinnaker set until the last possible moment.

Probably the most common error made by beginning racing sailors at a leeward mark is to cut the mark too close on the near side (the side of the previous leg). By the time the boat has rounded there's half to three-quarters of a boat length lost to windward, and often even more if the sheets aren't trimmed in snappily.

When one boat makes a sloppy rounding, room is available for another boat, without buoy room rights, to cut inside. Any skipper who rounds poorly will probably find a boat to weather controlling him and keeping him from tacking. If there is a boat dead ahead, he will be slowed down by its back-wind, and the boat to weather will probably sail right past.

The solution is to be prepared for the rounding early, with the spinnaker down, appropriate adjustments reset for windward work, and the crew ready to trim in. When the bow is even with the mark, there should be close to a boat length of open water between it and the mark. As you turn around the mark, you should come onto a closehauled course right next to it. When you are receiving room from outside boats, this can't be done, for they are only required to give you enough room to round safely, not to round in the fashion you'd like.

In Figure 150, boat A is rounding the leeward mark the best way. She loses a little distance as she drifts out, but this is negligible compared to the distance lost to windward when she rounds like boat B. If boat B tries to end up where A is by making a sharper turn, her speed will be decreased because of it and she'll end up making more leeway.

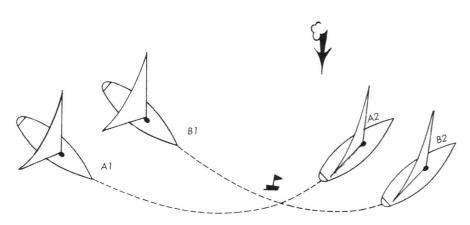

Fig. 150. Much can be lost by a wide mark rounding.

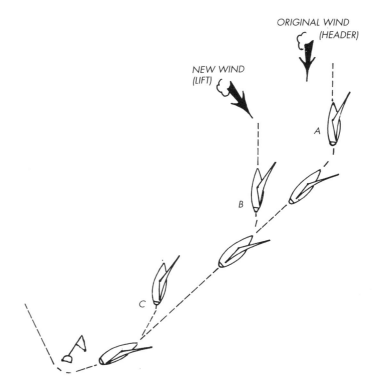

Fig. 151. Never sail off in a header after rounding the leeward mark. Later boats look good when the lift comes.

As soon as you round the leeward mark and go on the wind, it's of crucial importance to know if you're sailing in a header or a lift. Try to remember the port and starboard tack compass heading from the last beat and compare them. If you're sailing in a header, tack immediately. Figure 151 demonstrates through exaggeration what happens when three boats round the leeward mark and sail off in a header. When a lift comes, A looks around and suddenly sees that B and C are sailing up to weather. A can't afford to tack to consolidate (a normal, conservative racing tactic) because the port tack lift is a header on starboard tack. The skipper of A can only hope for a header to return so they can tack, but A has still lost the most because B and C sailed a shorter distance in the header before the lift came.

The Finish

The last few hundred yards upwind to the finish can be crucial. Many boats finish overlapped, and often the difference between winning and losing is a couple of feet—a second or two after hours of racing. As with the start, the finish line may not be absolutely square with the wind direction. If not, the downwind end is the favored end of an upwind finish. In Figure 152, boat A has crossed B on starboard tack. Because the line is not square with the wind,

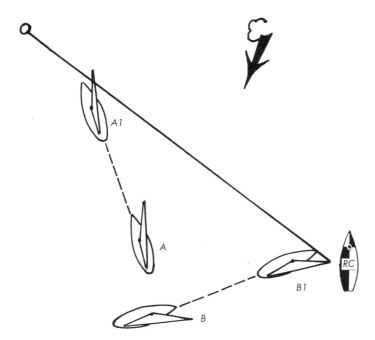

Fig. 152. Sail for the downwind end of the finishing line, as the boat on port tack is doing.

boat A is heading for the upwind end while B is going for the closer, downwind end. At position A₁/B₁ boat B has finished (any part of her hull, crew, or equipment in normal position crossing the line), but boat A, which was ahead of B, has not yet finished. Boat A should have tacked right in front and slightly to windward of B in order to be sure of beating B.

If two boats are approaching the finishing line, as in Figure 153, and one is obviously ahead (boat B, in this case), the other can try the last-ditch tactic of shooting directly into the wind. On displacement keel-boats in moderate

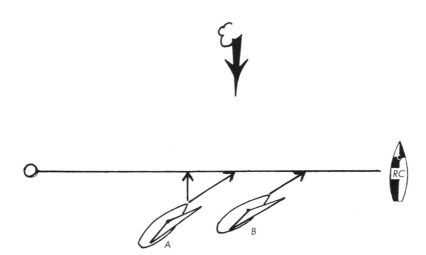

Fig. 153. By shooting into the wind, the windward boat goes a shorter distance and may beat the leeward boat.

winds and seas, not much speed is lost and the difference in distance can be considerable. Boat A shoots directly into the wind, a shorter distance to the line than sailing straight ahead, and beats B across the line. The timing has to be perfect. If you shoot too early, your forward momentum dies before crossing the line; too late, and you lose much of the distance advantage.

It's very hard to judge which end of the line is downwind when you're out there racing. We don't have the advantage we have at the start of being able to get both the compass bearing of the line and the wind. If there are no other boats or undesirable wind shifts to preclude it, the best approach is shown in

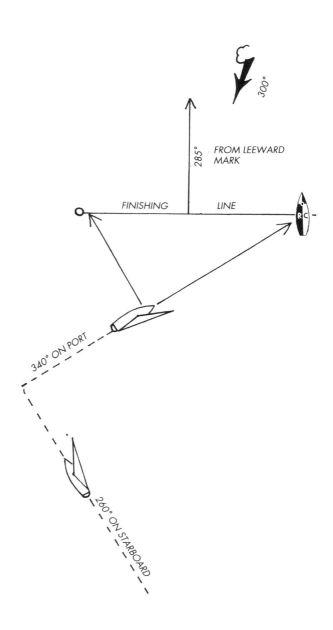

Fig. 154. If the wind has shifted to one or the other side of the course, the opposite end of the line to the shift will probably be downwind if the Race Committee sets the line properly.

Figure 154. When you are on the layline, tack to the committee boat or the buoy end, whichever comes first. When you can sight abeam at the other finishing mark, you are on both laylines simultaneously. Decide which mark appears closer and go for it. In the diagram, the buoy end is closer and the boat should tack for it.

Often, things don't work out so perfectly. Other boats may keep you from tacking when you want to. There are other ways of judging the favored end. Most Race Committees try to make the finishing line a compromise between right angles to the direction of the wind and right angles to the direction of the last leg (note Figure 154). The course from the last mark to the finish is 285°, you are sailing a boat that tacks in 80°, and your compass course on starboard tack is 260°. Therefore, you know the wind is 300°, or 15° to the right of square with the direction of the last leg. Since the line probably has been shifted 7 ½° toward the wind, the left end of the line is downwind and you should sail for it. This system takes faith in the Race Committee's doing things properly, and for that reason is suspect. They may decide to go the full 15° and make it square with the wind. Nevertheless, it is likely that if the wind has shifted to the right, you should finish at the left end of the line. If it has shifted to the left, finish at the right end.

◆ 7 ◆

Wind

Wind is the movement of air. All air movement comes from the fact that hot air rises and that the earth rotates. Without these two factors there would be very little wind on earth. When air is heated, it becomes less dense, lighter, and rises. Cooler, denser air comes in to replace the warm air, and wind is created. On a large scale this happens when air is heated at the equator. In the Northern Hemisphere, cooler air from the north moves in to replace the rising warm air.

If the earth didn't rotate, the resulting wind would be straight from the north. But surface friction from the earth's rotation causes the wind to become more northeasterly in the Northern Hemisphere. This can easily be visualized with the aid of a globe. Place a piece of chalk in the middle of North America and start drawing a line due south. At the same time, rotate the globe counterclockwise (looking down from above) with your other hand. When the chalk line reaches the equator, instead of being straight it will be a diagonal line with a great deal of east-to-west component in it. This rotation is the reason for the various trade winds we have on earth.

On a smaller scale, local winds are caused by local air temperature differentials. Land, for example, is heated up by the sun fast and cools off fast. The sea, however, changes temperature very slowly. When the sun shines brightly in the early spring and warms the land adjacent to a calm cold sea, the air rises over the land and cooler air above the sea moves toward shore to replace it. This is the typical "sea breeze," and occurs in the late morning or early afternoon, depending on the extent of the air temperature differential. In the evening, the reverse happens. The land cools off, and before long the air over land is cooler than the air over the sea. An offshore breeze results.

Since a class racing sailor's activities probably will be during daylight hours, the seabreeze is important. Consider staying near the shore on very light days and picking up a little onshore breeze. You may be laughing at others stuck farther offshore with no wind.

The vagaries of the wind are many, though, and the sailor who hugs the shore could be dismayed to find that others farther out are moving while he's becalmed. This is often caused by "lift-off" of the wind in front of a high shore, as shown in Figure 155. Though the "blanket" effect of such a high shore is obvious when the wind is blowing away from the land (Figure 156), many sailors don't realize how far away from shore the wind can lift off the surface to rise over cliffs when the wind is blowing toward the shore.

Near the shore, wind often has a different direction and velocity because of topographical influences. Wind blowing obliquely toward a high bluff along the shore often tends to parallel the shoreline (Figure 157), while wind blowing obliquely away from the shore tends to bend out at right angles to the shoreline before bending back to its original direction (Figure 158). This change in direction can be very helpful to a racing sailor. A port tack sailed toward the shore will result in a header as the boat gets near it. Then the boat flops to starboard tack and is sailing in a nice lift along the shore. Such a course is shown in Figure 158.

One big problem is to recognize wind. Wind is invisible, but its effect on our surroundings isn't. There are many signs that tell us where, in what direction, and how strong the wind is, or how it might change. Look at the land. Usually there's a smokestack that will show the wind direction and a possible change of direction. Compare the direction the clouds are moving with the surface wind. Given the right conditions, this higher level wind may come down to the surface and change the surface wind direction, as happens in gusts. Because wind aloft more often than not is veered (moves clockwise) in relation to the surface wind, such gusts may also be veered when they hit.

Look at the water surface. On light air days you can see ripples that indicate the presence of wind. Be careful not to confuse ripples caused by current

Fig. 155. The wind lifts in front of a high shore with an onshore breeze.

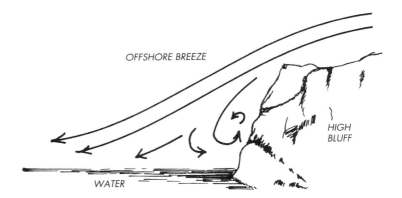

Fig.156. The blanket effect of a high shore with an offshore breeze.

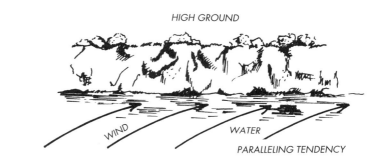

Fig. 157. An oblique onshore wind tends to parallel the shoreline.

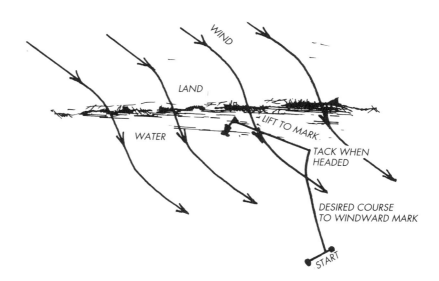

Fig. 158. An oblique offshore wind tends to bend at right angles to the shoreline before resuming its oblique course.

with those caused by wind. Even on windy days such ripples are noticeable on bigger waves and indicate even stronger gusts approaching. Some experienced racing sailors can see these dark patches approaching and can determine whether the gust is going to have an advantageous angle when it arrives. Seeing this takes a keen eye and years of practice, and even then there are only a few who can be so discerning.

Observe other sailboats off in the distance. Their direction and angle of heel can give you information about the wind they have, and what it will be like when it reaches you.

Be aware of tidal current direction. In many bays and sounds, an incoming current can bring in cool water that will set up a even greater temperature differential between the water and land. This, in turn, can set in motion a slight onshore breeze that you might be able to anticipate.

If you are sailing anywhere along the East and West Coasts of the United States in light winds coming from any direction except northwest, north, or northeast, you may expect that as the day goes by there will be a continual wind shift. In more than 50% of the cases, it is a veering shift (clockwise), one to the right as you face the wind. Since you always want to sail toward the next shift when beating, you should be on the right side of the course when the wind shifts so you'll be headed on port tack and have a starboard tack lift to the weather mark. By "right side of the course," we mean to the right of a line drawn from the start to the weather mark. The boat furthest to the right makes out best when the shift comes (unless the shift is so large she overstands the mark on starboard). However, if the shift goes the other way, she also has the most to lose—she's out on a limb, so to speak. When you have no idea what will happen to the wind, it's better to sail near the middle of the course, remembering that the right side will pay off more times than the left.

Be aware of wind shifts caused by fast-moving weather systems. Wind blows clockwise around a high-pressure system and counterclockwise around a low. When looking at a weather map to try to decide which way the wind is going to shift, I find it easier to move my position through the system in the direction opposite to which the system is moving, rather than trying to imagine the system as it moves past my position. Look at Figure 159 showing the winds around a low-pressure area. We expect the low to move to the northeast, in the direction of the arrow, and in twelve hours be at the point of the arrow. We draw a parallel line (dashed) from our position in the opposite direction and the winds we see along the length of the arrow are those we might expect during the next twelve hours. For us, the wind will back from the S and SE to NE and even N as the low passes to the south.

Local geographic and sea breeze influences mentioned above can upset the pattern. The weather system wind is called the "gradient" wind, and the

Fig. 159. Counterclockwise winds around a low-pressure system. Winds move clockwise around a high-pressure system.

closer the isobars (lines of equal pressure) are together, the stronger the gradient wind is. If we have a northerly gradient wind on a hot summer day, and later in the afternoon a southerly sea breeze comes in, they may nullify one another, leaving practically no wind at all. In this case, a racing sailor may try to avoid going for the sea breeze and stay offshore in the gradient wind.

Weather is a subject for many volumes. For a much more thorough study of weather, I recommend William P. Crawford's book *Mariner's Weather*, also published by W. W. Norton.

· 8 ·

The Spinnaker

When to Fly It

The spinnaker adds a great deal of sail area and power to almost any size boat, and an inexperienced skipper and crew inevitably get it all tangled and fouled up at first. For that very reason, it's a challenge to achieve smooth, trouble-free spinnaker work, and there is great satisfaction when the challenge is met.

First, you must always make a decision whether or not to fly the spinnaker at all. Is the wind too heavy or too light? Is the wind too far forward? Is the crew experienced enough? Usually these questions are interrelated. For instance, some spinnakers can be carried to advantage when the apparent wind is well forward on light to medium days (as close as 55° to 60° relative from the bow), but they would cause broaching (rounding up to windward out of control) and weather helm at the same apparent wind angle on heavy days.

The wind strength and direction weigh heavily on the choice of type of chutes, as they are often called (short for "parachute" spinnaker). There are close reaching, reaching, and running chutes. The former are flatter in cut and made of heavier cloth, while the latter are fuller and lighter.

In 5.5-meter sailboats, I've set a running chute in light air with the wind well aft only to find that the increased boat speed brought the apparent wind so far forward that a reaching chute was called for. Not long after, I set a reaching spinnaker anticipating the same true wind angle after rounding the weather mark, but I found that, since the wind now was heavier, even the increased boat speed failed to bring the apparent wind forward much. That day we should have set the running spinnaker.

Another factor in deciding whether to fly the spinnaker or not is its sail area relative to the jib. On some boats the jib is quite large, and if the wind is too far forward, or heavy enough to cause broaching, you may find the boat will go faster without the spinnaker. On others, the spinnaker has so much more area than the jib that even if you are broaching you will probably net out with a faster speed through the water with the spinnaker than without. When racing, go by the old axiom: "If in doubt, set."

On very heavy days it almost always pays to carry a spinnaker downwind if you're racing. Many times I've heard the argument on cruising boats that if the boat is already at hull speed, setting a spinnaker won't improve her speed. That's fallacious reasoning because, sailing in a trough of a wave and up the other side, the boat is rarely going near hull speed, and it needs the extra power a spinnaker provides. Furthermore, under surfing conditions there is no such thing as hull speed, for all sailboats can surpass it. The spinnaker will give just enough more power to start the surf earlier and make it last longer.

On very light days a chute can be set, and will fill well, if the spinnaker cloth is light enough and the apparent wind relatively far forward. But with the wind aft, particularly with leftover slop rolling the boat around, a jib may do just as well. The spinnaker will just flop back and forth, wrapping around the jibstay and catching on the spreaders. You're often better off without it in such conditions.

Spinnaker Lines

A spinnaker is a triangular sail. All triangular sails, including the spinnaker, have a head, tack, and clew. In the case of a jib, for instance, the tack is fixed forward and the clew is the free corner of the sail to which the jib sheet is attached. The tack of the spinnaker is also in a fixed position—at the end of a spinnaker pole. Just as with other sails, the edge of the spinnaker from the tack to the head is the "luff," from the clew to the head is the "leech," and from the clew to the tack is the "foot." When a spinnaker isn't set, the two edges are identical so we call them both "leeches" (and both corners "clews") until the luff is established by the corner at the spinnaker pole after setting.

Refer to Photo 143 and learn the various lines involved with spinnaker work.

The spinnaker is hoisted by the spinnaker halyard. One corner is held in place by the spinnaker pole, which is always set to windward opposite the main boom. Actually, the jaws of the pole snap over the line attached to the tack of the spinnaker. This line is called the "afterguy," or more commonly, the "guy." The free corner of the spinnaker has a sheet attached to it like the jib. The only tricky thing about the foregoing terminology is that during a jibe the pole is switched over to the new windward side, the old guy becomes the

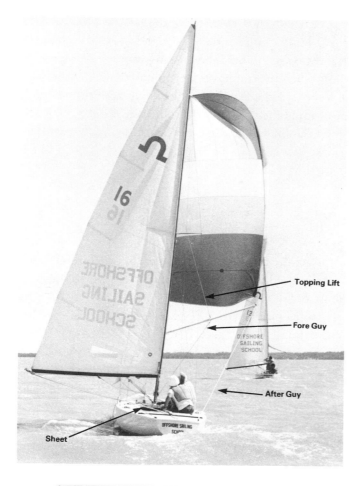

Topping Lift

Fore Guy

After Guy

Sheet

143. Spinnaker control lines on a small keelboat.

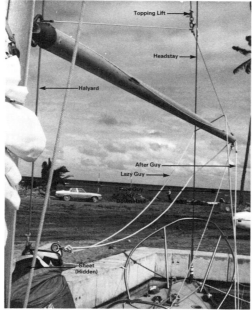

Topping Lift

Headstay

Halyard

After Guy
Lazy Guy
Fore Guy
or Down Haul

Sheet
(Hidden)

144. Cruising boat pole and spinnaker ready for setting.

new sheet (attached to the free corner of the sail), and the old sheet becomes the new guy (running through the jaws in the end of the pole).

There are two lines to hold the pole in position: the topping lift to keep it from falling when the spinnaker isn't full of wind, and the foreguy (some people call it the "spinnaker pole downhaul") to keep the pole from "skying" (pointing way up in the air) when the spinnaker is full.

The spinnaker lines on a cruising boat are identical except that two additional lines, the lazy guy and the lazy sheet, are often added to facilitate jibing. These are shown in Photo 144.

The Set

Now, how to "get the damn thing up." Ever hear these words before? Pretty much the same procedures are involved in both larger and smaller boats; they just have more or fewer people.

Some potential problems can develop before the boat even leaves home. If the spinnaker is improperly packed, it can get twisted as it is hoisted. Most spinnakers are packed in sailbags, buckets, deck depressions, or other containers. These are commonly called spinnaker turtles because the container originally used was a piece of plywood covered by an old inner tube, secured along three edges, under which the spinnaker was stuffed. Placed in the bow, this object looked like a turtle and the name stuck even though spinnakers are now stuffed into bags, buckets, or even cardboard boxes.

To properly "turtle" or "bag" a spinnaker, find the head of the sail. This is easily identified by the narrow angle, the many layers of cloth reinforcement, and the swivel attached to it. Grab one leech near the head and follow down the edge of the sail, folding it back and forth accordion-style, holding onto the material as you go. After you have followed down one side of the sail as in Photo 145, change hands and follow down the other side from the head to the other clew. Mark the location of the head with your finger in case the head gets lost in the folds of the sail. Since the spinnaker is triangular, it follows that if two edges are untangled, the third one has to be also. Have one person hold both of the folded edges and all three corners close together, as with the cruising boat spinnaker in Photo 146, while the other stuffs the spinnaker material into the bag or turtle. The edges go in last and the three corners are left on top outside the bag so that the halyard, afterguy, and sheet can be easily attached, They should be separated and, if a sailbag is used, the three corners are usually tied together with the head between the tack and clew, as in Photo 147. This will work 99% of the time, but sometimes the three corners get a 180° twist so that the tack and clew are reversed in relation to the body of the sail. The spinnaker might rotate itself out of such a potential wrap, but if the wrap tightens up, it will be the devil to get out. On a smaller boat one person can handle the whole packing job, with the result shown in Photo 148.

One of the best ways to picture how you set up for a spinnaker is to imagine a slow-motion movie of a spinnaker being hoisted, run backward. In other words, from out and drawing, the spinnaker will collapse and slowly fold itself back into the turtle. Imagining this will show that all sheets and halyards must

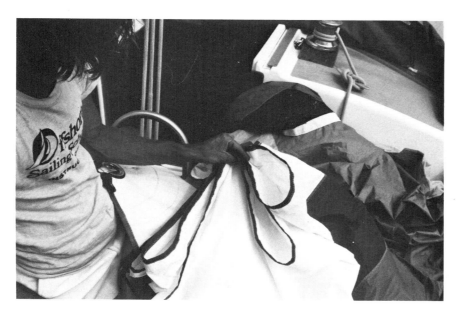

145. Folding the edge of the spinnaker.

146. Folded spinnaker ready for bagging.

be outside all shrouds, jib sheets, barber haulers, etc., in preparation for the set.

For a cruising boat set, the first step in preparation is to reave the guy and sheet. Both lines go outside all shrouds and the headstay, and should be long enough so it is unnecessary to use stop knots in the ends. If you have to let the guy go because of a broach, you want it to run completely free, without having a stop knot jammed in the turning block. In this case, the spin-

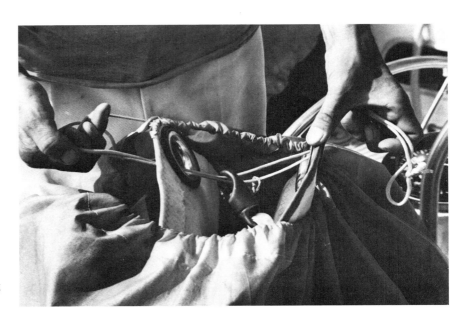

147. Tie the bag's drawstring through the three corners.

148. One of the many types of containers used for the spinnaker set.

naker could fill again way out over the water because the guy couldn't be released any further. The resulting knockdown would be far worse than the original broach. The sheet should be brought forward on the leeward side and attached to the lifeline in the middle of the foredeck. The afterguy (or just plain "guy") should be brought all the way around the headstay and back to the same location as the sheet. The halyard must be brought around behind the jib and in under the foot of the jib to the same location as the others. Next, set the spinnaker pole. First, attach the topping lift and lift the pole off the deck, attaching one end to the mast and snapping the jaw at the other end over the guy. The pole should be resting against the windward side of the headstay at about shoulder height. Now attach the foreguy or pole downhaul, whichever you prefer to call it. Bring your "bagged" spinnaker on deck and attach the guy, sheet, and halyard to the respective corners of the spinnaker. Make sure the bag is also attached somewhere on the boat so it's not lost overboard after the spinnaker leaves it. You are now ready for the hoist, and the spinnaker should come out of the bag without a twist,

Another way of preparing a spinnaker to avoid twists is by "stopping" it. This was the original method years ago and was replaced because it was too slow. Racing sailors found it faster to set it "flying," as described earlier. Stopping consists of furling the spinnaker with the two edges together on the outside and tying it at intervals with easily breakable twine. Racing crews still "stop" storm spinnakers or heavy-duty spinnakers used in high winds. The sail is hoisted in stops, and is "broken out" by pulling on the sheet which breaks the lower stops. Then the wind fills the lower part of the spinnaker and breaks out all the stops further up. This method tends to be a bit safer because the sail can't fill when it's only half hoisted (which can be disastrous in heavy winds).

Since stopping the spinnaker with "rotten" twine is time-consuming, a different method is sometimes used. Cut the bottom off a plastic bucket, stretch rubber bands around the outside of the bucket, pass the spinnaker through the bucket starting with the head and, keeping the luffs together, slide off the rubber bands onto the sail at desired intervals. This much simpler method is shown in Photo 149, but is not highly accepted, probably because of the difficulty finding just the right strength rubber bands.

For the set, the boat must be on a reach or a run. To avoid a twist on the way up, the corners of the sail must be separated quickly. It's a good idea to pull some of the spinnaker out of the bag toward the pole before setting. Photo 150 shows a Soling rounding the weather mark with the spinnaker ready to go. Be careful that the sail doesn't fill with wind or water and pull the rest of the spinnaker out. Then, with one person in the cockpit tending the guy on the windward winch and another on the leeward side with the sheet (or, if fewer crew, leave the sheet cleated), someone on the halyard starts

149. Stopping a spinnaker with rubber bands.

150. Prepared for an immediate set after rounding the mark.

151. Upside-down spinnaker set caused by inadvertently attaching the halyard to the clew and the sheet to the head.

to hoist away. Make sure that the halyard is attached to the *head* of the spin-naker or it will be hoisted sideways, as in Photo 151. As the halyard is pulled, the guy is trimmed so that the tack meets the pole and starts bringing the pole aft. The sheet is also trimmed moderately in order to further separate the corners.

A question often asked is how to know where to preset the sheet—when the pole is level? when the halyard is up? or when the pole is far enough back? The simple solution is to mark the lines with an indelible pen. When you trim to the mark, you know that the adjustment is correct.

Common Spinnaker Mistakes and Problems

There is only one sure way to avoid problems with the spinnaker—don't set one. But if you don't, you'll also lose almost all of the pleasure of sailing a boat on a run. The foredeck crew tangled up in the spinnaker in Photo 152

152. Sometimes it just doesn't pay to get up in the morning.

153. A sea anchor is dragged astern to slow the boat down during gales. It is usually a canvas bag (like a wind sock), not a spinnaker, as above.

may not agree at this moment, but in the long run it's true. Besides, there are certain procedures that can avoid or at least reduce the problems and others which will solve them faster.

For instance, the crew in Photo 153 will be able to get their spinnaker "sea anchor" aboard far easier if the skipper turns the boat right into the wind. The boat will stop and the water pressure filling the spinnaker disappears. By concentrating on pulling just one corner of the spinnaker, it can be brought aboard even with water resistance. The following are some other common problems—and the easiest way to solve them:

Halyard Tangled

Photo 154 shows what happens if the halyard is not clear all the way up before hoisting. When the topping lift was attached to the spinnaker pole, the halyard was between the pole and that line. Either lower the halyard and untangle it, or disconnect the topping lift from the pole, let it go, and grab it again after the spinnaker has filled. Always make a last-second check before hoisting to make sure that the halyard is clear all the way up.

154. Spinnaker halyard caught under the topping lift.

Wraps

This problem plays no favorites. Even large cruising boats can get spinnaker wraps. They happen when the spinnaker collapses for one reason or another and starts to rotate around itself. They can also occur as the spinnaker is hoisted if the corners of the spinnaker are not pulled apart quickly

155. A typical spinnaker wrap.

enough or if the bag has been inadvertently rotated before the set. When the wrap is very low in the spinnaker, it probably has to be lowered and sorted out. Never pull the pole back or head the boat up in order to fill the spinnaker on the assumption that the wrap will unwind if the spinnaker is full. It doesn't work and, in fact, makes the wrap tighter. Get the spinnaker in the dead air behind the main and jib and "blanket" it. Then shake it or pull down on the leech. The wrap shown in Photo 155 should come out with this method. If the wrap is high in the sail, releasing the halyard a few feet should allow the swivel, which may be jammed in the block, to rotate and unwind the spinnaker.

A bad type of wrap is one which winds around the jibstay. If it gets tight, it can be next to impossible to unwrap without cutting the spinnaker away. The problem is that a wire jibstay has strands that are twisted around each other. As the spinnaker is pulled down (assuming a crew member can reach the foot of the sail and pull it), it is rotated by the strands and gets tighter and tighter. (A rod or grooved jibstay, often found on cruising boats, is smooth and a wrapped spinnaker slides easily down it to be unwrapped.) Once a jibstay wrap occurs, there are only a couple of things that can de done: (1) send a person up in a bosun's chair to untangle it (if the boat is large enough), or (2) jibe the main boom so the airflow off the mainsail is in the opposite direction. Instead of wrapping tighter, the spinnaker starts rotating in the opposite direction and unwrapping itself. I've known of this method for many years but never had to resort to it, until one of our teaching boats developed a tight spinnaker wrap around the jib while running in a 25-knot wind. Nothing seemed to work, so we suggested (from a chase boat) that the crew jibe the

156. A very difficult wrap to solve.

mainsail. Within minutes this "impossible" wrap had completely unwound itself.

The type of wrap shown in Photo 156, which is low in the spinnaker and includes some extraneous lines for good measure, probably is incurable without lowering the spinnaker and starting anew.

Large cruising boats with wire rather than rod headstays that intend to have a spinnaker set for long periods of time prevent wraps by using a spinnaker net. This is a series of light lines tied to the jibstay at intervals and hoisted by the jib halyard, as in Figure 160. It fills in the area from the jibstay to the mast and prevents a collapsed spinnaker from passing through and wrapping. The end of each line is tied to the headstay with a bowline as the net is slowly hoisted. Though snaps would be faster, they can snag and rip the spinnaker.

An alternative type of spinnaker net which I invented in 1965 has gained wide acceptance. It's basically the same idea as the one in Figure 160, but with two vertical lines, one leading to each side of the boat rather than only one vertical line coming down in front of the mast. The horizontal lines run from one vertical around the headstay and back to the other vertical. This eliminates the need to tie each line to the headstay and saves a great deal of time. Plus, the spinnaker can be jibed with the net in place, which cannot be done with the first method. This is important, because it is during a jibe that a spinnaker has a good chance of collapsing and wrapping.

A third, extremely simple, and very popular type of spinnaker net uses shockcord (elastic rope). Imagine the middle two horizontal pieces in Figure 160 as two separate pieces of shockcord, one end fixed to the mast and the

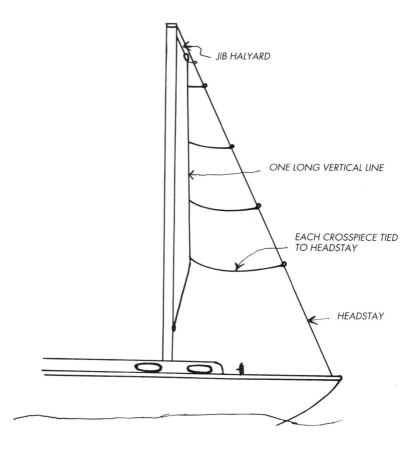

JIB HALYARD

ONE LONG VERTICAL LINE

EACH CROSSPIECE TIED
TO HEADSTAY

HEADSTAY

Fig. 160. A spinnaker net.

other end tied to a ring around the headstay. As the jib is raised, the top hank of the jib lifts the lower ring first and then the upper ring, and carries them both up to the top of the headstay. The shockcord just stretches and lays vertically along the mast. When the jib is lowered, both pieces of shockcord fall into place across the space between the mast and the headstay, closing it off from an errant spinnaker. The shock cord gets tired and has to be replaced a few times a season, but that's the only drawback to this otherwise neat little system.

Losing the Guy and Sheet

Often both the guy and sheet get free inadvertently. It sometimes happens during a jibe when one person is holding onto both and the spinnaker suddenly fills with a gust of wind. More often, it happens on the douse. The guy is released before someone has a hold on the sheet behind the mainsail on the leeward side. The sail goes flying out, as in Photo 157. One solution is to turn the boat dead downwind. In all but the heaviest winds, the spinnaker will come down within reach and can be gathered in. Another solution is to pull on just one line, either the guy or the sheet, and let the other trail free. As the

157. Someone released the guy and sheet prematurely.

corner gets close, ease the halyard. Premature halyard ease, however, runs the risk of having the spinnaker fill with air way out beyond the boat. When this happens the problem becomes serious. The boat may be pulled over so far that she fills with water and the heeling makes it impossible to turn the boat "into" the spinnaker to relieve the pressure, i.e., downwind. Freeing the halyard completely, or cutting it, may become necessary. If the guy and sheet are lost on a large cruising boat, send a person up the mast with a line leading down to the middle of the foredeck. He or she clips it into the head of the spinnaker and comes down. Now ease the halyard while winching down on the downhaul line. When the head of the sail gets about halfway down, the crew should be able to reach part of the spinnaker and gather it aboard.

Premature Filling

Another common error is having the spinnaker fill with wind before it is all the way up. On a small boat this can cause a capsize, and on a larger boat, such as a Soling, it may be difficult to raise the rest of the way because of the strain on the halyard. On a cruising boat, however, it can be downright dangerous to have the spinnaker fill prematurely. The proper way on such a boat is to haul on the halyard, hand over hand, quickly, until the sail is over halfway up and then wrap it around the halyard winch and winch it the rest of the way. What must be avoided is having the spinnaker fill with wind before the turns are put on the winch. If you put the turns on too early, the friction of the winch slows the process of hoisting and increases the possibility of the spinnaker's filling with wind prematurely. If the latter happens when the spinnaker is too low, the sail will be pulled out of the bag into the water and rip when it fills with water. If the wraps are put on the winch too late and the spinnaker fills with wind, the halyard could burn the skin off your hands as it zings out, and it will be a long, laborious process to winch the sail all the way up when you get the wraps. Once raised all the way, lower the jib on a cruising boat immediately so the wind can get at the spinnaker and fill it.

Losing the Halyard

Premature ease of the halyard before another crew member is prepared to gather it in, or inadequate securing (cleating) of the halyard after the spinnaker is raised, can cause the problem shown in Photo 158. If this halyard isn't caught and brought back up immediately, the spinnaker will either fill with

158. Halyard slipping can cause major problems.

159. The crew member on the halyard eased faster than the spinnaker could be gathered in.

water or be run through by the bow of the boat. Easing the halyard on the douse faster than it can be gathered in leads to the problems experienced by the crew in Photo 159. The head of the chute is about to fill with water, the weight of which will inevitably wrench the rest of the spinnaker from the grip of the crew. All this could have been avoided if the person easing the halyard had watched the person gathering and had tried not to get ahead of him.

Spinnaker Trim

There is no mystery about what makes a crew member a good spinnaker trimmer. It's experience and concentration, and neither of these can be taught. One is developed and the other innate. We can teach the basic rules of spinnaker trimming, but it depends on the person to eventually become good at it.

However, even the basic rules can be misleading. Nothing is hard and fast in sailing, and for every rule there's an exception or two. First, let's examine the general principles behind spinnaker trimming. When running, the spinnaker is fairly well stalled. It is dragging the boat downwind. True, there's a little flow around the backside of the luff (from a crew member's vantage point), but that doesn't result in much drive. Therefore, we want the greatest projected area possible.

Just as a large parachute will let a man down more slowly than a small one, the more area of spinnaker exposed to the wind, the greater its effectiveness. This is done by keeping the pole well squared (aft) and the sheet well trimmed. The dotted line in Figure 161 shows the amount of area exposed

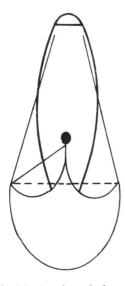

Fig. 161. Moving the pole forward gets the spinnaker away from the sail plan, but reduces its projected area.

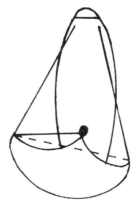

Fig. 162. Moving the pole aft increases the projected area, but pulls the spinnaker in close to the sail plan and the mainsail's turbulent lee.

to the wind with the pole forward. The dotted line in Figure 162 is much longer with the pole aft, indicating a greater "projected area."

If there weren't a price to pay for having the pole well aft, that's where we'd set it, but there is. As we square the pole aft, and also trim the sheet to keep the spinnaker from collapsing, it is drawn in closer and closer to the mainsail. This means that the spinnaker is in the bad air of the main and loses efficiency. So we ease the pole forward and ease the sheet to get the chute away from the sail plan. Somewhere there is a happy medium between starving the spinnaker behind the main and losing projected area through too much ease, and this is where experience comes in.

The next general aspect of spinnaker trimming to remember is that a spinnaker is a symmetrical sail and should look symmetrical when flown. Although there are a few exceptions to this, such as when close reaching or in light air, it is generally true. If the spinnaker is misshapen, as in Photo 160, because the pole is too high or too low, it will lose much of its effectiveness. keeping the above two general aspects of spinnaker trimming in mind, all the rest of the basic rules fall in place.

Following are some of the requirements for pole position. A good starting point is to set the pole square to the apparent wind. The masthead fly is in undisturbed air and is a good guide. Set the pole at right angles to it. As the boat sails further downwind, however, air over the main tends to flow forward and around the mast, making the spinnaker practically by the lee. This means that the pole will need to be squared back, past perpendicular to the masthead fly. Actually, it will be perpendicular to the shroud telltales. I would use the masthead fly until the wind is well aft and then switch to shroud telltales.

There are some unusual cases where the masthead fly isn't very accurate for spinnaker trimming, such as on a 12-meter yacht. Being a ¾ rig, the head of the spinnaker is considerably lower than the masthead fly and the apparent wind at the top of the mast is noticeably farther aft than that at pole height, due to increased wind velocity aloft. Another exception to setting the pole perpendicular to the apparent wind is when you are using a very short foot spinnaker. In that case, squaring the pole brings the clew near the jibstay and much of the projected area is lost.

The pole should generally be level, not parallel to the water as I continually hear people saying, but perpendicular to the mast. This means that if you raise or lower the outboard end of the pole, you should raise or lower the inboard end (the end attached to the mast) a corresponding amount. The idea is to get the spinnaker as far away from the sail plan as possible, but to insist on keeping the pole level to achieve this is overkill. A pole has to be cocked 25° from level to decrease its effective length 10% and during the first 20°, only 5% is lost, so a few degrees off of level really doesn't make much

160. A distorted spinnaker can be caused by improper pole height, reducing efficiency.

difference. Probably more speed is lost by fussing around with inboard pole height than is gained by having the pole exactly level. Also, a slight cock upward will put the pole in line with the guy and reduce the bending strain on the pole.

More important is the height at which the whole pole is set. The general rule is to keep the tack and clew of the spinnaker level with the plane of the deck (not with the water). But this really goes back to keeping the spinnaker symmetrical. When the two corners are level, the spinnaker is symmetrical, looks good, and flies well.

The exceptions to this occur mainly while reaching, and in either high or low wind velocities. While reaching, particularly when flying the spinnaker with the jib set, the tack of a normal reaching spinnaker on a class boat can be set higher than the clew. This opens the slot between the spinnaker and the jib. It also eases the luff of the spinnaker and flattens the chute. Photo 161 shows the tack and clew fairly even. There is little space between the jib and spinnaker luffs. The pole on the center boat in Photo 162 is quite high and the slot is open, but the spinnaker is misshapen. The boat on the right in the same photo has the best spinnaker set of all.

161. Here is a fairly tight slot between luffs of jib and spinnaker.

Once the pole is set correctly, it's fairly simple to play the spinnaker. The sheet should be eased until one sees a slight curl along the luff as in Photo 163, and then trimmed to make the curl disappear. This must be done constantly and is where concentration plays its biggest part. Quite often the novice over-

162. Raising the pole opens the slot.

163. Ease the sheet until a curl appears along the luff, then trim.

164. This spinnaker is "starved" for air. The sheet should be eased, the pole squared, or both.

trims the spinnaker, which gets in the disturbed air behind the mainsail and collapses in Photo 164. This is called a "starve." Pull the pole aft to correct the problem.

The spinnaker guy should also be played if the boat is small or if you are running in a slop. As the boat rolls to windward, the pole must be squared and the sheet eased. As it rolls to leeward, the pole should be eased forward and the sheet trimmed.

All changes in apparent wind direction necessitate changes in pole position and sheet trim. If the boat starts surfing, if it falls off a plane, or if the wind velocity changes, the apparent wind direction will be affected and the spinnaker trimmer will have to make adjustments. Moreover, he or she must learn to anticipate these changes ahead of time.

Halyard Ease

There are times when one should ease the spinnaker halyard, but when is it good to ease it off—and how much?

The next time you are on a reach with the spinnaker set, look up behind the mainsail on the lee side. Then ease the spinnaker halyard six inches or so while looking at the leech of the sail, not the head. It will become obvious how much the slot between the spinnaker and the main will open up to allow free air passage.

When running downwind in a breeze, easing the halyard has two effects. First, it gets the spinnaker away from the disturbed air of the mainsail, and second, it allows the spinnaker to be more vertical than it is when fully hoisted. In light air, however, the halyard shouldn't be eased, since the spinnaker will just come straight down. Nor should it be eased on a reach in heavy air, because the sail's center of effort will go out further over the water and possibly cause a broach. On a run in heavy air, an eased spinnaker will be more apt to roll from one side of the boat to the other (oscillate) than one fully hoisted. In short, easing the halyard is rarely done on a run and is really only beneficial on a medium air reach.

Spinnaker Broaching

No matter what size sailboat you sail, if you set a spinnaker in heavy air, you will probably broach at one time or another. Fifteen-footers broach and 80-footers broach. Size is no deterrent.

A mild form of broaching is shown in Photo 165. It is essentially an overpowering weather helm caused by a number of factors. When the weather helm (the tendency for the boat to round up into the wind) becomes so strong that the helmsman is unable to counteract it with the rudder, the boat will broach. Most of the time this means that the boat will just wallow broadside to the wind until steering control is regained and the boat can be headed back downwind.

A major factor causing broaching is heeling. When upright in the water, a hull is symmetrical, splits the water evenly, and is pushed in neither direction more than the other. When heeled, the bow wave on the lee side becomes quite large and pushes against the curve of the hull as it works aft. The helmsman has to steer the boat well to leeward to keep her sailing straight.

165. A broach.

Contributing to additional weather helm is the fact that the force in the sails is out over the water when heeled. Let's fantasize for a moment. Imagine that in Photo 165 we have tied a line around the mast just above the spreaders and have run it all the way to shore where we've tied it to the back of a car. Now, we drive the car inland, pulling the mast faster than the hull of the boat can keep up. By looking at the photo and using your imagination, it should be clear that first the boat will rotate until it is parallel to the shore, and then the car will be dragging the whole mess shoreward by the mast. The hull at this point will be dragging sideways through the water, creating such resistance that the mast will be almost lying in the water from the pull of the line. This is a more severe reaction to the same forces described in "Balance" in Part I, Chapter 6.

With the spinnaker out over the water, the total wind force affects the boat in exactly the same way as our imaginary line to the shore. The more the boat heels, the more it rotates into the wind. The more the boat rotates into the wind, the more it heels, until we have a full-fledged broach on our hands.

In a broach, the rudder becomes next to worthless. The boat is lying on its side, so the rudder is near the surface where it can't get a "bite." Since the rudder now is more parallel to the surface than vertical and perpendicular to the surface, steering to leeward has much the same effect as the elevators on the tail of an airplane. The stern and keel will lift rather than turn. So the more the boat heels, the less effective the rudder becomes in turning it back downwind to reduce the heel. In fact, the rudder will start to increase the heel after a certain amount of heel is reached.

If in the early stages of a broach the helmsman is able to turn the boat so that the hull is parallel to the direction of pull (on our imaginary line to the shore), the hull has less resistance and a better chance of keeping up with the sails. The tendency to broach will be reduced. To facilitate catching the broach before it develops, the skipper and crew can take certain precautions.

Since heeling is the enemy, they must hike out hard during gusts of wind that could precipitate a broach. The crew in Photo 165 have not done this and are about to pay for it. Another way to reduce heeling is to luff the sails. Since the spinnaker gives the boat a great deal of drive, it is the last sail to luff. First, luff the mainsail. Remember—if your boom vang is on tight, the boom is being held down. As the main is luffed, the boom end goes into the water and is pushed back toward the center of the boat. This is shown clearly in Photo 165. Since the main can't be eased, more heeling will occur and the boom will be pushed even closer to the hull by the water flow. This will cause even more heeling and another vicious cycle starts, until a broach occurs. So, ease the boom vang. In fact, Soling racers disregard the mainsheet and play only the boom vang to avoid a broach. The boom lifts as the vang is eased and the top part of the sail near the head luffs first. Since this is the part that causes most of the heeling, the sailor is reducing heeling without detracting much from the general drive of the sail.

The next sail to ease is the jib, if one is being used under the spinnaker. It is fallacious to think that trimming the jib will reduce weather helm by blowing the bow to leeward. Whatever lee helm could develop by this method is nullified by the weather helm caused by the additional heeling of the jib when trimmed tightly.

When it is obvious that drastic measures are needed to avoid a broach, the spinnaker can be collapsed by easing the sheet a couple of feet. The helmsman must anticipate the need for this and give the command to the spinnaker trimmer to "break" the spinnaker. When the boat has been steered back downwind and has straightened up, the spinnaker can be trimmed again to fill it.

There are a few other factors that can contribute to broaching. If the spinnaker halyard has stretched or is not all the way up, the center of effort of the spinnaker (its "pull") will be further out over the water and aggravate the turning moment. The tack of the spinnaker should be right at the end of the spinnaker pole for the same reason. If the pole is too high, as in Photo 165, the luff will have a large curve to leeward, causing the drive to be further out over the water. And if the leech of the spinnaker is cupped, as in the photo, rather than flat and free, the trapped air will cause more heeling.

Crew weight should be aft on reaches for two reasons. First, the forward force on the sails against the resistance of the hull will have a natural tendency to bury the bow and lift the stern. This tendency is pronounced in many catamaran designs when reaching. They tend to bury the bow of the lee hull and actually "trip" over it (capsize). The crew has to move way back near the stern of the weather hull. Second, crew weight aft keeps the rudder deeper in the water and increases its effectiveness.

Rolling or Oscillating

Photo 166 shows another problem in spinnaker work: rolling, or oscillating. The boat in the photo is rolling by the lee and will shortly roll in the opposite direction. In heavy seas this can become wildly exciting. Your boat is almost jibing as the mast rolls to windward, nearly broaching as it heels to leeward. Most of the problem is caused by allowing the spinnaker too much freedom.

In the photo, the sheet has been eased to near or beyond the jibstay (hidden from view), so the spinnaker is able to get completely around to the starboard side of the boat. It then pulls the mast over in that direction. As it heels, the starboard bow wave develops and shoves the bow to port, toward a jibe. The helmsman steers the boat hard in the opposite direction, the spinnaker

166. Rolling.

oscillates over to the port side of the boat, causing heeling and a strong weather helm which, again, the helmsman counteracts. Thus the rolling starts. If there is any ease in the halyard, the spinnaker is free to spin in a large arc. Pulling the halyard up very tightly and trimming the sheet reduces the rolling.

Off the wind in heavy air, the mainsail becomes a large factor in control, particularly on small boats. A powerful boom vang is a must. If the boom is allowed to lift in the air, the top of the leech will fall off so far that it may actually point forward of abeam, or at least be folding over the spreader and shrouds. Figure 163 is a cross section of the sail near the foot and near the head. Note that while the foot of the sail is stalled, the top part of the sail is getting airflow over the lee side, creating lift in the direction of the arrow. This tends to pull the top of the mast to windward, making the boat roll to windward. Once started, each subsequent roll is a little more severe. The apparent wind goes more forward and flow is picked up lower down in the sail each time the mast rolls to weather, and the faster it rolls, the more forward the apparent wind goes. The more forward the apparent wind goes, the greater the area of mainsail that develops airflow on the lee side, and the greater the lift. The greater the lift, the faster the mast swings to windward, and so on, until the boat is rolling madly. The solution is to vang down strongly and, if the vang can't handle the forces, to trim the mainsheet in a little so the top part of the sail is also stalled. Though the vang in Photo 166 appears to be fairly tight, we can see by the shadows in the mainsail that the top part is well forward of the bottom, so more vang tension would be helpful.

When rolling conditions exist, consider trimming the jib in flat. It will help to keep the bow downwind, and helps dampen the rolling like a baffle.

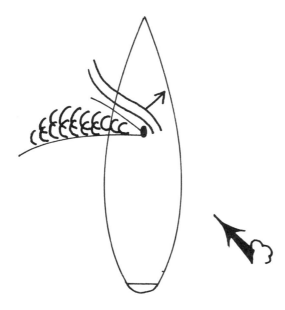

Fig. 163. Without a vang, the upper part of the mainsail falls off, picks up airflow, and creates lift to windward.

Changing course to more of a reach can also help. Further, in such conditions we want to reduce the effectiveness of the spinnaker. By easing the pole forward of square with the apparent wind and by overtrimming the sheet, we can roll part of the spinnaker in behind the mainsail, thereby partially blanketing it. This also keeps the spinnaker from picking up airflow on the lee side, which, like the main, pulls the spinnaker over to the weather side of the boat and rolls the mast to windward. Lower the pole to keep the spinnaker in closer to the sail plan of the boat, but don't overdo it. Lowering the pole excessively on a running chute makes the luff fuller in cross section and more likely to collapse. In heavy winds the jolt of the spinnaker filling after having been collapsed can easily break something. Make sure the pole foreguy is tight so the

167. Spinnaker flying out beyond the pole.

pole can't swing back as the boat heels to windward. Never let the tack of the spinnaker fly out beyond the pole end, as in Photo 167. It can cause wild rolling.

Place your crew weight on opposite sides of the boat (if it's small). Just as children can seesaw faster if they're closer to the middle of the seesaw then when sitting at the very ends, the boat will roll less if the crew weight is spread out wide apart. And, last, change helmsmen if it appears that the present one doesn't quite have the anticipation or timing to counteract the rolling.

As with all sailing, don't accept problems such as broaching and rolling as unavoidable. Certainly, they can happen to any crew, but one should work at reducing the problem to more acceptable and manageable terms.

Light Air Spinnaker Work

Spinnaker trimming in light air takes a great deal of patience. Lower the pole way down, but always keep the outboard end a little higher than the clew. Then, when a puff of air comes and fills the spinnaker, the pole will be at the proper height. In other words, keep the pole at the proper height for the 10% of the time that the spinnaker is filled and doing the boat some good, not the 90% of the time when it is drooping and not producing any forward drive. Another reason to keep the pole a little higher than the clew in light air is that a low pole will stretch the luff and fold it over (see Photo 168). When a puff arrives, the spinnaker is unable to fill because of the shape of the luff.

The same thing can happen with some very full-shouldered running spinnakers. The luff can collapse from a starve and though you know you must

168. An excessively low pole tightens the luff and causes the spinnaker to collapse more easily.

pull the pole aft, first you have to overtrim the sheet to unfold the luff. Only then can you pull the pole back with the spinnaker full. It is better in light air to have the pole too low rather than too high, as the latter causes the spinnaker to droop to leeward and it will take a much stronger puff to fill it.

Another light air problem is caused by the jib. Air flowing past the lee side of the jib causes a suction on a reach, and if the spinnaker collapses, it sucks into the jib and is very difficult to fill it again. The natural tendency is to trim the jib to get it away from the spinnaker, but actually the opposite should be done. The first time the spinnaker collapses, free the jib sheet to break down the airflow over the jib. If it happens a few more times, take the jib down or roll it up.

Jibing the Spinnaker

End for End

Spinnaker jibes seem to be a great bugaboo for most crews. Though almost any crew can get into trouble, sometimes it is very difficult to analyze the problem. A jibe happens fast and all crew members have tasks to perform. When you're busy with your own job, it is often hard to notice where things are going wrong. Most of the time the person on the foredeck who is all wrapped up in spinnaker cloth, lines, etc., is the butt of abuse when actually the fault lies with the person steering.

The skipper who turns the boat too sharply and who gives the crew inadequate time or directions will almost certainly cause a bad jibe. In heavy air, the helmsman must be sure to counteract the tendency for the boat to round up into the wind right after a jibe. The boom swings over with a great deal of force and, when it reaches the end of the mainsheet, it stops abruptly and the sail creates a wall to the wind. Something has to give until an equilibrium is found, so the boat heels over and a strong weather helm results. The forces in the sail out over the water turn the bow of the boat toward the wind. This combination of factors will cause a broach in heavy winds unless the helmsman heads the boat off decisively to meet the anticipated turning moment. Done properly, the boat, though being steered as if to jibe back again, just sails straight ahead. Nothing can make a crew look worse than a bad helmsman.

But, to be fair about this, some of the worst problems are caused by the crew handling the spinnaker guy and sheet. A "reach-to-reach" jibe is one in which the boat is turned from a reach with the pole on or near the jibstay on one tack to a reach with the pole near the jibstay on the opposite tack. It is a difficult type of jibe because the boat is turned so far, approximately 90°. The spinnaker has to get completely around to the other side, and problems occur if this is not done with alacrity.

Photos 169–171 portray the problem. As the boat heads down from the starboard tack reach in order to jibe, the pole should come aft and the sheet

169. Approaching the jibing mark on starboard tack, the sheet should be eased more.

170. At the point of jibing, the pole should be pulled aft. Here, it's still forward.

171. After jibing to port tack, the spinnaker should be on the starboard side of the boat. Here, it's still on the port side.

172. The spinnaker, on the windward side of the boat after the jibe, blows through between the jibstay and the mast.

should be eased. After all, the boat is on a dead run at the instant of jibing and the spinnaker should be trimmed properly for that point of sailing. The jibe of the main boom and spinnaker pole is then completed and the boat heads up to the new port tack reach. The pole should be on the jibstay and the sheet trimmed in. In Photo 170, nothing of the sort has happened. At the point of jibing, the spinnaker is still on the port side of the boat, the same side as the wind is about to come over. After the jibe, the spinnaker starts to blow through between the jib and the main as in Photo 172. When this happens, about the only solution is to head back downwind to blow the spinnaker forward around the jibstay.

During the jibe, the foredeck crew on a boat like a Soling should stand, back against the mast, facing forward, as in Photo 173. From this position, he or she has much more leverage for controlling the pole and getting it off the mast and can see the spinnaker and help keep it full. On a reach-to-reach jibe, the crew should take the pole off the mast and then off the old guy. This makes the spinnaker free-wheeling and the mid-cockpit crew can pull the spinnaker around the boat without the pole's restricting it in any way. The foredeck crew then connects the end of the pole that was previously on the mast to the new guy and snaps the other end of the pole onto the mast fitting. This is called "end for ending" the pole.

When the pole is not taken completely off the spinnaker, the foredeck crew has to be extremely quick not to end up in the situation shown in Photo 174. The crew here decided to snap the end that came off the mast onto the

173. During the jibe, the foredeck crew faces forward with his back braced against the mast.

174. The foredeck crew should have disconnected the old guy before jibing. Now the pole is against the starboard shrouds and the spinnaker cannot be pulled further around the jibstay.

175. A running jibe.

new guy before unsnapping it from the old guy. The cockpit crew has pulled the spinnaker around to the starboard side, but cannot pull it any further because the pole is against the shrouds. The jibe has been completed and the spinnaker is starting to blow in between the jib and the main. If the pole were not attached, the spinnaker could have been pulled all the way around to the starboard side even if the foredeck crew was having trouble getting organized.

176. A running jibe almost completed.

A running jibe is much easier. The boat's heading changes only slightly, so all we are basically doing is changing the pole from one side to the other while keeping the spinnaker full. Photo 175 shows a running jibe at mid-stage. The foredeck crew is in a good position, back braced against the mast and feet spread apart for balance. In light winds as shown, the skipper should hold the main boom in the middle of the boat for a short time to keep the spinnaker full while the pole is being transferred to the other side. In the case of a running jibe, the pole may be left attached to the old guy until the other end is snapped over the new guy. Thus, the foredeck crew can help keep the spinnaker full during the jibe. Photo 176 is taken at the point when the jibe is almost completed. The foredeck crew should have the pole on the new guy and should be attaching the other end to the mast, so he is a little behind schedule (or the skipper is a little ahead, depending on your point of view).

Dip Pole

On larger sailboats, the spinnaker pole is too heavy to take completely off the mast and end for end. Even though the topping lift is holding it up in the air, a sudden lurch of the boat could cause the foredeck man to lose control of the pole. A heavy pole dangling from the topping lift and swinging around the foredeck would be very dangerous, so the common jibe used on large boats is one that leaves the pole attached to the mast. It's called a "dip-pole" jibe because the outboard end is lowered (dipped) so the tip can pass aft of the headstay.

The spinnaker is usually equipped with two guys and two sheets, one of each on each side of the boat, with the lead of the guys well forward of the lead of the sheets. Let's say we're on starboard tack and want to jibe. The lazy sheet (not being used on the windward, starboard side) is trimmed to take some of the strain off the guy. The lazy guy on the port side (not being used before the jibe) is led forward to the bow to accept the pole end as it swings through. The inboard end of the spinnaker pole is raised on the mast to allow the outboard end swing through aft of the headstay.

On jibing, a crew member pulls the lanyard that opens the jaw of the pole, and the afterguy (the guy) falls out. This is called "tripping the guy." The topping lift is eased and the pole swings down to the bow, where another crew member waits with a loop of the lazy guy to snap into the jaw of the pole as it swings down inside the headstay. With the hail "made" from the bow person indicating the guy is in the pole jaw, the topping lift is hauled up to lift the pole back to a level position on the new side, and the new guy is tightened, which pulls the pole end out to the corner of the spinnaker. With the strain now on the new guy, the old sheet is released and becomes the lazy sheet, waiting for the next jibe. With this method, properly executed, the spinnaker never collapses during a jibe, so no speed is lost.

Dousing the Spinnaker

Small Boats

Taking a spinnaker down to leeward is quite simple—the only major problem is caused by letting it get out from behind the mainsail into strong, unobstructed wind. The crew gathering in the chute must have control of the sail by bringing the sheet forward to a spot just behind the shrouds. The guy is then eased and the halyard lowered, as the sail is pulled in behind the mainsail. On small boats, if someone lets the guy go before the sheet is under control, the chute will go flying aft to the stern and will be the devil to gather in.

There may be times when a windward douse is in order. If you are racing and are coming into a mark on the wrong jibe, a takedown to windward will be the new leeward side after the douse. Or, if you know you must set the spinnaker again and the next set is on the other tack, a windward takedown will prepare you properly for the next set.

Take the pole down before you intend to douse (Photo 177) and then just pull the spinnaker around to windward with the new guy as the halyard is lowered (Photo 178). In some larger class boats it's hard to do on a reach, but it can be done quite easily on a run. Many smaller boats set and douse the spinnaker to windward as a matter of course.

Large Boats

One of many methods to douse a spinnaker on a cruising boat is very much like that on a smaller boat. First, raise the jib so that the spinnaker will be blanketed. Let the pole forward and lower it so a man in the bow can open

177. Windward spinnaker douse —get the pole out of the way first.

178. Then gather in the spinnaker to windward, pulling on the guy.

the snap-shackle attached to the spinnaker. Another crew member should grab the spinnaker sheet just aft of the shrouds and gather in the foot of the spinnaker when the tack is released from the pole. The halyard is then lowered with care to avoid letting the spinnaker dip in the water. After the spinnaker is down, the pole is cleared away and the spinnaker prepared for the next set. It's frustrating to be ready to set a spinnaker only to find that it hasn't been bagged properly, so make a habit of preparing it right after the douse.

Asymmetrical Spinnakers

These are spinnakers that look and act more like reaching jibs. They are tacked on the end of a pole sticking straight out from the bow of the boat near deck level. The clew has a windward and leeward sheet like a jib. Asymmetrical spinnakers are easy to use and to jibe. They are very effective in light winds, because downwind speed is enhanced by sailing more on a reach than by sailing downwind. When the wind increases to 12 knots or more, the "crossover" wind speed, a regular symmetrical spinnaker becomes faster, because it is a more effective running sail. Nevertheless, asymmetrical spinnakers are gaining in popularity. Fewer crew members are needed to handle them, which give them a decided advantage for family sailing.

Racing in Various Wind Conditions

Helmsmanship in Heavy Weather and Light Air

Why is one skipper able to make a boat go faster than another? The key words are concentration and awareness. A good skipper concentrates not only on keeping the boat in the groove (the "groove" is an undefinable term that describes a feeling that the boat is sailing its fastest to windward), but is also aware of subtle changes in wind strength, wave direction, and the relation of his or her boat to others. Much of this information is transmitted by the crew, but the skipper is the one who has to sort it out, and do so without losing his ability to concentrate on steering.

The biggest problem for a beginning racing sailor is not paying adequate attention to steering. Steering is not an automatic thing, and when beginners look away at another boat or at the mark, they lose their orientation to the wind. The result is that they may bear off or head up. The boat will heel more or straighten up, respectively, but the helmsman's sense of awareness is not developed enough to feel the subtle change to the boat's angle of heel. A more experienced sailor will be aware of this change and will immediately correct it. Yet, the best sailors will rely on their crews to feed them information about the location of other boats or marks so they won't have to look around at all. Unfortunately, a novice racing sailor often gets a novice racing crew, since a better crew probably will want to be with a potential winner. This means that the novice skipper usually has to gather all the information alone, even while developing a sense of awareness.

Another common fault of the novice is to bear off before tacking. Why this happens, I don't really know, but one should continually try to avoid doing it. Still another is to use the tiller for a handhold. On a small boat, for example, if the skipper has been hit by a puff and has not feathered the boat up enough (pinching it to nearly a luff), the boat will heel over. This causes the skipper to slip to leeward and, without thinking, push against the tiller to keep from sliding further. The boat then rounds up sharply into the wind. You must learn that the arm you use to steer with can do nothing else but that. You must, in effect, spiritually detach that arm from your body. Hold the tiller firmly, neither too lightly nor so hard that the phrase "white-knuckled sailor" applies to you. The steering arm must do the brain's bidding with regard to steering, but it must resist the impulse to do any other functions.

A common habit the novice racing skipper must avoid is oversteering. When sailing upwind, there is a tendency to steer the boat first up and then down. As the boat heels over and develops some weather helm in a puff, the skipper should learn to let the tiller pull slightly to leeward. Don't push the tiller unless playing large waves.

When a boat is on a run, oversteering is most common and there are several reasons. First, there is no real feel to the boat since one has to steer in both directions. Second, the apparent wind direction shifts madly back and forth when sailing downwind. Third, the apparent wind speed is less than it is upwind and is hitting the back of your head rather than blowing in your face, making it more difficult to feel its direction. Finally, the sea tends to kick the boat's stern around.

Beginning racing skippers are likely to oversteer to avoid a downwind broach, but by doing so they usually cause one. On a windy spinnaker run, they will be late in anticipating a wave, the wave gives the stern a shove, and they have to push the tiller hard over to avoid a broach. Then the boat slews down the wave and they have to steer hard the other way to avoid a jibe.

A fine exercise for an inexperienced helmsman on a cruising boat is what I call "nonsteering." The next time you're on a windy spinnaker run and you're working madly to keep the boat on course, grit your teeth, tell yourself you're not going to steer, and simply hold the wheel or tiller amidships. It's amazing how most boats will settle down.

You may have to modify your resolve a little bit and compromise with half a turn of the wheel in either direction. But if you do this enough, you'll find yourself getting into the habit of steering only when it's necessary, and the result will be that your timing will improve greatly. Remember, too, that any oversteering brakes the boat. You can test this by steering the boat through a series of sharp turns while on a light reach or run. You'll be surprised at how much the boat slows down.

One other mistake a novice racing sailor often makes, particularly on a one-design keelboat, is to steer from the leeward side while beating. Though it is comfortable and easy to see the jib, you are unable to see and play the waves or see the ripples of a gust on the water as it approaches. When a 35–40 knot puff hits, the force is substantial and, since the apparent wind comes aft, the puff will have even more effect on a boat that hasn't been steered up to meet it. Your weight to leeward is detrimental, even for a keelboat. Furthermore, when it's blowing hard it's really not necessary to see the jib anyway, for most good sailors sail by the angle of heel. In short, though you may become good, you will never be a great sailor until you get used to steering from the windward side.

One final bit of advice on steering goes back to where we started—concentration. When some other boat is on your weather quarter and you want to tack, try forgetting about him and concentrate hard on steering. Recently, I found myself in that very situation in a pickup Sunfish race. I was being run out to the port tack layline by another boat, and I kept looking back anxiously at him to see if I could cross him on port tack. After about a minute of maintaining the status quo, I said to myself, "This is ridiculous. If I can keep looking around at him and stay even, what can I do if I concentrate?" So I hiked out further, played every wave and puff I could, and knew without looking I'd soon be able to tack. When we did finally cross, the distance he was left behind in that short period of time was amazing!

Light Air Racing

All skippers and crews can look good in winds from 8 to 15 knots. It's the heavy and light air conditions that really test you. Let's take a look at light air conditions.

On light, "fluky," drifting days, often you hear how "lucky" some guy was in a race because he got the wind first when it filled in. If you look at the record, though, you'll probably find that the same guy is "lucky" most of the time. Probably he has a little more patience and concentration than the others, he has studied the weather and currents better, and he may be more observant, noticing smoke, darkness on the water, or sails on other boats that might indicate a new breeze.

There are some things you can do to make your own boat sail faster in very light air. One of the most important techniques is to heel the boat slightly. At slow speeds, the friction of the water running past the hull is a greater drag factor than it is at higher speeds where wave-making drag becomes more important. Obviously, a clean, smooth bottom on the boat reduces friction, and that's a matter of hull preparation.

Reducing the amount of hull surface in contact with the water (the wetted surface) also reduces friction. Heeling the boat lifts more hull surface out on the windward side than is submerged on the leeward side (for most hull shapes). This net reduction in wetted surface reduces friction. Heeling the boat when closehauled has the added effect of allowing the sails to fall into their designed shape. For example, if three persons pick up a sail by the head, tack, and clew, it will take the shape designed into it. But hang the sail vertically and it's a mess of wrinkles. Of course, when a puff does come it will fill the sail, which then will start to pull for you. But if the boat already is heeled and gravity has shaped the sail to its designed contours, the sail will start to pull immediately as the puff hits. And it will work with the slightest zephyr.

Another advantage to heeling the boat on a beat is the slight weather helm it will create. This gives lift to the rudder, helps reduce leeway, and makes it much easier for the helmsman to steer well.

To heel a boat, simply put the crew on the leeward side, as in Photo 179. This can be done in everything from dinghies to 12-meter sailboats. It's worth trying on any boat. Make sure that the crew stays low and doesn't disturb the existing airflow. Remember, too, that any crew movement in light air must be made as though one were walking on eggs. Any thump or sudden movement can kill the forward momentum the boat has built up. Sails must be adjusted extremely slowly and carefully. A jerk on the jib sheet can separate the airflow over the lee side of the sail, and it will take a second or two for it to attach itself again. On a small boat, the winch handle often is used more in light air than in heavy to trim the jib just a "click" or two. Both the jib and mainsheets must be adjusted constantly in light air, because the skipper can't turn the boat fast enough to follow the changes in wind direction. And if the skipper did try to follow them, the boat speed would be hurt. In heavy air, the reverse is usually the case. The sheets remain trimmed pretty close to one

179. Heeling the boat when beating in light air to reduce wetted surface drag.

180. Heeling the boat to weather helps speed on a run.

location and the boat's course is adjusted to accommodate the change in wind direction.

When beating in light air, station the crew a little forward of their normal position on boats with a flat run aft, as this too can help reduce wetted surface. Shifting the weight this way lifts the wide transom out of the water, and submerges part of the narrow bow. It also helps create weather helm and, if there is a "bobble," increases the drive of the boat through the waves.

Another technique that can help drive a boat into a slop when there's no wind to speak of is to keep the crew low in the boat. This seems to reduce rolling, and the boat goes faster. It also reduces windage, which is an important drag factor in light air.

When running in light air, it is best to heel the boat to weather. This helps in a number of ways: (1) it reduces wetted surface, just as heeling to leeward does when closehauled; (2) it reduces any weather helm produced by allowing the center of effort of the sails to get out to leeward over the water (weather helm is of no benefit when running and only creates rudder drag); (3) it raises the main boom higher in the air and thereby puts more sail area higher where the velocity of the wind is greater (the increased velocity can be as much as 100% greater at heights of 35 feet than it is at 2 feet above the surface, though this does depend on the initial wind strength); and (4) heeling to weather on a run causes the spinnaker to come out from the disturbed air behind the mainsail. Photo 180 shows a crew heeling a Soling to weather, and gravity helps expose the spinnaker to nice clear air.

Heavy Weather Racing

Heavy weather (as in Photo 181) is the time when previously unimportant things become important. The helmsman who doesn't quite have the timing becomes a disaster in heavy weather, the mainsail that you're keeping for "one more season" stretches into a "bag," the spinnaker guy with the little chafe marks lets go, the little leaks in the hull become big ones, and the crew members with a tendency for seasickness become seasick.

The only way to really feel at home in heavy air and to have an edge on the competition is to practice in it. The person who sails in San Francisco Bay is going to feel more at ease in heavy going than the sailor from Long Island Sound. He or she knows what the boat and the crew can take. Once you are confident that there is nothing that you or the boat can't handle, then all the rest is just sound and fury. It's natural to be a bit apprehensive or frightened of heavy winds at first, but soon you'll find yourself really enjoying the heavy stuff as an exciting part of sailing!

If a lot of heavy air practice is impossible, here are a few things to remember about sailing in it when it occurs. Upwind, keep the boat flat to reduce

181. Heavy weather.

weather helm. This is usually done by easing the traveler out, bending the mast to free the leech, and tightening the cunningham on the mainsail to keep the draft from working aft in the sail. If the sea is lumpy and the wind quite strong, at some point you may want to ease the mainsheet, thereby allowing the boom to lift. The top of the mainsail near the head will be luffing in respect to the bottom of the sail and the result will be less heeling.

Playing the waves is of crucial importance in heavy air racing. If the waves are running in the same direction as the wind (about 40° to 45° off your bow), the best way to play them is to head up, perhaps even pinch slightly, on the front side of the wave, and then head off down the backside of the wave. This means that you sail a short distance up the front of the wave where the wave's "current," or "orbital flow," is against you, and you traverse along the backside where the current is with you. This reverse flow on the backside of the wave will help push you to windward.

With steep, short waves like the ones you can sometimes find in a current flowing against a strong wind, heading off the wind at the crest of a wave also helps avoid the bone-jarring pounding that results from the boat's literally falling into the next trough. Instead, the boat slides down the back of the retreating wave.

Tacking can be very difficult in heavy winds. The main problem is the wind resistance of the rigging, the flapping sails, and the resistance of the hull to the seas. If the boat isn't traveling fast to begin with, a skipper attempting to tack may end up "in irons," head to wind and dead in the water. The wind and seas quickly stop the boat, making the rudder useless. To avoid this, be sure you have adequate speed. Wait for a relatively calm spot (both wind and sea, if possible) before you attempt to tack. There are always areas of smoother water, though when you're sailing in heavy seas this is sometimes hard to believe. It's all relative; just tack in a less heavy area of sea. Tack at the crest of the wave when much of the bow and stem are out of the water. Less hull in the water means easier pivoting, very much like a skier making his turn on a mogul or mound of snow, when the ends of the skis are in the air.

The boat in Photo 182 has just fallen off the crest of a wave, as we can see by the splash. To tack at this point will put the bow right into the next wave coming along. The boat in Photo 183 is just about to go up, and over, a wave. If they want to tack, this is the best time to do it. When the conditions are very rough and you have to be sure of completing the tack because of some obstruction, have your crew delay releasing the jib sheet. Let the jib back momentarily when you tack, but do so just long enough for the wind to help push the bow over to the new tack.

Running downwind in heavy weather can be wildly exciting and more than a little tense for any new helmsman. In this situation, it helps to rationalize and think ahead. Think about the worst that can happen; then say to yourself that even the worst isn't so terrible, so why worry about little things like being out of control, jibing wildly, broaching, etc. If you've ever had the "worst" happen, as I have, you'll know that it's all pretty quiet after you've lost a mast or capsized. It's the wild speed and commotion short of the worst that scares you. If you think about it in those terms, you'll perhaps find yourself even enjoying being at the very edge of control.

Playing the waves when running is aimed at one goal: getting on a surf and maintaining it. As a large wave approaches from astern, head up a little toward a reach in order to pick up speed just as a surfboarder paddles furiously in front of a wave. If possible, pump the mainsheet. Pumping is the rapid trimming of sails. By pulling the mainsail in against the force of the wind, the boat gets a little extra boost of speed. When the stern starts to lift, head down the wave as boat U.S. 620 has done in Photo 184. Note in Photo 185 how U.S. 620 has left U.S. 622 far behind because of the good surfing ability of the helmsman. The bow wave is twice as high and the white wake indicates how fast she is moving. The trick is to aim your bow for the lowest part of the trough in the waves ahead. If it looks like you are going to overtake the wave ahead, start traversing the wave. When you lose the wave, keep an eye out astern for the next good one. When you see it coming, first head up for speed, then head off and start riding it.

When the winds get strong enough, even the racing sailor has to reduce sail. In the cruising section we covered shortening sail on large yachts. On small sailboats reefing is usually impossible, so a sail must be lowered. The sailor who is just out for an afternoon sail may decide to get some sail down when he sees a dark squall approaching. It's hard to judge, even with a great deal of experience, just how bad a squall will be. Sometimes a nasty-looking sky turns out to be only dark clouds and rain, but no wind. However, when

182. Don't tack while in the trough of a wave.

183. Tack at the crest of a wave.

184. Soling #620 is heading off to catch a wave . . .

185. . . . And it pays off with a high-speed surf that leaves the others behind.

a bad squall hits, the wind can go from 10 knots to 50 or 60 knots in seconds. If you hadn't reduced sail previously, you should have at least prepared for the possibility of having to. Halyards should be neatly coiled and ready to run. Each crew member should be briefed on responsibilities if the squall is a bad one so that not a second is lost in giving orders. This has the secondary advantage of decreasing the chance of panic. When the first blast hits and the boat is laid over on its side, the brain processes of even some experienced crew members may tend to become stupefied. If all know what is expected beforehand, they don't have to think.

On a small boat, the mainsail usually has greater sail area than the jib and should be the first sail to lower. If it isn't lowered, as the wind increases the skipper should release the mainsheet to reduce heeling. The boat, due to the weight of the wind and sea, will probably be on more of a close reach than closehauled. At some point, even with the main jib luffing completely, the wind force will be sufficient to lay the boat over on its side. The boom and mainsail will hit the water to leeward, which, due to the boat's forward motion, will force the sail in toward the center of the boat just at a time when you want to let it out. The drag on the end of the boom pivots a small boat without a spinnaker up to leeward just when you want to head up into the wind. The mainsail fills and over you go if it's a capsizable boat. So lower the mainsail first! The boat should sail well under jib alone.

When the jib is full and drawing, it is not necessary to head into the wind to lower the main. On small boats or on cruising boats in heavy air the jib will bend the wind direction aft so that the main, with the sheet eased a little, should come down with no problem, even on a reach. When the jib has been lowered first, then the boat needs to be headed into the wind to lower the main. If it's still blowing too hard, lower all sails and run before the wind "under bare poles" (no sail), unless there's a chance of running aground.

Your best friend in bad conditions may very well be your anchor. If the visibility is down to a few feet, you're not sure of your position, and you're afraid you may be blown ashore, get your anchor over the side. You may not have enough line to reach bottom, but you can be fairly sure that the anchor will hook before you get into water shallow enough for your boat to go aground or be swamped by breakers.

◆ 10 ◆

Current

Current, and how it affects the course of a sailboat, is often misunderstood. If three or four pieces of wood are drifting along in a current, they are essentially motionless with respect to one another. Now imagine these hunks of wood spread out in a long line parallel to the direction of the current. You could sail your boat in and out among the drifting wood much like skiing a slalom course.

If the wind were dead abeam, a boat sailing upcurrent would take no longer to complete the course than a boat sailing downcurrent. In other words, the existence of current has no real bearing on how fast a boat moves through the water.

One popular misconception is that current exerts more force on a deep-keeled boat than it does on a shallow-draft boat. Actually, a piece of wood would stay right alongside a large cruising boat drifting along on a windless day, even if the current were running at 5 knots. The stick of wood and the cruising boat are motionless in a moving mass of water. There are rare occurrences when the current a few feet under the surface is moving at a different rate than at the surface, but that's highly unusual.

Another common belief is that current on the windward side of a close-hauled boat pushes it to leeward and current hitting the leeward side of a boat pushes to windward through the water. This, too, is a lot of nonsense. The only effect current has on a boat is in relation to the bottom. Nevertheless, it is mandatory for every sailor to know the direction and speed of the current, and there are numerous ways of doing this. Tide tables are often used, though in certain areas they are notoriously inaccurate. They can be as much as an hour off the actual time the tide turns, so never become overly dependent on them. A strong westerly wind (a wind blowing from the west) can delay and reduce a westerly current (one that flows from the east to the west).

The most common way to check the current is to look at it flowing by a stationary object such as a buoy. As mentioned before, the buoy will appear to be moving through the water, leaving a wake; the direction of the wake will be, obviously, downcurrent. Also, watch bubbles or bits of wood or paper drift past the buoy.

If you're very familiar with a certain buoy's shape, you can tell the current direction by the way it's leaning. In my experience, however, some buoys lean upcurrent and some downcurrent depending on the nature of their underwater shape and ground tackle. You must know the idiosyncrasies of the particular buoy before using its attitude to determine current direction. In a really strong current, however, all buoys will lean down-current.

A quick look at anchored boats can also help. However, a powerboat, with its high superstructure and shallow draft, will usually be affected more by wind than current, so try to use an anchored, deep-keeled sailboat as a guide to current direction.

During a race, constantly check the current, using both of the previous methods where possible, and also use ranges. By watching land behind a buoy, you can determine whether you are holding your own against a current. Line the buoy up with an object ashore such as a tree or a house. This is called a range. If the buoy appears to be moving slowly to the left along the shore, you are being set to starboard, and vice versa.

Your heading may have to be well upcurrent, if the breeze is light and the current is strong, to stay on the range you've made for your boat. Ranges are used mostly on the reaching or running leg of a course. When there is no land behind the buoy to use for a range, take a compass bearing on the buoy and keep it constant. This is the same idea as a collision course. If the bearing doesn't change, you will collide, or in this case, reach the buoy by having sailed the shortest possible distance. If there is no land and you don't have a compass, look back at the buoy you came from, then look forward to the next one, and judge whether you're still on a straight line between them. If not, adjust your course accordingly.

The depth of water has a great deal to do with the speed of the current. There's an old saying: "Still water runs deep." But it is better to remember it in reverse—still water really runs shallow. The swiftest current is found where water is the deepest. The one exception to this is where water depth is only slightly shallower than surrounding deep water. Here, water will speed up to cross the shallow spot rather than find its way around it. If you look at the water depths on a chart, you can determine where to sail to get into faster current or where to sail to avoid it, depending on your own course relative to it.

Look at waves a few hundred yards offshore or where you know the water begins to get deeper. If they are shorter in length and choppier than waves further inshore, the current is running against the wind. Since you know wind direction, you easily can determine the current direction. Whether you want to stay in the chop depends on whether the current will be with you or against you and whether you are beating or running. On a beat, this chop may slow the boat enough so that the advantages of such a favorable current are actually offset.

Though current has no effect upon how a boat moves through the water in relation to another boat, it has a large effect on how the boat moves over the bottom. This causes confusion among some sailors about what "leebow" current does to a boat. Many feel that if they can point high enough to get the current on the leeward side of their bow, they will get a boost to windward with the current. Figure 164 shows why it appears that way. Boats A and B are even at the start. Boat A sails normally while boat B pinches. Thus, at positions A_1 and B_1 (without current), boat A is ahead of B, but B has squeezed out to windward a bit. Now, inject current into this picture. Boat A is dead into it, moving to position A_2. Boat B ends up in position B_2—the same amount behind and to windward of A as without current. If you draw in apparent wind vectors for the boats, you must first correct the true wind by the direction and speed of the current. The current is creating a new direction and velocity of true wind for all boats sailing in it and then the individual boat's course and speed create its own particular apparent wind. Therefore, Figure 164 isn't perfectly accurate, since it shows only one wind direction with or without current, but the effect is the same. About the only advantage boat B has over boat A is that if B, by pinching, has been able to fetch a mark, whereas A has had to make two tacks. In light air this can be very time-consuming.

If the wind is very light and you have a strong contrary current, be well aware that you may be sailing backward. At night it is particularly hard to know that this is happening, but when you've made the correct diagnosis, it's extremely rewarding (in relation to other boats) to anchor. Many times we've anchored and found ourselves moving "up" past the running lights of other competitors who have failed to anchor. The current is setting them backward in relation to us, and their reaction is that we have a little more wind than they. A range of a buoy against the land, two lights ashore, a GPS fix, or a compass bearing to a known landmark will help tip you off that you're losing ground against the current.

When it becomes necessary to anchor during daylight hours in a small-boat race, slip the anchor over the side as surreptitiously as possible, preferably to leeward. If your competitors don't see you do it, you may gain quite a margin on them by the time they figure it out and sort out their anchorline. When anchored, lend all credence possible to the fact that you are still sailing the

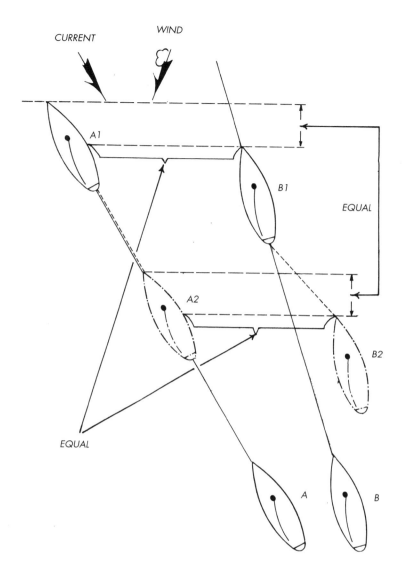

Fig. 164. A "lee-bow" current has no real positive effect. Boats A and B are in the same relative position to one another whether or not there is a current.

boat as fast as you can make it go. The crew can sit to leeward on the anchor-line as it leads over the side from the cockpit. The main and jib are tended properly, and the skipper steers with the appearance of utmost concentration.

The time to get the anchor up is before the line tends aft. When there's enough wind to sail forward and get slack in the anchorline, make the decision whether it's a temporary puff or a lasting breeze. If the latter, get the anchor up in a hurry. You just don't want to wait so long that the boat is past the anchor so that by raising the anchor you slow down the boat.

Keep in mind what current does to your tactics at marks. A current setting you to windward across a starting line will cause boats to be on the line early, so there will be a jam-up at the starboard end (don't barge) and a lot of boats bearing off to avoid going over early. Stay well to leeward, upcurrent, and make your final approach relatively late. If you are forced over the line early, it may be very difficult to stem the current downwind in order to recross the line and start correctly. With current in the same direction as the wind, stay very near the starting line or even on the wrong side, upcurrent of the line, until the appropriate moment. There is apt to be space at the starboard end of the line, so you may be able to get away with a barging start.

Allow for current when tacking on the layline of the windward mark. Current with you will make you overstand the mark unless you tack early, and current against you may set you below the mark, unable to get around it without a couple more tacks.

At a leeward mark, the crucial decision in light air is when to douse the spinnaker. If you are sailing against the current, the spinnaker may be giving you just enough power to move slowly over the bottom. When you douse the spinnaker, even 20 feet from the mark, you may start losing distance on the mark. This is aggravated by the fact that other boats behind you with spinnakers set will catch up and take away what little wind you had. So fly your spinnaker until the last possible moment when fighting against a current.

Running downcurrent creates less acute problems. Just remember that you are closing with the mark much faster than normal, and must douse the spinnaker early.

Sailing Attitudes

One of the most important aspects of racing is the attitude with which you approach the sport. It is natural for beginning racers to be pleased with getting around the course without fouling another boat, hitting a mark, capsizing, wrapping the spinnaker, experiencing an equipment failure, or coming in last. They may never make it into the upper half of the finishers and have subconsciously accepted a "pecking order" that keeps them out of a higher position. These persons are not racing as I define it, but just sailing around the race course. Racing is the active desire to beat the others in the race and having the confidence to do it. Luckily for the leaders, there are many sailors on the race course who defeat themselves. Races are won by those who make the fewest mistakes. When the mistakes are foolish ones, start questioning whether your attitude is conducive to winning. Do the most mistakes occur when you are leading or near the front of the fleet? Are you a little concerned that you'll be the one everybody shoots for if you win? Do you do well in one race only to flub up in the next? Do you take flyers—go out on a limb—the "palace or outhouse" syndrome? If the answer to any of these questions is yes, you may not be sailing with a winning attitude.

What we have said in this section should go a long way toward improving your basic racing skills, but cannot change your attitude. That's up to you if you see the telltale signs.

The main thing about sailing, cruising, and racing is that they are fun, relaxing, and challenging. Sailors have a traditional kinship that may suffer from the callousness of the modern world but I hope is never lost. The fraternal feeling is both a personal identity with other sailors and also a respect for the sea and seamanship. While the former may diminish, the latter is sure to persevere. May this book help be an entry into the deeper fulfillment one can derive from the sport of sailing.

TEST QUESTIONS ON PART III

1. Which comes first, the warning signal or the preparatory signal?
2. Which represents the true time, the gun or the shape?
3. What is the "favored end" of the starting line?
4. What is a current stick?
5. What is a dip start?
6. If you are on a closehauled course to the starting line, can you be barging?
7. What is the draft of a sail?
8. Are full sails for power or for speed?
9. What is a cunningham for?
10. Does backstay tension "free" the leech of the mainsail?
11. Does raking the mast aft effectively move the jib lead forward or aft?
12. What is the sign of too much mast bend?
13. What is a safe leeward position?
14. What is a loose cover?
15. What relation should the spinnaker pole have to the apparent wind?
16. When is it beneficial to ease off the spinnaker halyard a little?
17. Where should crew weight be in drifting conditions?
18. Does current run faster in deeper or shallower water?
19. When is a boat legally tacking?
20. When must a leeward boat stop luffing a windward boat?

PART I Answers

1. Length overall, the distance from bow to stern excluding a bowsprit or boomkin.
2. Wires that hold up the mast. Lines that adjust sails.
3. Stays keep the mast from falling fore and aft. Shrouds keep the mast from falling over the side of the boat.
4. Halyards raise and lower the sails. Sheets adjust the trim of the sails.
5. Tack, head, and clew.
6. Luff, leech, and foot.
7. A series of tacks.
8. Turning toward the wind.
9. A wind shift toward the bow. A wind shift toward the stern.
10. Changing direction clockwise. Changing direction counterclockwise.
11. It goes aft.
12. The jib lead is too far aft.
13. Change the balance by luffing or trimming the mainsail.
14. Skimming across the surface of the water.
15. Being pushed along by waves when reaching or running.
16. Stay with the boat.
17. The bearing doesn't change.
18. The zone from dead ahead to two points abaft the starboard beam (for motorboat right-of-way.)
19. The boat with the right of way:
    1B, 2B, 3A
    4B, 5B, 6A
    7B, 8B, 9B

PART II Answers

1. Docking lines that keep the boat from moving forward or aft and, therefore, keep it parallel with the dock.
2. A valve-type through-hull fitting.
3. Anchor.
4. Puckers at each jib hank indicating inadequate halyard tension.
5. To pull on the line leading from it.
6. Turn the boat directly downwind.
7. A line from the end of the boom to the bow to prevent the boom from flying across in an accidental jibe.
8. A reef using tack and clew grommets spaced a few feet up the luff and leech.
9. A wave filling the foot of a low-cut genoa.
10. A downhaul and a safety line bypassing the shackle.

11. A tug with a tow behind.
12. CNG (compressed natural gas).
13. The relation of the depth of the water plus freeboard to the length of the anchorline.
14. The crew takes turns staying on deck throughout the night to make sure that the anchor doesn't drag.
15. A line to pull the anchor out backward if it gets jammed.
16. The angular difference between true north and magnetic north.
17. The error the boat's compass assumes because of metal aboard.
18. Yes, by lining up two points of land.
19. 60.
20. As a courtesy, to keep the halyards from slapping the mast and disturbing the rest of others.

PART III Answers

1. The warning signal.
2. The shape.
3. The upwind end.
4. A stick dropped in the water near a fixed object to determine the direction and amount of current.
5. A start made after dipping from the course side of the starting line.
6. Yes, if there's a boat to leeward of you with luffing rights.
7. The maximum depth of the sail as measured from an imaginary line drawn from the luff to leech.
8. For power.
9. To increase luff tension.
10. Yes.
11. Aft.
12 Wrinkles emanating from the clew toward the mast.
13. A position to leeward and slightly ahead of a nearby windward boat.
14. One which doesn't disturb the air of the covered boat.
15. The pole should be roughly square (90°) to the apparent wind.
16. On a medium air reach.
17. Usually to leeward and low in the boat.
18. Deeper.
19. From head-to-wind to a closehauled course if beating.
20. When the helmsman of the windward boat in his normal position is abeam or forward of the mainmast of the leeward boat and the windward skipper has hailed "mast abeam" or words to that effect.

Index

International Sailing Federation
(formerly International Yacht
Racing Union), 32, 278–87
International Yacht Racing Union (IYRU),
see International Sailing Federation
isobars, 318

"Jibe ho," 47
jibes, jibing, 40, 46–50, 79–80
    accidental (flying), 49, 81, 164
    commands for, 46–47
    cruising boats, of, 147–48
    definition of, 279–80
    drills, 100–101
    racing, in, 303–5
    spinnaker, with, 348–54
    vs. tacks, 49–50, 58
    see also specific jibes
jib hanks (snaps), 32–33
jib lead angle, 271–72
jib leads, 20, 33
    placement of, 66–67, 149, 269–71
jibs, 22, 23, 127
    backing the, 35–36
    bagging of, 33
    blanketed, 48, 66, 71
    dousing sail, 150–51
    folding of, 28–29
    genoa. *see* genoas
    jibing of, 148
    light air sailing, in, 348
    racing, adjustments to, 260,
        268–72, 276, 343
    raising of, 32–35, 129, 133–39
    reacher, 177
    roller furling, 129, 133, 149–50,
        177
    shortening sail, in, 172, 177–78
    tack of, 32–33
    telltales on, 63–67
    trim of, 63–67
    winging of, 66, 164–66
jib sheets, 22, 33
    easing of, 140–41
    sailing wing and wing, in, 165–66
    tacking, in, 51, 141–45
jibstays, 22
jiffy reefing, 173

kedging off, 189
keelboats
    stability of, 32, 86–87, 96
    stopping, 53
    see also keels
keels, 20, 31, 88
    leak source, as, 191
    leeway reduction of, 63, 70, 85

kerosene lanterns, 205
ketches, 127, 170
kinking, 134–36
knives, use of, 184
knots. *see* specific knots
knots (speed), 75, 211

lanterns, kerosene, 205
Lasers, 96
lateen-rigged sailboats, 26
laylines, 290, 296–300
lazy guys, 322, 354
lazy sheets, 322, 354
lead, in boat balance, 91
leaks, sources of, 191
leeboards, 63
lee-bow currents, 370–71
leech cords (pucker strings), 24
leeches, of sails, 23, 320
lee helm, 88
lee rail, buried, 70–71
leeward, definition of, 280
leeward end, in racing, 243
leeward marks, rounding, 308–10
leeward side, of boat, 48
leeway, 62
    adjusting compass course, in, 220
    reduction of, 63, 70, 85, 88, 92–93
leeway angles, 88
length overall (LOA), 19, 20
lever arms, 86–87
lifesaving equipment, 96–97, 167–68
life-sling method, lifesaving, 171–72
lift-off, of wind, 315
lifts (suction), 59–62, 67–68
lifts (wind shifts), 72–74, 304–5
light air racing, 82–83, 359–62
    sail shape, 269–71, 274–76
    spinnaker work, 347–48
    starts for, 250, 253
lighthouses, on charts, 212
Light List, 191
Lightnings, 96
lights, navigation, 191–93
line of position, 218
line-of-sight bearings, 223
lines, 22
    chafing of, 182–83
    coiling of, 126, 134–37, 139–40,
        157–58
    docking, 116–17, 118, 123–26,
        153–59
    fouling of, 32
    safety, 185–86
    spinnaker, 320–22
    see also specific lines
lines of equal position, 295–96

load waterline (LWL), 19
LOA (length overall), 19, 20
logs, keeping of, 222
long-range navigation (loran), 224–25
loose cover, in racing, 290
loran (long-range navigation), 224–25
low vs. high, meaning of, 45
lubberlines, compass, 142, 195
luff and foot round, for draft, 256–57
luffing, 35, 43
    definition of, 279
    right-of-way rules, in, 282–85
    sail trim and, 63–64
    stalls vs., 64
luffs, of sails, 23, 43, 320
    tensioning of, 260, 271
lulls, 81–83
LWL (load waterline), 19

magnetic bearings, 107–8
magnetic meridians, 214
magnetic rose, 209, 215
mainsails, 22, 23, 127, 128
    backing of, 55, 101–2, 104–5
    construction of, 256–57
    dousing sail, 151–52, 367
    folding of, 27–29
    need for, 173
    racing, adjustments to, 260–69,
        274–76, 342–43
    raising of, 32, 35, 129
    reefing of, 93, 172–77
    rolling of, 154
mainsheets, 20, 266–67
    care of, 159–62
    jibing, in, 147–48
    pumping of, 364
    reefing, in, 173–75
make colors, 226
make leeway, 62
making land, in racing, 300
man overboard, 167–72
man overboard poles, 168, 169
Mare Nostrum, 83
Mariner's Weather, 318
mark
    definition of, 280–82
    rounding, in racing, 297–310,
        371–72
    rules for rounding, 285–87, 301
markers, anchorline, 203
MARPOL (Marine Pollution) Protocol,
    Annex V, 226
"Mast abeam," 283
masthead, 22
masthead fly, 39–40, 75, 304, 336